The Economics and Politics of Racial Accommodation

The Economics
and Politics of Racial
Accommodation

THE JAPANESE OF LOS ANGELES, 1900–1942

John Modell

UNIVERSITY OF ILLINOIS PRESS

Urbana Chicago London

LIBRARY OF CONGRESS CATALOGING IN PUBLICATION DATA

Modell, John.
   The economics and politics of racial accommodation.

   Includes bibliographical references and index.
   1. Japanese Americans—California—Los Angeles—His-
tory. 2. Japanese Americans—California—Los Angeles—
Social conditions. 3. Japanese Americans—California—
Los Angeles—Economic conditions. 4. Los Angeles—
Race relations.   I. Title.
F869.L89J35   301.45'19'56079494   77-6749
ISBN 0-252-00622-4

Contents

Preface

The incorporation of diverse immigrant groups into the American population is one of the grand themes of our national history. The details and the nature of this process make a difference to many. To a degree—and this is the truest for the history of the Afro-American—the intensity of interest has led to scholarly dialogue. From this dialogue has emerged a sense of the complex reality of minority-group experience in America. Neither wholly autonomous nor simply passive recipients of the malign initiatives of majority Americans, minorities have evolved varied attitudes and institutions appropriate to their circumstances.

To date, most study of the Japanese Americans has not reflected this dialectical perspective. Typically, Japanese in America have been treated as victims. And no wonder, in view of the uniquely palpable discrimination the Japanese in America suffered in World War II. Thus, our leading historian of the Japanese in America some years ago suggested that we ought to now turn our focus from the "excluders" to the "excluded," from those who oppressed the immigrants to the immigrants themselves.[1]

Yet the corrective, too, oversimplifies the problem facing us. For in the history of the Japanese in America, excluders were includers, of a sort; and the fact that most Japanese immigrants accepted the inferior ticket of admission which the "excluders" extended to them is perhaps the most interesting part of the whole story. Indeed, to those contemplating race in America from the vantage point of today, the very ambiguities of the historical Japanese-American situation, the blurring for most people of both races of the "exclusion" line, should make the Japanese-American story of more than passing significance. It is the task of the present volume to venture beyond a mellow acceptance of the magnificent economic achievement of the Japanese Americans since the war. However marked our shared

---

[1]Roger Daniels, "Westerners from the East: Oriental Immigrants Reappraised," *Pacific Historical Review* 35 (1966): 375.

admiration of the immigrants and their children, we must not simply concur when former Ambassador Edwin Reischauer maintains—somewhat thoughtlessly—that "no immigrant group has encountered higher walls of prejudice and discrimination than did the Japanese."[2] The view from the relocation camps of World War II clouds the view from beyond. We have higher purposes than to praise and blame.

American prejudice against the Japanese, though vicious enough, did not lack elements potentially compensatory to those against whom it was directed. We must respect the Japanese Americans' demonstrated ability to sense these elements, and to develop them assiduously. To recognize that "white racism" can be almost as varied as its practitioners will permit the Japanese-American story to contrast with other situations where racism has wreaked a more awful damage. Yet it would be equally shortsighted to overlook the intense emotional discomfort and very real material cost suffered by the "successful" Japanese Americans at the hands of the white majority. Within the Japanese-American community there has been a tendency to permit the constitutional monstrosity of relocation to erase the memory of the less dramatic but more insidious results of the discrimination that preceded it.

The comparative study of ethnicity in America reveals that the incorporation of immigrants and their descendants into the American nation has ever been a trying task to the assimilated. There is more than enough pain to go around. But these pains, in their *precise* historical context, constitute a part of the story of a group that must not be lost—not by forgetfulness, or by nostalgia, or by exaggeration. My attempt will be to portray the developing situation of an ascriptively unassimilable ethnic group in its place of highest concentration, Los Angeles, California, before Pearl Harbor and its aftermath added an unprecedented note to the Japanese-American story.

To be sure, Los Angeles is better known for more dramatic matters than the steady growth of a quiet, hard-working ethnic community. The formative period of Little Tokyo there coincided with Los Angeles's arrival as the most populous city of the Golden State, and as the nationally prominent center of the motion picture industry. Most of what has been written of the Japanese Americans, in fact, has examined them in other contexts: behind barbed wire; in their rural California colonies; in the San Francisco Bay area, where the

[2]Edwin O. Reischauer, "Foreword," in Bill Hosokawa, *Nisei: The Quiet Americans* (New York: William Morrow, 1969), p. xi.

"excluders" were centered during the period in which exclusion was being written into national law; or in their other major urban center, Seattle, where the University of Washington paid considerable attention to them.

But from several points of view, Los Angeles is where the Japanese Americans ought to be studied. The most obvious reason is the connunity's size and growth rate. A quarter of the growth of the Japanese population in the United States between 1900 and 1920 can be accounted for by gains in Los Angeles County; so can the *entire* 1920–40 growth, with some to spare. The "modal" Japanese American moved to Los Angeles if he moved anywhere, because it was in Los Angeles that the group achieved its most successful accommodation.

I use the word "accommodation" quite intentionally to indicate a group response to external pressures born partly of white resentment of Japanese resourcefulness in exploiting local opportunities. Accommodation on quite unequal terms was a responsible strategy because the opportunities were so visible. It was not an unrewarded pattern, but it had its costs. Both sides of the story would have been different had Los Angeles and California been less underdeveloped than they were when the Japanese arrived.

The themes of the book are straightforward, developing the general notion of racial accommodation, with emphasis upon the economic setting and responses of the group and upon its internal and external politics. Opportunities potentially available to the immigrants are examined, as are the uses they made of those opportunities. Anglo resistance to the group is laid out, and the Japanese response to it is analyzed. The internal structure of the Japanese community, as it developed over the period before the relocation, is understood with special attention to its relationship to opportunities and to white opposition. In this context, the differentiation of the second generation is interpreted.

In structure, the book mixes chronology and a topical approach. Chapter 1 suggests what "the economics and politics of racial accommodation" were in the Japanese-American case, with a consideration of the special variant of racism they faced, and their equally special response. According to this view, the local economic and political context in which they acted was critical. Chapter 2 discusses Los Angeles and the nature of Japanese immigration there. Both the place and its immigrants had distinctive qualities; so did the white reaction to the Japanese newcomers. Chapter 3 analyzes the evolution of discrimination against the Japanese in Los Angeles, paying attention to the statewide political issues in which the discrimination was enmeshed, and to highly localized neighborhood and class resentments which gave the "Japanese question" life.

Chapters 4 and 5 shift the focus to the Japanese themselves, treating community organization and the ethnic economy. The distinction, though helpful, is somewhat artificial, for the two were highly interdependent. Their amalgam represented the local Japanese accommodation to the blend of opportunities and antagonism which Los Angeles offered. As discussed below, the most substantial penetration I have been able to make beneath the surface of "accommodation" is in the matter of intergenerational relations. These are discussed in Chapters 6 and 7, on the "Nisei dilemma." The first emphasizes economic matters, indicating a growing though usually suppressed breach between the generations. The second treats the politics and outward symbolization of the American-born generation, a story increasingly impinged upon by tensions between Japan and America as the two approached Pearl Harbor. Chapter 8 briefly examines the local buildup toward the relocation of the Japanese Americans, and suggests that their sadly futile responses to the oncoming catastrophe were characteristic products of their particular accommodation.

The relocation, though a catastrophe, was not (as some had hoped) a "final solution," The Japanese Americans passed through the period changed—especially in the generational balance of power— but neither broken nor outwardly embittered. A host of signs indicate their success since. Whether the elements of their prewar accommodation have been recapitulated or shunned is a subject for another book. But neither students of current or historical ethnic behavior, nor the Japanese Americans themselves should allow themselves the luxury of forgetting.

The notion of accommodation has a problem that I must acknowledge. Specifically, I examine community behavior with evidence drawn largely from the actions and statements of the overt leaders of the group. It would be an exaggeration to say that I treat the Japanese community as a monolith, especially in view of the prominence of intergenerational differences in my account. But neither can I honestly claim to have always seen beneath the public surface of the Japanese community.

The reasons are two; the first is my inability to read Japanese. Of course, I recognized this as a shortcoming when I carried out my research, and I was fortunate to have many documents scanned and translated for me by colleagues at the Japanese American Research Project, University of California, Los Angeles. Still, I naturally tended to request the translation of the "most important" documents—that is, the quasi-official ones. I could not myself pore over the superb, infinitely varied resources offered by the vernacular newspapers, as I did pore over their English-language sections. Most observers who wrote of the immigrants in English, too, lacked a comfortable ability in Japanese. Like theirs, my account of the first generation accordingly must understate variety within community.

The second reason is more complicated. A part of it may best be seen in the light of the "insider/outsider" academic controversy so characteristic of the period when this book was conceived and when I carried out the research.[3] In the late 1960's (as now, but less acutely), scholars not of a group were much perplexed about whether they could successfully study it, lacking the perceptions of the insider. I am neither a Japanese American nor a Californian, and though I did not (and do not) subscribe to the academic position that would proscribe me from studying them, in retrospect I can see that I set limits to what I even hoped to understand of the Japanese-American mentality. This is not to say that I did not read sensitively; rather, my most central concern was accommodation as a *public* position. A piece of empirical research inevitably bears the mark of its original conception. The strongest qualities of my research, I think, are alertness to the complexity of human behavior, and energy and versatility in the collection and analysis of documents. I now wish there were, added to this, more effort directed to achieving a less external view of group process.[4] To accomplish much in this direction, however, would require a command of Japanese, and will take a scholar who is willing to take on and make sense of the undoubtedly disparate recorded viewpoints of first-generation participants in the evolution of a community.[5]

I carried out research for the present volume while living in Los Angeles and employed by the Japanese American Research Project,

[3]Robert K. Merton, "Insiders and Outsiders: A Chapter in the Sociology of Knowledge," *American Journal of Sociology* 78 (1972): 9–47.

[4]My current work on Japanese Americans (a study of the relationship of the ethnic economy and the ethnic community, done in collaboration with the sociologist Edna Bonacich) moves in the opposite direction, toward further abstraction from experienced reality. There are several ways of responding to the dilemma of divergent inside and outside views, each solution with attendant benefits and drawbacks.

[5]For example, the Japanese American Research Project has collected vast numbers of oral histories from immigrants. For a description of some of the JARP holdings, see Yuji Ichioka et al., comp., *A Buried Past: An Annotated Bibliography of the Japanese American Research Project Collection* (Berkeley and Los Angeles: University of California Press, 1974).

UCLA. The Project, which included sociological, historical, and archival aspects, was the grateful recipient of grants from the Japanese American Citizens League, the Carnegie Corporation, and the National Institute of Mental Health. My work at the Project, and my understanding of the Japanese Americans, was aided by Project research funds, by the Project as an ongoing research enterprise, and by Michael Edlen, Young K. Hahn, the late Joe Grant Masaoka, Yasuo Sakata, Ronald Tsukashima, and Robert A. Wilson. The Japanese American Citizens League generously provided funds for the typing of the manuscript. The indexing is the work of Vicki Haire.

As a dissertation in history at Columbia University, this study was aided immeasurably by Professors Robert D. Cross and Sigmund Diamond. My interest in immigration and ethnic behavior has since then been enriched and encouraged by my colleagues Edna Bonacich (University of California, Riverside), Edward P. Hutchinson and Dorothy Swaine Thomas (University of Pennsylvania), and Rudolph Vecoli (University of Minnesota). To Gene N. Levine of the Japanese American Research Project and UCLA and to Roger Daniels, then of UCLA, I owe the inestimable debt that younger scholars incur when their elders offer them encouragement, sponsorship, insistence on precision and honesty, and friendship. To Ann Lowry Weir, of the University of Illinois Press, I owe the special thanks of an author to a truly helpful editor.

The kindness shown to me by officials and employees of the following institutions has been one of the happy by-products of my research: Bancroft Library, California State Archives, The Haynes Foundation, The Hoover Institution, The Huntington Library, Los Angeles City Archives, Los Angeles Public Library, Stanford University Library, and the Library of the University of California, Los Angeles; American Legion (California Department), Americanism Educational League, California Intelligence Bureau, Los Angeles County Board of Supervisors, National Opinion Research Center, *Rafu Shimpo,* Local 770, Retail Clerks International Protective Association, and United Presbyterian Church in America.

—J. M.

1

The Ambiguities of Race: The Japanese in America

In 1937 the Los Angeles chapter of the Japanese American Citizens League, a leading association of American-born Japanese, invited radio actor Eddie Holden to be a guest of honor at the League's annual Nisei Day festival. White celebrities, of course, appeared quite regularly at ethnic-group functions in the large Los Angeles "Little Tokyo." And in none did they play a more integral role than in Nisei Day, for that affair was a paean to cultural pluralism. The basis of Holden's invitation was somewhat peculiar, however, since his radio role was that of Frank Watanabe, Japanese-American houseboy. The "Watanabe" show was the Japanese-American counterpart to the genially racist and hugely popular "Amos 'n Andy," with Holden's lines those of a crude Japanese-American stereotype: "Well, grand morning all right," he would chirp, "but from what glimpse point please?"[1] The Nisei somehow embraced "Watanabe," in no small measure because of the virtues embodied in the stereotype: Watanabe is loyal, competent, childishly guileful, and—outstandingly—eager to participate in the life around him. Only an excess of these virtues makes him outlandish, along with a sense of language that becomes most bizarre at frustrating moments. "My egg are just as good as the next fellow if not further," he insisted when his cooking was questioned.

To appreciate some of the practical advantages for Japanese

[1] *Rafu Shimpo* (Los Angeles; all references to English-language section), Aug. 5, 1937; "Frank and Archie," episode #110, Dec. 27, 1939, one of three scripts supplied to me by Ruth Preston, Central Records, National Broadcasting Company. This was not the first time that the Watanabe character had appeared as a guest at a Nisei affair; he was among the attractions at a benefit dance as early as 1932, in an event involving only Japanese Americans, *not* the white community. Both "Frank Watanabe" and Eddie Holden were rather obscure and are distinctly difficult to trace. The daytime slot and brief appearance of the show on network radio beginning in 1939 suggest that its fame was mainly local. *Rafu Shimpo*, Mar. 20, 1932; *Variety Radio Directory*, I-IV (1937/38-1940/41).

Americans of the muted appreciation implied by the Watanabe figure, one need merely reflect on the stock Negroes in "Amos 'n Andy": strident, slow witted, and, above all, lazy. Watanabe and some of his literary ancestors provide clues to the extraordinary patience and the faith in the eventual rationality of the white American which were shown by the Japanese Americans for so long as to almost defy belief; these elements compose an important part of their story in Los Angeles and elsewhere. As happens when accommodating to any stereotype so short of the complexity of life, accepting Frank Watanabe had its costs. But let us momentarily defer consideration of these costs and look more deeply into Watanabe's ancestry.

The standard interpretation of the Japanese-American stereotype has been conceived in a sense of shame and horror at what America did to the group in World War II. According to Floyd W. Matson in *Prejudice, War and the Constitution,* the stereotype "gradually congealed," mainly as a legacy of earlier viciousness toward the Chinese immigrant—especially since the Japanese, like their Asian predecessors, were heavily concentrated in the West, mainly in California.[2] The stereotype reinforced the legislative response to newcomers which Daniels has described as "a sort of racist conditioned reflex"; it so demeaned the Japanese American in the eyes of the white majority that indignities like relocation could ultimately take place. To be sure, the relocation of American citizens—the Nisei—could not have taken place except with the rationale of blood being thicker than water.

Yet the documents tell a different story. Indifference, rather than either contempt or hatred, usually characterized Los Angeles public opinion toward the Japanese Americans. And like the radio personality himself, the stereotypical ancestors of Frank Watanabe possessed remarkably redeeming characteristics.

Of Watanabe's literary ancestors the most famous was Wallace Irwin's popular Japanese-American houseboy. Hashimura Togo was the best-remembered vehicle of a humorist thought by many contemporaries to be the peer of Finley Peter Dunne, Don Marquis, or FPA. Togo's adventures, recounted in the form of his unsolicited and unanswered letters to the editor of a New York newspaper, were published in book form in 1909, with several sequels. *The Letters of a Japanese Schoolboy,* earliest and best in the series, takes the form of a gradual unfolding and skillful savoring of an ethnic stereotype—not the "deliberate use of the stereotype in its harshest aspects," as

[2]Jacobus ten Broek, Edward N. Barnhart, and Floyd W. Matson, *Prejudice, War and the Constitution* (Berkeley and Los Angeles: University of California Press, 1954), pp. 22ff.

Matson would have it, but a character in keeping with the humor of the day who was rounded enough to develop a life beyond that which its author originally had intended.

Togo is ever buoyant and fascinated by what goes on around him. Irwin ironically shows how the houseboy has wider ambitions for his fellow immigrants (although these are hardly presented as a realistic threat to America). To his editor-correspondent Togo explains that "derby hat, American pant, Tuxedo overcoat have rendered [resident Japanese] completely white of complexion and able to vote for President when asked to know how. . . . Let Japanese help to do push-out to all-coloured Yellow Perils coming to this country together with other patriots of star-stripe banner Yankee-doodle dandy, banzai!"[3]

This desire to be part of America, ridiculed by Irwin in the first installment, is thereafter treated more concretely, with considerable indulgence, and even with satirically qualified affection. Baseball catches Togo's fancy when "Yoni Hashimoto, Japanese boot-cobble" gets up a team which, at the suggestion of an Irish salooner, plays the Old Soldiers' Home team. The aliens had little trouble besting their disabled opponents, until the Japanese sense of deference permitted one especially maimed batter to score; then the Japanese sense of obligation forbade the Hashimoto squad to get *anyone* out. "After that . . . it were a very pleasant outing for them Hon. Vets. Each Old Soldier what go batt are some kind of delicious cripple & other hon. wounds, so we must also aid *him* to enjoy several homeruns."

A sense of melancholy, of the cost of eagerness thwarted, and of human dignity challenged is present beneath the buffoonery required by the literary conventions of a racial stereotype. Togo's New Year effort, an English-language poem entitled "O Joyful Newness of Year," reveals his mixed emotions. "I rejoice, legally, I intoxicate, I syndicate my thoughts to all humanity-races," Togo writes bravely. "And yet, to tell you honest true, [I do not care much for New Years time,] Because I do not."[4]

Even when Irwin tried, he could not paint a completely negative

---

[3]Wallace Irwin, *Letters of a Japanese Schoolboy* (New York: Doubleday, Page, 1909), p. 22.

[4]*Ibid.*, pp. 161–65. If Matson is right, this not unsympathetic character evolved from the "heathen Chinee" stereotype, which occupies a bigger part in California literature. To read Irwin's *Chinatown Ballads*, published two years before the first "Togo" letter appeared in *Collier's*, should be sufficient to disabuse one of this simplistic notion. The *Ballads* involve a descent by a white and disapproving narrator into the Inferno of San Francisco's Chinatown. Its tone is one of horror, unredeemed by ethnic virtues.

picture of the Japanese in America. Popular demand brought further Togo volumes in 1913 and 1914, and a final volume in 1923. By the last volume the vehicle had lost all its charm: Togo was neither stereotype nor human character, but a pasteboard excuse for the author's expatiations upon current events. Irwin had said his real farewell to the Japanese in a 1920 novel, *Seed of the Sun*. Daniels has correctly characterized this novel as "directed toward a single end—congressional enactment of Japanese exclusion."[5] Yet even in this basically propagandistic piece, Irwin cannot simplify the Japanese race to the point that their stereotype becomes as one-dimensional as Sambo. Although the Japanese figures in *Seed of the Sun* are unlovely, they are also more complex than Hashimura Togo.

The simple fictive structure of *Seed* is intended to persuade those who did not share white California's racial attitudes about the dangers of Japanese immigration. The book's basic elements are presented early: the seemingly innocuous Japanese-American farmers, "the most industrious people on the face of the troubled earth"; the heroines, the brave but naive Brand sisters from the East; the brilliant and distinguished Baron Tazumi, a family friend of the Brands; and Bly, California, a town being taken over by Japanese-American farmers. The unfolding of the tale involves the revelation of the threat posed by Tazumi and his racial fellows to the heroines and to California. Tazumi turns out to be a special agent of the Mikado, deputed to colonize Bly as a nucleus for Japanese expansionism, and with tremendous power over the Japanese-American population. As a sympathetic white figure puts it (too early in the story for the heroines to understand), the Japanese are "the greatest real-estate men in the world. They took Shan-tung for the good of the humanity, and they're keeping it for the good of Japan. . . . There's standing room only in Japan, and the race is suffocating."[6]

Despite all this propagandistic freight, *Seed of the Sun* does not present an entirely negative stereotype. When not enthralled by Tazumi, most of the Japanese-American figures are not unsympathetic, although they are distinctly foreign. Except for interludes in which the sense of Japanese mission possesses him, Tazumi himself is a subtle figure of considerable dignity. The theme is separate but (as Irwin clearly intended to stress) *equal*.

[5]Roger Daniels, *The Politics of Prejudice* (Berkeley and Los Angeles: University of California Press, 1962), p. 92.

[6]Wallace Irwin, *Seed of the Sun* (New York: George H. Doran, 1921), pp. 144–45.

The words from his high-pitched voice came sonorous and devout, but they were quite indistinguishable. Then Anna understood. His command of English had failed. He was praying in Japanese. What a prayer that might have been! Prayer to an Almighty who had set a gulf of race, wider than any ocean, between peoples equally human and yet equally unable to understand! Prayer of Asia for some answer to the yearnings of two alien worlds held apart by a law as immutable as that which keeps the planets in their courses.[7]

It is not facilities that are to be equal: the *races* are equal. A stereotype in which the stereotyped are acknowledged to be as deep, as capable of suffering, as civilized, as foresighted as the Anglo-Saxons, and more industrious, buttressed the nagging fear that the Japanese were not merely as good as white Americans, they were better. In this quality, indeed, lies the fundamental distinction between the stereotypes borne by Japanese Americans and by Afro-Americans.[8]

Sexuality is a point of marked distinction. Californians, of course, saw parallels between the South's race problem and the one they feared, and occasionally they applied the formulas of superiority that worked in the South. The state's ban on marriage between whites and Orientals, for example, followed from a similar ban on marriage between whites and blacks, at first by judicial interpretation and later by statute.[9] Interracial sexuality is a much more diffuse threat than

---

[7]*Ibid.*, p. 300.

[8]Although I have attempted to portray the central tendency of California anti-Japanism, I have omitted an explicit discussion of its variation. Relevant to the Japanese/black comparison is the novel most often coupled with *Seed of the Sun*, Peter B. Kyne's *The Pride of Palomar* (New York: Cosmopolitan, 1921). In this romance the far-too-good-to-be-true hero, a California white, easily defeats the Japanese heavy who appears briefly as a foil, and with only slightly more difficulty he overcomes the offstage Japanese menace to his lands. In strong contrast with Irwin's restrained treatment of the Japanese stereotype, Kyne viciously exposes Okada, his fictional "potato baron," to repeated physical humiliation. *The Pride of Palomar* tells the reader in no uncertain terms which is the master race. It also shares with its ideological inspiration, Montaville Flowers's *Japanese Conquest of American Opinion* (New York: George H. Doran, 1917), the ability to talk about Japanese Americans without quite recognizing them as human beings.

[9]Anti-miscegenation legislation in California dates from statehood. Originally applied to prohibit intermarriage between whites and Indians or blacks, it was extended four years later to forbid white and Chinese intermarriage. In 1910 "Mongolians," including Japanese, were added to the statutory prohibition of miscegenation. California's anti-miscegenation legislation was ruled unconstitutional in 1948, in the first such action by a state court; the provision was removed from the lawbooks in 1959. *Perez* v. *Sharp*, 32 C. 2nd 711, esp. pp. 719–20; B. E. Witkin, *Summary of California Law*, 7th ed. (San Francisco: Bender-Moss, 1960), III, 1948; Andrew D. Weinberger, "A Reappraisal of the Constitutionality of Miscegenation Statutes," *Cornell Law Review* 42 (1957): 208–22.

interracial marriage, but not even the most fervent anti-Japanese could conjure up a credible spectre of any sexual threat posed by the Japanese. While the blacks were imagined to be full of lust, the Japanese seemed inoffensive, perhaps even slightly underendowed.[10]

Although *Seed of the Sun* argues the Japanese threat to American racial integrity, Irwin was too much the novelist to challenge the usual image of the asexual Japanese. The book's dramatic climax revolves about this very point: Baron Tazumi's proposal of marriage to one of the Brand sisters is greeted by hesitation as the heroine's rationality argues against emotional repugnance. "He touched her hand for an instant, but she withdrew it. His fingers were soft as silk, but cold to the touch." Rejected, Tazumi's anger bursts out—but as an exhortation of his followers, not in front of the whites: "Seed of Yamato, germinate anew! Beget, beget, beget!. . . Now [after immigration was stopped] it is the more important still that we marry into this American stock. Prove your race equality in the blood of your children. Choose white women if you can. Where this is not practicable, marry negroes, Indians, Hawaiians." In other words, Japanese were not a threat because of their sexuality per se, but because their sexuality—attenuated as it might be—was, like all else, directed by policy. As the omniscient character in *Seed of the Sun,* a mixed-blood marginal man, explains: "They cannot change their bodies without one thing—intermarriage. Don't you see? Four feet six wants to become six feet four. Then Japan will have everything."[11] Japanese men didn't want white women; Japan wanted California. While white Southerners warned about one's sister, the clinching arguments of anti-Japanese were rhapsodies about "California—the Paradise of the White Man," which without constant vigilance would ultimately become "the paradise of the yellow man."[12] Interracial sex was less a threat than the purported enormous fertility of Japanese women, when mated to persons of their own race and living in California.

Within the Afro-American image lay the pervasive threat of blackness. The sinister Mikado, on the other hand, was imagined to lurk

---

[10]To be sure, the spectre was raised occasionally, especially by such crude anti-Japanese spokesmen as Clarence Hunt of the Native Sons of the Golden West, who maintained in 1911 that "the greatest permitted evil in this state to-day is that which allows Japanese MEN to attend our public schools, in company with white GIRLS." Hunt, "Exclude Japanese from Public Schools," *Grizzly Bear,* Jan., 1911, p. 6. But even Hunt's monthly column rarely repeated such concerns, finding other lines of attack which were more persuasive.

[11]Irwin, *Seed of the Sun,* pp. 217, 233, 234.

[12]Clarence Hunt, "Grizzly Growls," *Grizzly Bear,* Sept., 1935, p. 17.

behind the humblest Japanese American. Californians' respect for Japan exceeded their contempt, and their fear exceeded both. The competence, diplomatic skill, ambition, and pride of the Japanese nation were attributed to her citizens in America and to their progeny, while the political power of the mother country was thought to be at the immigrants' disposal. The racial and political threats to America were bound up in a strange mystico-biological bond connecting the Mikado and his subjects. Thus Montaville Flowers, among the vilest of the anti-Japanese in the first quarter of the century, dated America's "*acute* Japanese problem" from the Russo-Japanese War, "when Japan, swollen with pride, and conscious of the power of conquest, announced herself as a World Empire."[13]

Not only Flowers, but most white California chauvinists viewed their state as a racial frontier where, according to Senator James D. Phelan, "the civilization of East and West have met for a great trial of strength. One must dominate."[14]

Californians' fears were kindled more by an unyielding suspicion that, although the white men had prevailed more than amply on earlier racial frontiers, in California the Japanese were destined to win—an anxiety remarked on with some irony by shrewd contemporary observers.[15] Here we return to that striking component of the Japanese-American stereotype: the glimmerings of superiority it contained. The State of California in 1923 submitted a brief to the Supreme Court arguing that "If the Oriental farmer is the more efficient, from the standpoint of soil production, there is just that much greater certainty of an economic conflict which is the duty of statesmen to end."[16]

Whether through its lesser appeal to white cupidity and self-esteem, or simply because there were just not that many Japanese in America, the myth of Japanese-American superiority was much less widely or deeply held than the myth of Negro inferiority. California's really active racial frontiersmen were a small and self-selected lot,

[13]Flowers, *Japanese Conquest*, p. 11.

[14]Los Angeles *Examiner*, Oct. 17, 1920.

[15]Josiah Royce, "Race Questions and Prejudices," in Royce, *Race Questions, Provincialism and Other American Problems* (New York: Macmillan, 1908), p. 14; Lincoln Steffens, "California and the Japanese," *Collier's*, Mar. 25, 1916, p. 5.

[16]Brief for *Porterfield* v. *Webb*, 1923, quoted in *Oyama et al.* v. *California*, 322 U.S. 633, p. 657, n. 10. Justice Murphy's rejoinder to Webb's point, twenty-five years later, is perfect; "It would indeed be strange if efficiency in agricultural production were to be considered a rational basis for denying one the right to engage in that production. Certainly from a constitutional standpoint, superiority in efficiency and productivity has never been thought to justify discrimination." *Ibid.*, p. 670.

much given to windy sermonizing to one another about the glories of their state, and seldom achieving positions of power from which to accomplish much against their foes. Their victorious effort to close off Japanese immigration was achieved through luck and riding the coattails of a national movement against overseas immigration in general. Inseparable from the inadequacies of the active persecutors of the Japanese Americans was the fact that the stereotypical traits of the group—efficiency, reliability, eagerness, and hard work—were attractive to those people who had the most to say about whether the Japanese in California would succeed or fail: the state's employers, landowners, and consumers. In Los Angeles, for example, Japanese floral and fruitstand businesses proliferated, simply because the Japanese were widely believed to provide their customers with superior flowers and produce, at prices no higher than those of their white competitors. The farms that produced these crops were on close-in land rented by Japanese. Such land was available because white California farmers had "got out of the husbandman class," according to the lament of George P. Clements, head of the Agricultural Department of the Los Angeles Chamber of Commerce. People who "buy a small farm acreage but don't depend on it for life"[17] were quite ready to take on eager Japanese as short-term tenants. Likewise eager were Southern California suburban developers waiting for urban land values to engulf their speculatively held properties, big oil companies practicing comparatively generous spacing of their wells, Southern California Edison with its expensive power-line right-of-way, and the whole range of holders of agricultural land.

Before the outbreak of World War II, 1,500 Japanese farmers in Los Angeles County operated 5.2 percent of the farmland, dominating large areas of the southwestern portion and enjoying a near-monopoly on the production of such garden crops as celery, peas and beans, cauliflower, and berries. Much of this produce, in turn, was jobbed by Japanese-American wholesalers and brokers, and retailed at the perhaps 1,200 Japanese-American-run fruitstands and small groceries in the county.

Though these numbers indicate an important economic position, they by no means imply a fully healthy one. For every ten or eleven adult male Japanese Americans in Los Angeles in 1940, there was a

[17]Chester Rowell, "Orientphobia," quoted in J. S. Steiner, *The Japanese Invasion* (Chicago: A. C. McClurg, 1917), p. 79; "Survey Interviews: Southern California No. 2," Box 2, Survey of Race Relations Papers, Hoover Institution, Palo Alto, Calif. (henceforth SRR Papers); Clements, "The Japanese Problem," typescript, n.d., folder 63, George P. Clements Papers, University of California, Los Angeles.

fruitstand or grocery. About two-thirds of the Japanese-American labor force was dependent upon raising, catching, preparing, distributing, and retailing food.[18] That Japanese Americans were willing to develop along such narrow lines was an apparent source of relief to their white opponents; sometimes this development was even taken as a sign that the Japanese were not superior after all. The brawny all-American white hero of *Seed of the Sun* explained that the whites would eventually prevail in California because "the Jap is a one-horse farmer; the American is a thousand-horse farmer. Our imagination takes in the whole landscape, while a Jap gets down on his haunches and rubs a dinky piece of dirt between his hands." The Asiatic Exclusion League in its 1905 constitution incorporated the same desperately invidious comparison: "The labor of today in North America is a machine, as distinguished from a manual process. That race, therefore, which by its nature is best suited to complement the machine as the essential factor of production, is in that respect the superior race, and therefore best adapted to the conditions of American industrial life."[19]

If we abandon the notion that a race is unsuited to modern methods of production "by its nature," as the Exclusion League put it, we must examine the question of motivation. Why did the Japanese Americans continue to accept the niche allotted to them by the white Californians? For one thing, of course, their position was weak—the more so since they were proprietors with a stake in the status quo. For another, "cultural factors" hardly encouraged other than acquiescence; in fact, a Japanese-American social psychologist has recently proposed an "enryo syndrome," or ability to defer to the wishes of superordinate persons, to explain the mildness with which Japanese Americans accepted their assigned niche.[20]

Communities which have been socially situated between a clearly dominant group and its clear inferiors are historically not known for militancy. However, many of these middle groups are known for their successful, specialized entrepreneurial development. Just as the Japanese Americans became dominant in a small way while remaining on the whole subordinate, so the Indians in South Africa, the Lebanese in West Africa, and the Chinese in Southeast Asia occupied positions that partook both of servility (especially toward the white

---

[18]See the fifth and sixth chapters.

[19]Irwin, *Seed of the Sun*, p. 135; Asiatic Exclusion League constitution appended in Eliot Grinnell Mears, *Resident Aliens on the American Pacific Coast* (Chicago: University of Chicago Press, 1928), p. 435.

[20]Harry H. L. Kitano, *Japanese Americans: The Evolution of a Subculture* (Englewood Cliffs, N.J.: Prentice-Hall, 1969), pp. 103–5.

colonial populations) and of prosperity. There were differences, of course; yet the imperfect analogy should still alert us to the fact that much as the white majority did not feel themselves superior to the Japanese, so the Japanese did not see the whites as hated exploiters. Members of the middle group may align themselves more with the top than with those below.[21] On the whole, Los Angeles Japanese— particularly the immigrant generation—saw whites as their customers, and viewed Mexicans and Filipinos as employees. As long as these arrangements satisfied enough of their ambitions, they could comfortably adopt the assumptions of the dominant group about the worth of people, at least as operating values.

To understand the mild Japanese-American response to racism, we must also look to the social structure of the minority group itself— which was, in part, the result of its middle position. Only unusually successful modes of social control could enforce the self-discipline necessary to the group's continuing progress on its side of the color line. The Japanese-American community was always a remarkably organized one, including churches, purposive voluntary economic groupings, the Japanese Association (partly a defense organization, partly an institution for internal supervision of the Japanese-American community), vernacular newspapers, and an extensive network of less formal groups, based often on common place of

[21]R. C. McKenzie, "Cultural and Racial Differences as Bases of Human Symbiosis," in Kimball Young, ed., *Social Attitudes* (New York: Holt, 1931); Leo Kuper, Hilstan Watts, and Ronald Davies, *Durban: A Study in Racial Ecology* (New York: Columbia University Press, 1958); R. Bayley Winder, "The Lebanese in West Africa," in Lloyd A. Fallers, ed., *Immigrants and Associations* (The Hague: Mouton, 1967); Victor Purcell, *The Chinese in Southeast Asia,* 2nd ed. (London: Oxford University Press, 1965); Edna Bonacich, "A Theory of Ethnic Antagonism: The Split Labor Market," *American Sociological Review* 37 (1972): 547–59, and "A Theory of Middleman Minorities," *American Sociological Review* 38 (1973): 583–94.

The ambiguity of this position is nowhere better expressed than by Albert Memmi: "Like all other Tunisians I was treated as a second-class citizen [by the French]. . . . But I was not a Moslem. . . . The Jewish population identified as much with the colonizers as with the colonized. . . . Unlike the Moslems, they passionately endeavored to identify themselves with the French. To them the West was the paragon of all civilization, all culture. The Jew turned his back happily on the East. He chose the French language, dressed in the Italian style and joyfully adopted every idiosyncrasy of the Europeans. . . . For better or for worse, the Jew found himself one small notch above the Moslem on the pyramid which is the basis of all colonial societies. His privileges were laughable, but they were enough to make him proud and to make him hope that he was not part of the mass of Moslems." Albert Memmi, *The Colonizer and the Colonized,* trans. Howard Greenfield (New York: Grossman, 1965), p. xiv.

origin. Indispensable to Japanese-American organizational ability (and another striking contrast to the blacks) was the strong position of their leaders. The mutual obligations of leader and led were deeply ingrained in Japanese culture and reinforced by the unfamiliarity of the American situation. Moreover, the criteria of honor in the Japanese-American community were clear, and they did not differ from those of white Americans. The duly constituted leaders enjoyed the active support not only of the Japanese consulate, but also of a prestigious group of white Japanophiles: churchmen, educators, and international businessmen.

Japanese Americans could be motivated to persevere quietly in the tantalizing position of men in the middle, partly because their leaders (and white supporters) could effectively promote these desires.[22] The Japanese-American elite was for the most part a conservative group, with a heavy stake in the existing order of things, in terms of both wealth and prestige. To these men the niche already achieved seemed gradually expandable, even presupposing no major breakthrough along the color line. Although there were some would-be protest leaders, notably labor radicals,[23] they had to cope not only with the entrenched position of the respectable leaders, but also with the rank-and-file belief that the distinctly positive aspects of the Japanese-American stereotype boded well, despite racist irrationalities.

The classical policy of the Japanese-American community toward discrimination is nowhere clearer than in the memorial addressed to President Wilson by the Japanese Association of America, upon the occasion of his 1919 visit to San Francisco. More generally, the document addressed itself to California opinion. In outline it had two main imports, expressing first the accomplishments of the California Japanese and then their hopes. In bridging these two themes, the Japanese Association took special notice of the fact that white hostility emphasized the favorable qualities of the Japanese Americans,

[22]This is not an effort to indict the white Japanophiles as hypocritical exploiters of the Japanese-American rank and file, but only an attempt to indicate that their agreement with the Japanese-American leadership about the hopeful possibilities of the current situation had a conservative effect. The virtues, and not the needs, of the Japanese Americans are emphasized in their writings.

[23]James Gray, "The American Civil Liberties Union of Southern California and the Imperial Valley Labor Disturbances: 1930–1934" (Ph.D. dissertation, University of California, Los Angeles, 1966), p. 27; Stuart Marshall Jamieson, "Labor Unionism in Agriculture" (Ph.D. dissertation, University of California, Berkeley, 1943), I, 168–69; Hyman Weintraub, "The I.W.W. in California: 1905–1931" (Master's thesis, University of California, Los Angeles, 1947), p. 297.

even while attacking them. The Association discussed the charge that the immigrants worked too hard: "The Japanese nation is characterized by industry and perseverance, so naturally the Japanese who are here possess the power of endurance and the habit of industry. But it appears rather strange that Americans should complain of these facts, for they themselves take pride in these very characteristics." Guilty as charged, but having committed no real wrong, the Japanese asked for sympathy, not opprobrium: "The Japanese, as they have been conditioned upon arrival in this country, have found that the best asset they possessed consisted in those characteristics that have helped them get on an independent footing. So they worked and worked hard." Even their overwork will have what whites ought to consider a happy outcome. The Japanese in America "struggle so hard . . . so that they can give their children a chance to get education. It is a well known fact that the Japanese will do anything to get an education or enable their children to get it." Thus understood, the Japanese-American stereotype might perhaps be turned to the advantage of those who bore its burden. But the Japanese Association was willing to go further, to attempt to mold their constituents to avoid those qualities explicitly resented by whites. "We are advising them [the farmers] as best we know how, not to work so hard as to cause their neighbors to criticize them, and to create some leisure for self-development." The Japanese Association would inculcate these notions through an "Americanization" program, designed to convert immigrants who were already "at least fifty percent" American to hundred-percenters. "We tried to impart to our fellow countrymen elementary facts of American civilization so that they could better fit themselves for American life. We tried to teach them that assimilation was the first step in their success."[24] The policies of economic advancement and making oneself acceptable to white opinion were thus, in conception at least, unitary. The memorial stressed that the movement for acceptability was no matter of idle words; in more or less formal ways, the Japanese community suppressed vice and other scandalous activities, succored the destitute, found or created jobs for the out-of-work, healed the sick, and returned the incompetent to Japan. Hostility on the part of whites, even when the latter opposed such acceptably middle-class motives as the desire to move into a better neighborhood, led Japanese Americans not to outward protest but to self-censorship.

---

[24]Open letter from the Japanese Association to President Woodrow Wilson, in California, State Board of Control, *California and the Oriental* (1920), pp. 203–15; "Letter of Warning of Sei Fujii," Major Document 207, SRR Papers.

By any rational standards, including those of the time, the Japanese Americans unquestionably deserved the respect of white America. The very clarity of this fact made it that much harder for the immigrants to doubt that, with standard English, American education, and legal citizenship, their offspring would gain full acceptance. When college presidents, scholars, and clergy spoke and wrote of the marvelous achievements of the California Japanese, the praised could not conceive of other elements of the white population taking such testimony merely as further proof of the authors' abstraction from reality. With unquenchable hopes, the first generation grew increasingly comfortable in their niche, investing more and more psychological capital in their offspring.

The new generation, however, had been raised to expect a more varied reward for their toil; for them deferred gratification could no longer be an unquestioned virtue. Manifestations of strain abound, and the problem of motivation became ever more acute among the Nisei. Particularly to the point were increases in juvenile deliquency and in less dramatic departures from the straight and narrow, coupled with even more open and vigorous efforts to control such deviant behavior on the part of those who kept the faith of their parents. By the late 1930's, one immigrant characterized the Japanese community as like "a bear cooped up in a cage"; a white observer saw that the second-generation Japanese were "suffocating in Little Tokyo."[25]

With their talents, educations, and even energies being denied full scope of expression, Nisei struggled to change things. But change did not come easily, for their parents' ideas of Japanese-American propriety were nearly as restrictive as the constraints imposed directly by the white majority. The prewar struggle of the second generation displays many ironies; none is more indicative of the strains of being a "successful" colored minority than an episode involving the Japanese-American citizen leadership in Los Angeles. These young leaders, who celebrated Frank Watanabe, came of political age during a strenuous effort intended to demonstrate that if they weren't quite like the whites, at least they were more similar than some other

[25]Togo Tanaka, "Journal," typescript in folders A 17.06 and A 17.07, Japanese Evacuation and Resettlement Study Collection, Bancroft Library, Berkeley, Calif. (henceforth JERS Collection), esp. entry for July 14, 1941; *Rafu Shimpo,* esp. the prewar feature called the "Police Blotter"; Dorothy Swaine Thomas and Richard S. Nishimoto, *The Salvage* (Berkeley and Los Angeles: University of California Press, 1946), case histories; Daisuke Kitagawa, *Issei and Nisei: The Internment Years* (New York: Seabury, 1967), p. 12; Carey McWilliams, *Prejudice* (Boston: Little, Brown, 1944), p. 105.

groups. They joined in the promotion of a new housing development from which all but whites and Orientals would be excluded.

It is unclear whose idea the Jefferson Park development was. The subdividers, all white, incorporated in 1938; by February, 1940, they had submitted to the Los Angeles city engineer a plan for a 191-lot area in one of the less impressive parts of the middle-class Baldwin Hills section. At the same time, they took the unusual step of appointing a Japanese American as sales manager, suggesting some kind of departure from the typical "Caucasians only" pattern of restrictive residential covenants in better sections of the county. The "official" viewpoint of the Nisei leadership was well expressed in an editorial in the English-language section of one of the vernacular newspapers. With moderation reminiscent of the Japanese Association's memorial to President Wilson, the editorial conceded that "valid reasons for race restrictions and discrimination against the first generation Japanese may or may not have once existed." However this question might be decided, the second generation had by now proven their propriety: "conditions . . . are sufficiently advanced," as the editorial put it. If the Nisei could manage to lay "the facts and figures" before "the public at large," whites would agree "that the nisei is deserving of equality in housing."

Very few Japanese-American voices were raised against proposed deed restrictions that would exclude from Jefferson Park all races considered undesirable by the more genteel Japanese Americans— including Negroes and Mexican Americans. Fearing for their property values, white developers with interests in Baldwin Hills pressured the city council into rejecting the city engineer's favorable recommendation; in response, an ironically named "Equality Committee" was formed within the Los Angeles Japanese American Citizens League to secure approval for the project. (The name "Civil Liberties Committee" was explicitly rejected.) The committee's approach was drawn quite narrowly, since their legal case was watertight: the city council had no right to reject a recommendation of the city engineer without cause, and no show of cause had been made. The committee won its legal battle, but Japanese simply did not flock to buy lots. By early 1941 the project had collapsed.[26]

Although the color line separating them from black and brown

[26]"Articles of Incorporation of Buena Park Development Co.," filed July 14, 1938, and amended Mar. 6, 1940, Corporation No. 176,337, California, Department of State; *Rafu Shimpo,* Apr. 21, May 5, July 14, 15, 21 (editorial), Aug. 12, 15, Dec. 1, 1940, Jan. 8, Feb. 12, Mar. 5, 9, Apr. 3, 1941; *Kashu Mainichi* (Los Angeles, English-language section), Jan. 22, 1941; *Doho* (Los Angeles, English-language section), June 15, Aug. 15, 1940; Los Angeles *Illustrated Daily News,* Aug. 13, 19, 1940.

people had been reemphasized, the brief but unrestrained outburst of racial antagonism that accompanied the council's temporary rejection of the Jefferson Park plat was better remembered by the Japanese. Of these attacks, the most absurd is worthy of quotation; made by a Los Angeles city councilman, it shows that Japanese Americans were a marginal group that could easily be made the butt of gratuitous insults. Councilman Evan Lewis inveighed against Jefferson Park on the grounds that "the people of this district might rise up against the Japanese [residents of Jefferson Park] in a body, and there might be a bloody fight. There's a lot more to this movement than appears on the surface. Japan is promoting a war with the United States, and is ready to stab us in the back. Any excuse would do—a race riot would be as good as anything else.''[27]

The Equality Committee, in any case, survived both its irrelevant legal success and the fruitless aftermath. By 1941 it had evolved into a more or less permanent group dedicated to exposing sources of defamatory propaganda and bettering relations with the white community. Whatever their skills in dealing with ticklish situations, its members were put to severe tests after December 7, 1941, when essentially the same group appeared among the leaders of the newly formed J.A.C.L. "Anti-Axis Committee."

By 1942, of course, a once somewhat permissive color line had become impervious even to the demands of constitutionality. But behind that line was a vital and sturdy group, paying a price in inner tensions for its position. Japanese Americans constituted a "subnation," in William Petersen's suggestive terms;[28] however wronged

[27]Los Angeles *Illustrated Daily News*, Aug. 13, 1940. The Nisei of 1940 had come a long way from the 1920's image of the yellow invaders of white America without yet being acceptable neighbors. One letter in the Council files indicates local concern about Jefferson Park: "Surely you can do something to keep these Japs from moving in on us. We save so hard and read all the books on how to choose a desirable homesite. . . . We thought we were being so wise. . . . Now instead of being proud of our new home, we will probably get panned for living practically in a Jap district. You wouldn't like it at all, if you were in our place." Mr. and Mrs. Maurice L. Young to City Council, Aug. 13, 1940, Vol. 3366 (1940), File 1337, Council Communications.

[28]William Petersen, *Japanese Americans: Oppression and Success* (New York: Random House, 1971). I find that Petersen's formulation of "subnation" doesn't entirely ring true for the pre–World War II Los Angeles Japanese community. In particular, two of his criteria strike me as questionable in the light of my research, however true they may have been rendered later by the internal and external changes wrought by relocation and return. Petersen's criterion (3) holds that "as subnations acculturate in some respects, they thereby attain the status and the self-confidence to maintain or reassert their independence in other respects." His criterion (6) states that "a people that enjoys cultural unity is not shattered by internal divisions, but sometimes the contrary" (pp. 221–32). These notions are too roseate.

they were, they are certainly a group to which the category "downtrodden" cannot be applied. This book attempts to examine the local context in which the outstanding Japanese-American accomplishments of the prewar period occurred, and to assess as completely as possible (and from a viewpoint divorced from the perspective of the relocation) the economic and political thrust of a group of "superlatively good citizens," middlemen in a society in which racial categories have worked their ambiguous influence.[29]

[29]I wish to emphasize the notion of "ambiguities" with this book. My notion owes much to the joint influences of the two people with whom I have most intensely discussed the Japanese in America: Roger Daniels (the quotation is from *The Politics of Prejudice*) and Edna Bonacich.

2
Los Angeles

Growth has been the most striking fact of Japanese demographic history in Los Angeles, and one of the most crucial. The first census of Japanese in Los Angeles dates from 1893; in that year what was purportedly the entire Japanese population of the city was counted as they gathered for a celebration. The forty-one people enumerated were all young men straying a bit from the more common (though still scarcely developed) centers of Japanese life in America, especially Seattle and San Francisco. A second informal Los Angeles census was taken two years later by a Japanese-American yearbook. It revealed a tenfold growth, and a population largely headquartered in cheap hotels and roominghouses in downtown Los Angeles, but working in outlying agricultural areas, or for the railroad.

A faulty federal census denies us a fully trustworthy measure of the 1900 Japanese population. If we rely upon the same Japanese yearbook, though, we arrive at an estimated 1,200 Japanese in Los Angeles County in 1900, a growth of about 20 percent a year. A very meticulous census by another Japanese-American yearbook in 1904 counted some 4,000 residents in the county; we may have some confidence in that figure, since the California Bureau of Labor Statistics estimated 6,000 residents in 1907, while the U.S. Census, finally having discovered how to enumerate Japanese, counted 8,461 in 1910. Even if we doubt the detail of these figures, we can see a spectacular increase from the late 1890's through 1905, after which the growth rate settled down to a steady 10 percent per annum, or more, for the balance of the decade. In any case, within twenty years an imposing and visible colony existed where none had been before. The very explosiveness of this growth in many ways defined characteristics of the Japanese-American community, both as experienced by those who were a part of it, and as perceived by outsiders. This rapid growth continued through the 1920's, as Table 2.1 shows.

Immigration data are notoriously thorny to interpret—especially in the case of the Japanese, because many who came to the mainland of North America did so after remaining for some period of time in

TABLE 2.1.   Growth of Japanese and Total Population, Los Angeles County, 1900–1940

Year	Japanese population	Percentage intercensal gain: Japanese population	Percentage intercensal gain: whole Los Angeles population
1900	1,200[a]		
1910	8,461	ca. 600	193
1920	19,911	136	86
1930	35,390	79	136
1940	36,866	4	26

[a]Estimated; the census figure for 1900 is almost certainly an underestimate.

Source: *Census 1900 P1*, p. 571; *Census 1910 P2*, p. 36; *Census 1920 P1*, p. 109; *Census 1930 P2*, p. 266; *Census 1940 P2*, p. 567.

TABLE 2.2.   Characteristics of the Japanese Community, Los Angeles and United States, 1910

	Los Angeles City	Los Angeles City	United States
	Number	Percentage of total JA population	Percentage of total JA population
All Japanese Americans	4,238		
Males	3,546	84	87
Females	692	16	13
Immigrated before 1896	143	3	5
Immigrated 1896–1900	532	13	13
Immigrated 1901–5	1,665	39	35
Immigrated 1906–10	1,399	33	33
Not reported	198	5	8
Born in United States	301	7	6
Under 5 years old	245	6	5

Source: *Census 1910 P2*.

Hawaii. It is clear, however, that until the Gentlemen's Agreement between the American and Japanese governments went into effect in 1908, Japanese immigration was heavily male (11:1 before 1900, almost 7:1 until the Agreement) and was composed mainly of "birds of passage," often agricultural laborers. The migration of "coolies" was by and large banned by the Gentlemen's Agreement; for the balance of the migratory period females outnumbered males 1.5:1, and four out of five immigrants came to join relatives. The bulk of the immigrants, about two-thirds in most years, intended to settle in California.

Because the 1910 census asked immigrants when they had arrived in the United States, we are able to gauge some of the more salient characteristics of the Los Angeles Japanese community shortly after its establishment. (See Table 2.2.) It was slightly newer to America than were most Japanese communities on this continent. Women were slightly, but only slightly, more common; children were rare, but slightly less rare. While 26 percent of all Japanese male immigrants fifteen or older were married, 28 percent in Los Angeles were married. Any signs of permanence in the American Japanese community were slightly accentuated in Los Angeles. By taking some liberties with immigration and census data we can infer some sense of the permanence of Japanese in America—a finding that contrasts strongly with what the immigrants themselves had declared and thought when they migrated. Total Japanese immigration to Hawaii and the mainland was approximately 65,000 between 1900 and 1904; of these immigrants, fully 38,500 (59 percent) were counted in the 1910 census. Of those who migrated in the next five years, about 45,000 (69 percent) were there in 1910. Of the 1910–14 immigration cohort, a slightly lower proportion (45 percent) remained in 1920, and of the 1915–19 arrivals a like percentage stayed and were counted. The proportion remaining of the final 1920–24 cohort declined to only 23 percent in 1930. When the commissioner of immigration and naturalization began questioning returnees to Japan on how long they had been in the United States, he found that the average stay was eight years, a figure that was fairly steady from before 1910 until the 1930's.[1]

The Japanese had come to America—and moved to California and Los Angeles—for the usual reasons.[2] Like the Southern Italian immigrants who arrived in America at about the same time, most Japanese at first sought short-term economic gain which might be transported back home. Hence the high proportion of males among Japanese immigrants in 1910, and the low proportion married. The figures also reveal that a majority of married Japanese in America as

[1]U.S., Commissioner of Immigration and Naturalization, *Annual Reports,* 1900 et seq. *Census 1910 P2, Census 1920 C1, Census 1930 P1* present data for foreign-born persons on place of birth by date of immigration; these permit one to infer patterns of immigrant persistence.

[2]For the notion of the economic niche as a basis for population and its application to California early in the twentieth century, see Margaret S. Gordon, *Employment Expansion and Population Growth: The California Experience, 1900–1950* (Berkeley and Los Angeles: University of California Press, 1954).

of 1910 had their wives elsewhere. Most, obviously, had been married when they left Japan; of these, a goodly number anticipated an early return home.

As late as 1910, then, Japanese immigration had just begun to take on those aspects of family life which would ultimately imply real permanence. Like the Eastern European Jews, whose peak of immigration was also at about this time, the trip to America was both a demonstration of and a component in the ongoing process of receiving the widest influences of Western culture. A passion for education was a component in both the Japanese and the Jewish "enlightenment," and would eventually serve very well in America. Yet the Westerners from the East were Easterners nonetheless, and their immigration had certain characteristics that would differentiate the Japanese from other immigrant groups. Most notable in this respect were the resilient institutions which were implanted in America, in adapted form. Under stress from hostile Americans, these flowered into a degree of organization unmatched among other ethnic groups.

What was peculiar about the Japanese immigrants in Los Angeles? Their most striking characteristic was the likelihood that they were "secondary migrants," persons who had lived somewhere else in the States before coming to Los Angeles. Table 2.3 reveals that Los Angeles was capturing larger proportions of immigrants from all cohorts; for example, in 1910 only 5 percent of pre–1900 immigrants lived in Los Angeles, but by 1930 13 percent of those remaining did. Yet Table 2.3 also reveals that Los Angeles was and continued to be preeminently a city of relative newcomers, as well as of secondary migrants. For the Japanese in Los Angeles, their booming community was in a sense a frontier which had only begun to emerge into a settlement. At this point San Francisco exceeded Los Angeles in settled quality; the former had been the port of entry for most Califor-

TABLE 2.3.   Percentage of Japanese Immigrants in Continental United States Living in Los Angeles City

	1910	1920	1930
Year of immigration:			
Pre-1900	5	8	13
1901–10	6	11	16
1911–14		11	17
1915–19		11	19
1920–24			25

Source: *Census 1910 P5*, p. 1031; *Census 1920 P4*, pp. 787, 795; *Census 1930 P1*, pp. 500, 562.

TABLE 2.4. Birthplace in Japan for Selected Areas of Residence in Los Angeles, Males,* 1930

| | Little Tokyo | | | | | |
	S. of East First (%)	N. of East First (%)	Tenth St. (%)	San Pedro (%)	Hawthorne (%)	Gardena (%)
Hiroshima	18.0	15.6	5.1	1.8	19.0	31.6
Wakayama	12.3	5.7	6.4	69.2	3.7	6.1
Kumamoto	6.6	9.4	7.7	0.4	19.6	18.4
Tottori	—	1.0	29.5	0.7	1.6	1.0
Fukuoka	8.2	4.2	6.4	0.4	16.4	7.1
Yamaguchi	1.6	1.0	1.3	0.7	10.6	5.1
Others	53.3	63.1	43.6	26.8	29.1	30.7

*Females essentially duplicate pattern for males. All prefectures are shown which accounted for 10% or more in any single Los Angeles area.

Source: Edward K. Strong, Jr., *Japanese in California* (Stanford: Stanford University Press, 1933), p. 53.

nia Japanese and, as an older, more established city in American California, had attracted permanent Japanese residents earlier than had Los Angeles.

Strong's 1930 survey of California Japanese, excerpted in Table 2.4, is representative enough and was taken late enough to give a good view of the places from which the Los Angeles Japanese had emigrated, and how much difference these origins made in where they would settle within the county. Four prefectures contributed most heavily to the several Los Angeles areas which Strong surveyed. Hiroshima, a prefecture on the Inland Sea whose capital, later atombombed, was of substantial proportions at the time of the emigration, was the largest contributor of immigrants to America, as to Los Angeles. Little Tokyo and its environs had a plurality of Hiroshima natives—almost one-fifth of the Japanese immigrant population. A similar proportion was also found in the semi-rural Hawthorne district, while about one in three Japanese in agricultural Gardena came from Hiroshima. Yet both the Tenth Street Japanese residential district (a zone of emergence from Little Tokyo) and the San Pedro fishing community had almost no Hiroshimans.

Wakayama prefecture, on Honshu's Kii Peninsula, instead provided over two-thirds of San Pedro's Japanese population; a goodly representation was also found in Little Tokyo. Strong's data show that the Tenth Street district had a plurality of immigrants from Tottori prefecture—an idiosyncratic concentration indeed, since the investigators found almost no other Tottori natives elsewhere. Tottori was on the Japan Sea side of Honshu and was separated from

TABLE 2.5.   Composition of the Los Angeles County Population, 1890–1930

Year	Total population	Percentage non-white	Percentage foreign-born white	Percentage native-born white
1890	101,454	6.3	19.1	74.5
1900	170,298	3.7	16.2	80.1
1910	504,131	4.1	17.5	78.4
1920	936,455	4.5	17.8	77.7
1930[a]	2,208,492	4.1	16.6	79.3

[a]Mexicans computed with whites for consistency with earlier censuses.
Source: *Census 1890 P1,* pp. 586–87; *Census 1900 P2,* p. 575; *Census 1910 P4,* p. 173; *Census 1920 C1,* p. 28; *Census 1930 P2,* p. 242.

Hiroshima and Wakayama, and from major urban concentrations, by a mountainous region. Finally, Kumamoto was the home prefecture of the largest group of Japanese immigrants in Hawthorne and provided as well the second-largest concentration in Gardena. Kumamoto was a large and prosperous agricultural area on the island of Kyushu; its emigrants were also found scattered throughout Japanese Los Angeles, except in San Pedro.

In Los Angeles County, overall population growth centered in the incorporated city of Los Angeles. Between 1890 and 1920 the population of unincorporated places in the county declined from about 40 percent to about 15 percent of the total. The difference was made up by the central city, which grew from containing half to three-quarters of the county population. The total Los Angeles County population increased ninefold during those thirty years. Already by 1920 Los Angeles was a spread-out city, the first of its kind in the country. But its population concentration in the center, its tightly built-up residential neighborhoods, and its transportation system radiating from the center are all factors which point to a city, with semi-satellite suburbs.[3]

For some time the Japanese fit quite smoothly into this civilization. Table 2.5 shows that, after a sharp drop between 1890 and 1900 (due to the death and return home of many Chinese), the proportion of all nonwhites in the total population of Los Angeles leveled off at about 4 percent. The growth of the Japanese population, roughly keeping pace with the huge overall growth, largely accounts for the steadiness of this figure. Among all nonwhites in the county, the percentage of Japanese grew from less than 3 in 1900 to 41 in 1910 to 47 in 1920, gradually declining thereafter, until in 1940 the figure was only 29

[3]Robert M. Fogelson, *The Fragmented Metropolis* (Cambridge: Harvard University Press, 1967).

TABLE 2.6.   Composition of Los Angeles City Nonwhite Population, 1890–1930

	1890	1900	1910	1920	1930
Japanese-American					
Total	26*		4,238	11,618	21,081
Foreign-born		152*	3,937	8,519	11,865
U.S.-born			301	3,099	9,216
Chinese	1,871	2,111	1,954	2,062	3,009
Mexican-born	493	817	5,632	21,652	51,026 **
Negroes	1,258	213	7,599	15,579	38,894
Other non-white	35*	5*	100	550	4,376
TOTAL population	50,395	102,479	319,198	576,673	1,238,048

*Probably a considerable undercount.
**Not including a nearly equal number of "Mexicans" of American birth.
Source: *Census 1910 P5*, p. 854; *Census 1930 P1*, pp. 62–63; *Census 1930 P2*, p. 69.

percent. Even from 1920 to 1930, as the Japanese made their largest absolute intercensal gain in population, their proportion of the total nonwhite population declined.[4] The Japanese had had the good fortune to enter the county at a fairly early stage in its growth, when menial jobs were to be had without particular competition except from Mexicans, who were generally considered to be lackadaisical workers.[5] But when the Japanese-American economy entered its own entrepreneurial period, cheap labor from outside their own community was available to Japanese businessmen. Table 2.6 provides a finer breakdown of the minority race composition of Los Angeles (unfortunately, for the city only). Yet it demonstrates the stage of "racial succession" within that population, and the quantitative impact of the Japanese.

Los Angeles in 1890 was only a few years removed from its first great boom, which, according to its historian, had "wiped out forever the last traces of the Spanish-Mexican pastoral economy."[6] To be

[4] Another non-white minority from across the Pacific, the Filipinos, began to enter the population in sizable numbers at this time. Bruno Lasker, *Filipino Immigration* (Chicago: University of Chicago Press, 1931), pp. 21–25, 347–49.

[5] See the tabulations and quotations from employers of agricultural labor in California State Board of Control, *California and the Oriental* (1920), and in Governor C. C. Young's Mexican Fact-Finding Committee, *Mexicans in California* (1930).

[6] Glenn S. Dumke, *The Boom of the Eighties in Southern California* (San Marino, Calif.: Huntington Library, 1944), p. 276.

sure, much of the boom had been based on specious argument and questionable finance, a search for a lifestyle offering "an Italy nearer home—an Italy without the Italians," in Carey McWilliams's words.[7] Yet it bequeathed to the area an agriculture based on crops rather than livestock, transportation facilities, schools, population, and national fame. Growth between 1880 and 1890 had been spectacular and highly uneven, but the development of the region was not halted by the puncturing of the boom. In the closing decade of the century Los Angeles County enjoyed a 39 percent gain in population, to 170,000. The eastern end of the huge county was developing its citrus economy, while the western and southern beach communities were adding tourism and then oil to the general agriculture already there. Interurban rail linkage and Los Angeles's great man-made harbor were projects of the late 1890's and early 1900's.[8]

Los Angeles was neither a commercial nor an industrial metropolis; indeed, detractors would say it was no metropolis at all. "Expansion became the major business of the region, the reason for its existence." Industrial and mechanical pursuits occupied relatively few laborers, in contrast with the heavy concentration of workers in the building trades. Service, clerical, and trade occupations accounted for almost half of all male employees.[9] The sizable growth of the county in the first decade of the century (growth which for the first time attracted substantial numbers of Japanese) continued and even exaggerated these same tendencies.

The nature and rapidity of Los Angeles's growth is reflected in an economic structure highly encouraging to newcomers as ambitious and hard-working as the Japanese, who were willing to take advantage of the somewhat unusual orientation of the bulk of Los Angeles's domestic newcomers. "Instead of promising prospective immigrants material prosperity, southern California promoters offered them an easier, more varied, less complicated, and well-rounded life."[10] To judge from employment data, the promise was often fulfilled. People of virtually every age, race, and sex were less likely to be at work in Los Angeles than in San Francisco, or in other Pacific Coast cities. In 1900, at the beginning of the big Japanese push into Los Angeles, 40.8 percent of all Los Angelenos were in the labor force; the figure

[7]Carey McWilliams, *Southern California Country* (New York: Duell, Sloan & Pearce, 1946), p. 96.

[8]Dumke, *Boom of the Eighties;* Fogelson, *Fragmented Metropolis,* pp. 85–134.

[9]McWilliams, *Southern California Country,* p. 134; *Census 1900 Pl,* pp. 571, 573; Oscar Osburn Winther, "The Rise of Metropolitan Los Angeles, 1870–1900," *Huntington Library Quarterly* 10 (1947): 391–405.

[10]Fogelson, *Fragmented Metropolis,* p. 72.

TABLE 2.7. Percentage in the Labor Force, Selected Groups, Los Angeles and San Francisco, 1890–1920

	Males 65 + Years		Foreign-born white males	
	L.A.	S.F.	L.A.	S.F.
1890	57.8	74.4	86.9	93.4
1900	61.3	66.6	88.2	91.5
1910	NA	NA	87.7	91.6
1920	47.1	56.4	85.5	91.0

Source: *Census 1890 P3*, pp. 124, 130, 682–83, 728–29; *Census 1900 P2*, pp. 134, 143; *Census 1900 P3*, pp. 590–93, 720–25; *Census 1910 P3*, pp. 560–61, 600–601; *Census 1910 P4*, p. 163; *Census 1920 P2*, pp. 1129–32, 1226–30; *Census 1920 P4*, pp. 294, 304.

for San Francisco was 47.8 percent, and even that figure was on the low side among Pacific Coast cities. Each working person in Los Angeles supported about one-fourth again as many people as in the other cities; and, assuming (as was assuredly the case) that Los Angeles residents wanted as many goods and services as did residents elsewhere, there were more job openings in Los Angeles.

Although differences in background and in age structure contributed to the relative ease of the Los Angeles population, they do not offer the complete explanation. For example, although persons over sixty-five worked less frequently than their juniors, and the foreign-born worked more frequently than natives, persons in each category were more likely to be in the labor force in San Francisco than in Los Angeles. (See Table 2.7.) In fact, with only one consistent exception, all significant age-sex and ethnic categories show that San Franciscans were more likely to be in the labor force than Angelenos. The single exception is noteworthy: "other non-white" males, a category increasingly dominated in Los Angeles by Japanese, invariably had the opposite city-to-city tendency. In Los Angeles, "other non-white males" had a higher proportion in the labor force than any other category; females, though often in the labor force, were less often working than were Negro women. Los Angeles offered the Japanese an opportunity for quick penetration into the occupational system, and they accepted that opportunity with alacrity.

Rapid population growth and a consumer orientation encouraged a huge and speculative investment in residential real estate, keeping a high proportion of the Los Angeles labor force engaged in construction and services. At the same time, it opened certain niches into which the Japanese Americans could fit. The first sizable number of Japanese had entered the county in the late nineteenth century as section hands on the Southern Pacific and Santa Fe railroads. In the early 1900's, the railroads, preferring Mexican workers, began to lay

TABLE 2.8.   Los Angeles County Farms, 1890–1920

	Number of farms	Average acres per farm	Average value per farm
1890	3,828	199.0	NA
1900	6,577	136.2	$11,300
1910	7,919	95.7	$25,200
1920	12,444	70.9	$31,800

Source: *Census 1890 A1,* p. 200; *Census 1920 P3,* p. 76.

off Japanese hands. Seeking alternatives, the Japanese began turning to the evolving agriculture of Southern California. Especially important at first were the openings for gang-type labor.[11]

In Los Angeles, total farmland was shrinking sharply between 1900 and 1910. At the same time, the number of farms and their values increased substantially, as did the rural population, for progressively more intensive use was made of farmland. (See Table 2-8.) Farms of under ten acres (about a third of all Los Angeles County farms in 1910) almost doubled in number as larger farms were divided and put to new uses.[12] With farmland valued at $238 per acre in 1910, five times the state average and three times the 1900 values, the economics of the farm situation clearly called for highly intensive labor applied to high-profit crops.[13] The applicability of small-unit non-owner operation is apparent, given these conditions—and this was exactly what developed, much to the advantage of the Japanese.

Agriculture was to provide the backbone for an ethnic economy that sustained the Los Angeles Japanese-American community until

[11]Grace Heilman Stimson, *Rise of the Labor Movement in Los Angeles* (Berkeley and Los Angeles: University of California Press, 1955), p. 267; U.S. Immigration Commission, *Reports:* XXIII, *Japanese and Other Immigrant Races in the Pacific Coast and Rocky Mountain States,* Senate Doc. 633, 61st Cong., 2nd sess. (1911), part 1 (*Japanese and East Indians*), pp. 37–38; Immigration Commission, *Reports:* XXV, *Japanese and Other Immigrant Races in the Pacific Coast and Rocky Mountain States,* part 3 (*Diversified Industries*), pp. 7, 13, 449; Joyoshi Uono, "The Factors Affecting the Geographical Aggregation and Dispersion of the Japanese Residences [in Los Angeles City]" (Master's thesis, University of Southern California, 1927), p. 12; Chotoku Toyama, "The Japanese Community in Los Angeles" (Master's thesis, Columbia University, 1926), p. 6; *Census 1910 P3,* p. 561.

[12]*Census 1890 A1,* pp. 124–25; *Census 1900 A1,* pp. 60–63; *Census 1910 A1,* pp. 150, 156.

[13]This was also a statewide and long-term trend. Taylor and Vasey indicate that in 1899 43.3% of California crops were intensive, as compared with 49.5% in 1909 and 63.4% in 1919. Paul S. Taylor and Tom Vasey, "Historical Background of California Farm Labor," *Rural Sociology* 1 (1936): 283, 286; *Census 1910 A1,* pp. 148, 150.

World War II. But it was not agriculture alone that permitted the Japanese-American economy to grow alongside that of the whites. Other occupational developments will be treated at greater length in later chapters, along with their relationship to agriculture, but the general role of agriculture in Los Angeles County, and in the white occupational structure of Los Angeles City, should be stressed at this point. The favored Japanese-American self-image is congratulatory: hard work has paid off, say the celebrants of the group. And indeed, a combination of hard work, initiative, and trained skill played a necessary role. But the opportunities of the Los Angeles environment cannot be overlooked in explaining their great penetration there. Japanese-American economic enterprise followed the traditional pattern of minority enterprise in this country; it started out by exploiting the fringes of Caucasian economic enterprise, where initiative, hard work, and the willingness to put up with a great deal of discomfort can make a substantial difference. Los Angeles had many "fringes," as Japanese Americans discovered.

The ability of the Japanese to locate and develop such fringes explains why their community grew to 34,141 just prior to relocation;[14] it was then by far the largest such community on the American continent. But, as Louis Wirth has so eloquently shown, a ghetto is still a ghetto, even in the absence of poverty, and the Japanese Americans of Los Angeles were in the larger sense ghettoized. The peculiar characteristics of Los Angeles—its growth, its climate and the way of life associated with it, the comfort and prosperity so openly displayed—affected the resident Japanese. The size, economic security, and group aspirations of the Japanese community contributed to a large and communally vibrant ghetto. The phenomenon tells us a great deal about "separate but equal"—or, more precisely, somewhat separate and in some ways equal.

[14]U.S. War Relocation Authority, *The Evacuated People: A Quantitative Description* (Washington: Government Printing Office, 1946), p. 61.

3
The Japanese Problem

Historical justice cannot be done to California if we attribute all its excesses to base motives, or forget that the state is huge, naturally beautiful, varied, and—in important ways—different from the rest of America. People could, and still do, love California as a special place.

California entered the Union in 1850, providing the occasion for one of the periodic struggles between North and South that ultimately led to the Civil War. Though entering as a free state, California easily took over the predominant attitudes of the day, by which some races were thought to be naturally inferior to others. Meanwhile, Chinese joined those journeying to the rich gold mines which chance had uncovered shortly before the Golden State was brought into the Union.[1]

Even as Chinese immigrants began to upset white American newcomers, California Indians and Californios (Spanish-speaking natives) were suffering the depredations of the white miners from the East, their hangers-on, and the governments they established. As Mexican and Chinese miners arrived to compete with the whites, they found themselves subject to discriminatory taxation. As the mines' easily accessible wealth was taken up and California's economy began to assume a more conventionally "American" shape, its labor force assumed a "split" form, with those deemed racially inferior being held generally to the tasks considered more noxious by the dominant white majority.[2] Where transgression of the racial line

[1]This point is especially well developed in Alexander Saxton, *The Indispensable Enemy: Labor and the Anti-Chinese Movement in California* (Berkeley and Los Angeles: University of California Press, 1971), ch. 2. On the history of race and ethnic relations in California, see Roger Daniels and Spencer C. Olin, eds., *Racism in California* (New York: Macmillan, 1972), and Charles Wollenberg, ed., *Ethnic Conflict in California History* (Los Angeles: Tinnon-Brown, 1970).

[2]Saxton, *The Indispensable Enemy,* ch. 1; Bonacich, "A Theory of Ethnic Antagonism: The Split Labor Market," *American Sociological Review* 37 (1972): 547–59, with specific reference to the Japanese Americans.

seemed to threaten, symbolic violence resulted, such as cutting the queues (ponytails) of the Chinese. And more bloody violence was not absent: although most accounts of racial persecution come from San Francisco, Central California, or the diggings, the single most bloody event occurred in the sleepy city of Los Angeles, where the anti-Chinese movement was not really organized or politically potent. Here, in 1871, eighteen Chinese were massacred in one night.[3]

California had already passed twice from the hands of one race into those of another: from the Indians to the Spanish, and from Mexicans to Americans. Such a prize might well be coveted by yet another race. The Chinese represented 9 percent of the entire California population from 1860 to 1880, despite the fact that the state's population more than doubled during those years; this clearly suggested a threat. Like others of their generation, white Californians saw the "Negro problem" as the archetype of race relations, and they had no wish to repeat it with yellow people from across the Pacific. Although Chinese labor played a very important part in the building of the state, the Chinese were excluded from further immigration to the United States in 1882. Ominously, the Exclusion Act (which was to be renewed and ultimately made permanent) stated that continued Chinese immigration would endanger "the good order of certain localities." As John Higham has pointed out, the anti-Chinese movement was distinct from previous and subsequent nativistic episodes involving white immigrants, in that "Americans have never maintained that every European endangers civilization . . . [while] opponents of Oriental folk have tended to reject them one and all."[4]

The obvious richness of California, particularly of its agricultural potential, made Chinese labor or something very much like it highly desirable for many Californians. If California's history to 1850 had been one of racial succession in authority, its subsequent history has been one of racial succession in the commercial agriculture of the state, a process brilliantly described by Carey McWilliams in his *Factories in the Field*.

> In all America it would be difficult to find a parallel for this strange army in tatters. . . . Sources of cheap labor in China, Japan, the Philippine Islands, Puerto Rico, Mexico, the Deep South, and Europe have been generously tapped to recruit its ever-expanding ranks. As

[3]William R. Locklear, "The Celestials and the Angels: A Study of the Anti-Chinese Movement in Los Angeles to 1882," *Historical Society of Southern California Quarterly* 42 (1960): 239–54.

[4]Edwina Austin Avery, ed., *Laws Applicable to Immigration and Nationality* (Washington: U.S. Government Printing Office, 1963); John Higham, *Strangers in the Land* (New York: Atheneum, 1963), p. 25.

one contingent of recruits after the other has been exhausted, or has mutinied, others have been assembled to take their places. . . . In substance, it is the same army that has followed the crops since 1870.[5]

It is obviously a historical crudity to pretend that the sophisticated, educated, and peacefully organized Japanese immigrant was equivalent to the far less individualistic Chinese, or to the often uneducated and poverty-stricken Mexican laborer who preceded and followed him. Yet such was the role that the Japanese filled for a period, with majority attitudes and the nature of the job market determining their position.

As such, the Japanese immigrant was the recipient of much of the ambivalence that characterized reactions to the Chinese, which Gunther Barth has analyzed: "Strike and acculturation were the opposite poles of the reaction toward the Chinese sojourners, the varied manifestations of which crystallized around work camp and Chinatown. Both reactions existed side by side like the set of conflicting notions sustaining American California."[6]

Between 1880 and 1890, when Japanese immigration to North America became numerically significant, the Chinese population in America held roughly stable at 100,000. In the 1890's Chinese departures approximately equalled Japanese arrivals; only between 1900 and 1910 did the total number of Orientals increase substantially, as Japanese arrivals outnumbered Chinese departures.[7] In this period, too, important anti-Oriental agitation resumed for the first time since 1882. It was now directed against the Japanese.

The first sign that the new Oriental immigration would not be accepted without incident came in early 1900. In San Francisco a bubonic plague scare led to an organized protest against Chinese and

---

[5]Bogardus describes early acceptance but subsequent hostility as part of a "race relations cycle" which seems to be part of the natural history of racial antagonism, at least in California. Among the many who have employed this schema, McKenzie expands it in empirical application and theoretical relevance. "The plantation and pioneer belts of the world" have typically attracted and briefly encouraged Oriental immigration. But "as a region passes from a pioneer to a settled condition, the human material that was once of value becomes a source of annoyance and trouble." Emory S. Bogardus, "A Race Relations Cycle," *American Journal of Sociology* 35 (Jan., 1930): 612–18; R. D. McKenzie, *Oriental Exclusion* (Chicago: University of Chicago Press, 1928), quotation on pp. 11–12, application to Japanese Americans on p. 30; Carey McWilliams, *Factories in the Field* (Boston: Little, Brown, 1939), pp. 7–8.

[6]Gunther Barth, *Bitter Strength: A History of the Chinese in the United States, 1850–1870* (Cambridge: Harvard University Press, 1964), pp. 129, 131.

[7]U.S. Bureau of the Census, *Historical Statistics of the United States, Colonial Times to 1957* (Washington: U.S. Government Printing Office, 1960), p. 9. As with the Japanese, Chinese population clustered in California.

Japanese, in whose quarter the plague was thought to center. Reacting to this agitation, Japanese in America created their first strong central organization, formulated with consular advice, to present a unified strategy with which to meet white hostility and deal with other problems.[8] This defensive move was an important step in the self-definition of the group as a unit apart. Conflict heightened as the accelerating threat of Japanese labor competition led the Labor Council of San Francisco to found the Japanese and Korean Exclusion League. Political scandal and ferment in that city and the scrambling of residential patterns following the famous earthquake contributed to the animosity toward the Japanese. The Exclusion League emphasized the menace presented to white schoolgirls by older male Japanese students; their solution was segregation. By 1907 the agitation had become so respectable that Theodore Roosevelt, previously annoyed at the crudity and impolitic approach of the San Franciscans, now admitted that the reaction to the Japanese was "complicated by genuine race feeling."[9] Racial issues were serious issues, and the Gentlemen's Agreement was achieved only by much heady diplomacy, domestic and international. According to its terms, Japan would voluntarily forbid unskilled laborers to emigrate to the United States.

The international implications of domestic anti-Japanese agitation were never again quite so threatening. But California passions became more general and more excited, as the Gentlemen's Agreement failed to prevent wives and others not affected by the agreement from swelling California's Japanese population. A new spectre appeared: the second generation, Oriental in guile, spirit, and blood, but possessed of American citizenship and American English. These new Americans would in many cases not be children of poverty: the Japanese were doing well.

Japanese progress was particularly apparent on the land, and it was here that whites sought to defend their heritage. In California the anti-Japanese forces had formed an invaluable alliance with small farmers and the Progressive movement. They succeeded in pushing an alien land bill through the California legislature, despite federal efforts to avoid this embarrassment to American-Japanese rela-

[8]Michinari Fujita, "The Japanese Association in America," *Sociology and Social Research* 13 (1929): 211–28; Hidesaburo Yokoyama, "The Japanese Association in America" (Master's thesis, University of Chicago, 1921). A repaginated version of this thesis, from which I have taken information, is Major Document 279, Box 6, SRR Papers.

[9]Roosevelt to Kermit Roosevelt, Feb. 4, 1907, quoted in Raymond A. Esthus, *Theodore Roosevelt and Japan* (Seattle: University of Washington Press, 1966), p. 149.

tions.[10] California's Alien Land Law of 1913 forbade aliens ineligible for citizenship (essentially a euphemism for alien Japanese) to own land for agricultural purposes, though it did permit three-year leases.[11] Agitation resumed again in earnest at the end of World War I. The first triumph of the anti-Japanese forces was a new California Alien Land Law, passed in 1920; as an initiative measure, it gave California voters a chance to demonstrate to one another their solidarity on the racial question. Even greater was the triumph of 1924, when a section of the Immigration Act recapitulated the national solution that had ended the Chinese menace. With passage of the exclusion measure, agitation again subsided. The ultimate then conceivable under the Constitution had been achieved. The proscribed group was now free to develop as best it could, given the disabilities placed upon it.

Not the Japanese but the Japanese question was treated differently in Los Angeles. The agitation in the north had repeatedly struck sympathetic but muted chords in Los Angeles, each time failing to establish the lasting and respected organization needed to keep the question before the people. To the extent that the history of the Japanese in California is one of active persecution, Los Angeles is the exception; to the extent that this history is one of quiet but distinct subordination, Los Angeles is the rule. Los Angeles betrayed no lingering doubt of the correctness of racial discrimination; rather, it displayed an uncertainty about how to draw a line that could exclude Japanese from some endeavors but not from those which were important to the economy and to the smooth functioning of business in the area. They would permit the Japanese certain freedoms without also extending these freedoms to the Mexicans, Negroes, and Filipinos; and they would barely broaden the range of permissible activities for the new generation of Japanese Americans when they came of age as citizens. The fact that the line grew increasingly sketchy as the Nisei approached maturity points to the tacit collusion of the immigrant leadership in the earlier operation. The arrangement as it evolved was not a stable one: the life of a ghetto is dependent upon the mainte-

[10]George Mowry, *The California Progressives* (Chicago: Quadrangle Books, 1963), pp. 154–55; Spencer C. Olin, "European Immigrant and Oriental Alien: Acceptance and Rejection by the California Legislature of 1913," *Pacific Historical Review* 35 (1966): 303–15; James B. Kessler, "The Political Factors in California's Anti-Alien Land Legislation, 1912–13" (Ph.D. dissertation, Stanford University, 1958).

[11]California was by no means alone in thus restricting landownership. Alien land legislation eventually obtained in eleven other states, most notably Washington, Oregon, and Arizona. Milton R. Konvitz, *The Alien and the Asiatic in American Law* (Ithaca: Cornell University Press, 1946), p. 161.

nance of attitudes that surrounded its creation and sustained its members.

When San Francisco labor first took up the cry against the Japanese in the schools,[12] two organizations were spawned: the Anti-Jap Laundry League and the broader Asiatic Exclusion League. Both of these early anti-Japanese groupings made efforts to organize themselves "in the various communities that are suffering from Japanese competition." The Laundry League failed to create a local branch in Los Angeles, in spite of the State Federation of Labor's request that the local councils provide "at least their moral support." Although the Exclusion League won monetary support in Los Angeles (and the purchase of 25,000 "Fire the Jap" stickers), cooperation was ineffective and short-lived.[13]

Los Angeles lacked many of the elements which made the Chinese and Japanese "problems" exposive in San Francisco. Most notably absent was a well-organized labor movement based on white immigrant groups which used racial rhetoric to develop its side of a conflict over jobs and within which tenuous alliances in part depended upon "the indispensable enemy."[14] In the formative years, organized labor in Los Angeles had very seldom come into conflict with Japanese laborers, whose confrontations were usually with Mexican agricultural laborers.[15] Los Angeles labor read of the Japanese in the labor force before having first-hand contact. Two kinds of opinions set the poles between which the labor movement vacillated before finally settling upon an orthodox anti-Japanese position.

[12]The year 1905 saw an explicitly discriminatory piece of legislation, according to the terms of which Japanese would have to pay tuition to attend California public schools. It passed the almost completely Republican Assembly by a 39–13 vote, later to die in the Senate. Quite consistent with their strong indebtedness to the powerful Southern Pacific machine, which opposed the San Francisco agitation, three of the five Los Angeles assemblymen opposed the bill. San Francisco's representatives, by contrast, voted 14–0 for it. California, *Journal of the Assembly,* 36th sess. (1905), p. 1789 (vote on A.B. 837); Franklin Hichborn, "California Politics, 1891–1937" (unpublished manuscript in Haynes Foundation Library, University of California, Los Angeles), III, 1227–30.

[13]*Los Angeles Citizen,* July 2, Aug. 20, 1909 (minutes of Central Labor Council, June 25 and Aug. 15), Apr. 2, 1909, Apr. 22, 1910 (minutes, Apr. 15), Dec. 22, 1911, May 10, 31, June 7, 1912; Anti-Jap Laundry League, *Pacific Coast Convention,* first (1908), second (1909); California, *Journal of the Assembly,* 38th sess. (1909), p. 426 (motion to reconsider A.B. 79); Roger Daniels, *The Politics of Prejudice* (Berkeley and Los Angeles: University of California Press, 1962), p. 28.

[14]This is the central thesis in Saxton, *The Indispensable Enemy.*

[15]Marginal whites were also involved in some of these conflicts, especially among citrus pickers. Stuart Marshall Jamieson, "Labor Unionism in Agriculture" (Ph.D. dissertation, University of California, Berkeley, 1943), I, 131–32; Letter of John Knoit, Alhambra, *Los Angeles Socialist,* Feb. 22, 1902.

The San Francisco–oriented State Federation of Labor championed a pure racial-frontier outlook: "The Japanese, by adopting our forms of dress only outwardly conform to the Western standard of civilization, in their customs and morals remaining essentially Japanese; that is [,] men of a lower standard of morals, of a lower standard of wages, men of a race that has never assimilated with the Caucasians, but which race has always pulled down and pulled down irresistibly, the men of the Caucasian race that have been forced into contact with men of the Mongolian race."[16]

This viewpoint was challenged in Los Angeles by accounts of a two-month Japanese agricultural strike in nearby Ventura County. So successful were the Ventura Japanese against the sugar beet planters that in 1903 the Central Labor Council of Los Angeles memorialized the AFL executive board in Washington, professing that the heroic fight in Ventura "against starvation wages and iniquitous conditions" had allowed the Japanese to prove "their courage and manhood." Since they had now "emerged from their ordeal with unbroken ranks," the Japanese were obviously worthy of organization by American labor. Although the Council favored exclusion of further Japanese immigrants, "we heartily favor the thorough organization of those already here."[17]

Nevertheless, isolated outbursts by local whites became more frequent as Japanese migration to Los Angeles continued; at least one confrontation involved a near shoot-out, squelched by the law after considerable bloodless swaggering.[18] But before Los Angeles labor would adopt an outspoken anti-Japanese position, San Franciscans had to make an active propaganda effort. The vehicles were the publications of the labor-sponsored Japanese and Korean Exclusion League and the communications of its leading spirit, Olaf Tveitmoe.[19] By late 1906 Los Angeles labor took up the fight with verbal

[16]California State Federation of Labor, *Proceedings, 1904,* p. 47. Two years earlier, similar views had been expressed by the Federation; the year before that the Los Angeles Central Labor Council had approved the formation of a State Federation committee to study the advisability of general Asiatic exclusion. Grace Heilman Stimson, *Rise of the Labor Movement in Los Angeles* (Berkeley and Los Angeles: University of California Press, 1955), pp. 216–17.

[17]Quoted in Norman Lowenstein, "Strikes and Strike Tactics in California Agriculture: A History" (Master's thesis, University of California, Berkeley, 1940), pp. 22–23, 97–98.

[18]Los Angeles *Times,* Dec. 6, 1904, Mar. 27, 1905; *Common Sense,* Dec. 10, 1904, Apr. 15, 1905 (letter of J. B. Rutherford).

[19]As late as June 1, 1906, a large signed editorial in the *Union Labor News* of Los Angeles came out in favor of exclusion, but insisted that exclusion did nothing to solve the other immediate Oriental problem, that of the Japanese already here. "The only logical course to pursue under the circumstances is to organize him, and teach

ferocity, giving its "hearty" and unqualified endorsement to the lobbying activities of the Japanese and Korean Exclusion League. In June, 1907, the Los Angeles Central Labor Council trumpeted the demise of its earlier ambivalence in the columns of its official newspaper, the *Citizen*: "Japs to the right of them, Japs to the left of them, Japs in front of them. . . . Japanese have not only taken the place of girls [in domestic service], but are also putting the negro and chink out of business on the Pacific Coast. *Compact organization* is the only way to fight these people *and their employers*. There is now being waged, all along the Pacific Coast, the *fiercest struggle in labor history between organized capital and the trades unions*."[20]

A week later the *Citizen* printed a darkly humorous canard about the Japanese, one which would have remarkable parallels a generation later. The *Citizen* had happened upon a Japanese-language street map of Los Angeles which provided proof of the immensity and immediacy of the Yellow Peril: the map was a clear military asset to the Imperial hordes. The patent ludicrousness of the charge did not embarrass the *Citizen*: "To be sure a Japanese caught with such a map as this in his possession could easily assert that he used it purely for commercial purposes, or to find his way to the houses of friends. . . . But the fact remains that for war purposes . . . nothing more scientific than this same map could have been developed."[21]

After one more week, the entire history of the Japanese in America was rewritten in Yellow Peril imagery, and imaginatively connected with the plight of Los Angeles labor.

IN CASE OF WAR WITH JAPAN. . . . Henry E. Huntington would seek safety behind several regiments of carmen, and the thousands of Japanese that he has gathered upon his [railroad] "system" would be as dangerous to the Pacific Electric as they are now a menace to the American working class. It is not for nothing that thousands of Japanese have been employed laying rails all over the Pacific Coast: How long would it take these same oriental constructors of road beds to destroy the lines of communication which they have helped to build? America will pay the penalty of [Los Angeles *Times* publisher, Harrison Gray] Otis' hate by a war which may lay waste the Pacific Coast. The Huntingtons and the Otises come dear![22]

him the love of luxury. . . . The Jap is willing to be organized, and has demonstrated on numerous occasions that he appreciates organization." Z. W. Craig, in *Union Labor News,* June 1, 1906. On the efforts of northern labor to bring the agitation against the Japanese to Los Angeles, see *Union Labor News,* Feb. 2, 23, Mar. 23, Dec. 14, 1906.

[20]*Los Angeles Citizen,* June 7, 1907.
[21]*Ibid.,* June 14, 1907.
[22]*Ibid.,* June 21, 1907.

Self-consciously, at the behest of the rampant and politically involved labor forces of San Francisco, Los Angeles labor leaders drew a caste line between themselves and the Japanese and identified the latter with labor's class enemies.

Los Angeles had other organs of opinion which were themselves uncertain about how to react to the Japanese. The business community's chief voice was the staunchly anti-labor Los Angeles *Times*. Like most others, businessmen thought in racial categories; but their outlook on the Japanese was informed as well by their economic role. And to the extent that San Francisco organized labor opposed the Japanese, Los Angeles businessmen saw some virtue in them.

Over the first decade of the new century, business's outlook on the Japanese became less distinct, as familiarity with the Japanese bred doubts about their tractability. Initially the Japanese seemed a fully acceptable substitute for the excluded Chinese, and "the gist of all this [anti-Japanese] agitation is to be found in the action of the labor union leaders at San Francisco . . . [who] are trying to involve the entire state in their little controversies." But the marked entrepreneurial tendency of the Japanese raised doubts in the minds of the businessmen who had sponsored them as docile laborers. By 1907 Los Angeles businessmen and their press opinion would neither associate themselves with the anti-Japanese bandwagon, nor actively oppose it.[23]

In the previous year the business-backed superintendent of schools had defied local labor opposition[24] in declaring that "there is no Japanese question here" and no need for segregated schools for Orientals.[25] But within three months the Los Angeles *Times* had adopted a new tack, in response to the economic progress of the local

[23]Secretary of Merchants and Manufacturers Association late in 1906, quoted in Herbert B. Johnson, *Discrimination Against Japanese in California* (Berkeley: Press of the Courier Publishing Company, 1907), p. 18. The Los Angeles *Times* expressed the identical position on Dec. 5, 1906. On press opinion more generally, see Eleanor Tupper and George E. McReynolds, *Japan in American Public Opinion* (New York: Macmillan, 1937), p. 28; see also "Real Attitude of the Pacific Coast toward the Japanese," *Literary Digest* 34 (1907): 43–44.

[24]"If the working people had chosen and elected to office school trustees and superintendents of their own class there would be no questions as to what would be done—but, as it is, the employers have decided that the Japs shall be admitted to the public schools, for our employers have elected the officers in charge" (*Union Labor News*, Nov. 23, 1906). Note that this statement slightly preceded labor's full conversion to the San Francisco position.

[25]Superintendent E. C. Moore, Los Angeles *Herald*, Feb. 3, 1907; U.S. Immigration Commission, *Reports: XXXI, Children of Immigrants in Schools, General Tables Vol. 3*, Senate Doc. 633, 61st Cong., 2nd sess. (1911), pp. 566–603, 613–14.

Japanese and to California's chauvinistic reflex to Japan's anger at insults suffered at San Francisco. "The Times has frequently expressed the opinion that the exclusion of Japanese children of proper age from San Francisco schools was foolish, that it is a labor-union subterfuge to force exclusion of Japanese laborers from the country. . . . But . . . the Japanese government should be impressed with the fact that an education for aliens is a privilege to be sued for, not a right to be demanded."[26]

Originally having ignored the racial frontier idea, businessmen now chose to take it up. Such spokesmen for business as the Los Angeles Chamber of Commerce could not afford to voice outright support for Japanese immigration. Instead, they dreamed of the readmission of rational, temporary, unaggressive, Chinese coolie labor. Non-white, non-permanent immigrants were unquestionably needed for the citrus and produce industries of southern California: "For this work we need the Chinese and Japanese and essentially the former. To all practical intents a discussion of the immigration problem in Southern California is synonymous with a discussion of the Chinese question. . . . We feel that reciprocity between our country and China is the key to our immigration problem."[27] Thus, a "Japanese question" of nominally local application had with some effort been defined in Los Angeles. By 1910 the racial frontier had been clearly impressed upon the minds of defenders and opponents of the Japanese.

Within three more years the *Times* had become dubious about the virtues of the Japanese, wishing that they (like the Chinese) would "cultivate their gardens, and clean clothes, and make and sell kimonos." The article continued: "We have tolerated if not invited Japanese to acquire and cultivate a trifling quantity of land, and engage in a limited amount of commercial and industrial pursuits in our midst. They are, as a rule, peaceful and law-abiding, though

[26]Los Angeles *Times*, June 19, 1907. The Los Angeles *Examiner,* the recently established Hearst outlet then appealing to labor, declared that "the Japanese are a great people, a wonderful people, but they must not be allowed to run this country or any part of it. Any suggestion to the contrary coming from Japan, or even the White House, insults every American worthy of his citizenship in the republic. . . . The lesson of the San Francisco agitation is . . . that *we should hasten to acquire a navy adequate to safeguarding our interests and upholding our honor*" (Los Angeles *Examiner,* Feb. 5, 1907).

[27]Los Angeles Chamber of Commerce, *Members' Annual, 1910*, pp. 62–63. In the previous year the Chamber had opposed efforts to exclude Japanese—a statement officially "deprecated" by the Central Labor Council, which by now sought a definitive confrontation with business on the Oriental question. *Members' Annual, 1909*, p. 35; *Los Angeles Citizen*, Mar. 4, 1910.

inferior to the Chinese in these qualities. They engage in no labor to the detriment of any American who is willing to work.''[28] But the *Times* came out against the Alien Land Laws, partly for commercial and developmental reasons, but particularly because of its contempt for [Governor] ''Holy Hiram [Johnson] and his freak legislature.''[29] Even Hearst's *Examiner,* which held that the California Japanese ''live encysted in their orientalism as a foreign growth within the American body politic,'' fulminated mainly against Japan rather than against the Japanese Americans.

Los Angeles was almost without agitators at this time, when Japanese agricultural development of local resources was at its most brilliant.[30] With politics to which the Japanese issue was peripheral, with a labor movement which declared that it was ''not . . . especially interested in the present Japanese agitation'' (although the Central Labor Council did petition the California legislature in behalf of the bill), without the class of avocational anti-Japanists that it would eventually develop, Los Angeles made little effort to dissent from the *Times.*[31]

The Alien Land Law of 1913 was ineffective, but it was not until 1919 that agitation again broke out in California. James D. Phelan of San Francisco, Democratic senator and anti-Oriental of long standing, was up for reelection in 1920. During speaking appearances he found that in California the Japanese issue had suddenly developed life. References to strong Japanese demands at Versailles meshed neatly with recitals of the failure of the Gentlemen's Agreement to stabilize the Japanese population and the failure of the Alien Land Law to prevent increasing Japanese farm proprietorship. Phelan's biographer concludes that ''what perhaps started as an incidental

[28]Los Angeles *Times,* Apr. 20, 1913.

[29]Los Angeles *Examiner,* Apr. 22, 1913.

[30]One letter to Governor Johnson expressed the agony which this development caused for some: ''In the name of every one of the thousands of small ranch owners in the state, whose land had been his hope for a living but now is unproductive—whose income has been cut off by the killing competition of the Japs & Chinamen we demand of the state that the land shall *not be leased* for more than one year. . . . The year lease to Japs & Chinks has *already* cost us our home market and we cannot exist if our small homes are ruined by these aliens who have driven us out of the business of raising small fruits and vegetables on our ranches. I have protested in print and by letters to our representatives. . . . If we are to till the soil and produce these small fruits & vegetables at all the alien must be frustrated from using the land at all.'' H. F. Nelson, Gardena, to Johnson, May 2, 1913, folder ''N. Misc.,'' Box 37, Hiram Johnson Papers, Bancroft Library, Berkeley, Calif.

[31]*Los Angeles Citizen,* May 2, 1913; California, *Journal of the Assembly,* 40th sess. (1913), p. 2463; Clarence Hunt, ''Grizzly Growls,'' *Grizzly Bear,* May, 1913, p. 8, July, 1913, p. 2.

argument soon became the major issue itself."[32] To take advantage of this heightened public awareness, a stronger alien land bill was proposed. For somewhat complex reasons,[33] it eventually reached the 1920 ballot as Initiative Proposition 1.

As officially presented to the electorate by its proponents, the new land law "simply closes the loopholes in the 1913 law." But no aware Californian could have been ignorant of the fact that the 1920 Alien Land Initiative was a referendum upon Phelan's slogan, "Keep California White," and served as a rehearsal for the final push for exclusion. Opponents of Proposition 1 were traitors to California, "white Japs."[34] Phelan put his version of the Japanese question quite explicitly to the respectable City Club of Los Angeles: "Time has shown that there is no assimilation by marriage of Asiatics and our people. The Japanese remain permanently a foreign colony. . . . Where races cannot mingle there is no democracy, and incidentally the situation results in a lowering of the standards of the civilization. . . . Of course, we would not submit to that, so the situation would result in local more or less sanguinary conflicts."[35] In Los Angeles, Phelan claimed, the "dread" of the Japanese was "just as pronounced as in central California."

Support quickly gathered. The most important voice belonged to the Native Sons of the Golden West, a group which defined itself in a recruiting advertisement a few years later: "If for no other reason than to be identified with a group of men willing to make any sacrifice for the welfare of California," they exhorted, "every White native-born son should be affiliated with this organization."[36] In October, 1919, a Los Angeles "joint Anti-Asiatic Committee" was convened

[32]Robert Edward Hennings, "James D. Phelan and the Wilson Progressives of California" (Ph.D. dissertation, University of California, Berkeley, 1961), p. 346.

[33]These had to do with the alternating sessions employed at the time by the California legislature, the peculiar nature of Governor Stephens's tenure as the inheritor of the governorship following Johnson's departure for Washington in 1919, and the concern of the federal government lest Japan be offended by California's actions.

[34]*Amendments to Constitution and Proposed Statutes with Arguments . . . General Election . . . November 2, 1920* (n.p., n.d.). Hunt, "Los Angeles Bulletin," *Grizzly Bear*, Dec., 1920, p. 20, is the first known use of the "white Jap" notion.

[35]Los Angeles *Examiner*, March 12, 14, 1919. The City Club had earlier shown an interest in the Japanese question, hearing major spokesmen on behalf of the Japanese during or after agitations of the question. A man of appearance as dignified as his office, Phelan obviously had entree to this sounding board of respectable Los Angeles opinion which had been denied to his predecessors among the anti-Japanese. City Club of Los Angeles, *Annual Programs, 1907–17.*

[36]*Grizzly Bear*, Dec., 1933, p. 24.

by the Native Sons, in order to hold weekly meetings and to encourage other like-minded groups. On November 15, 1919, the committee formally reorganized itself as the Los Angeles County Anti-Asiatic Society. Chief components of the Society were the Native Sons, the American Legion, and (briefly) organized labor. Chairman, both at its organizational meeting and subsequently, was Sheriff William I. Traeger, a potentate in the Native Sons. The other officers were either Native Sons or persons professionally involved in law enforcement. By August, 1920, the Society, now attached to the statewide Asiatic Exclusion League, had a working alliance with the senatorial campaign of James D. Phelan, himself a leading Native Son.

Although Los Angeles finally had an organization of avocational anti-Japanists, the Society failed to gain the steady adherence of some likely allies. The Los Angeles Farm Bureau Federation had been at the forefront of a state federation campaign to deny farm proprietorship to Japanese, but it preferred to remain independent of the County Anti-Asiatic Society.[37] Organized labor was likewise lukewarm in its relations. At first represented, labor edged away from the Anti-Asiatic Society and seems to have rejected membership in January, 1920, after "considerable discussion," although the *Citizen* eventually gave weak support to Phelan and Proposition 1. A *Citizen* editorial in favor of the initiative measure explicitly stated that the devotion of Los Angeles labor to the anti-Japanese cause was less than it once had been: "The present agitation against the Japanese once more forcefully illustrates the fact that nothing is ever done for Labor unless it is done by labor. Years ago the trade unionists of San Francisco, operating through the Asiatic Exclusion League, started the agitation against the Japanese which is now being seized upon by politicians of every degree."[38]

[37]Floyd William Matson, "The Anti-Japanese Movement in California: 1890–1942" (Master's thesis, University of California, Berkeley, 1953), p. 52; Los Angeles *Evening Herald*, Oct. 26, 1920; Los Angeles *Times*, Jan. 17, 1920; House Committee on Immigration and Naturalization, *Hearings, Japanese Immigration* 66th Cong., 2nd sess. (1920), pt. 3, pp. 940, 970. Phelan was a substantial contributor to the treasury of the Los Angeles Society. Los Angeles *Times*, Feb. 9, 1920; telegram, Phelan to Traeger, Dec. 31, 1919, Box 13, James D. Phelan Papers, Bancroft Library, Berkeley, Calif.; Phelan, press release, Feb. 21, 1920, folder "Japanese file 1917–1919," carton 15, *ibid.;* open letter, unsigned but on Asiatic Exclusion League letterhead to Fred F. Bebergall, folder 2, Box G II, JERS Collection; *Grizzly Bear*, Oct., 1920, p. 20, Nov., 1919, p. 22, Dec., 1919, p. 22; Los Angeles *Times*, Nov. 2, 1919.

[38]*Los Angeles Citizen*, Jan. 16, 1920 (minutes of Central Labor Council, Jan. 9), July 23, Sept. 17, Oct. 1, 22, 1920.

Another potential ally not realized was the prosperous business class of Los Angeles, for by the 'teens such men had discovered that the Japanese threatened their image of racial dominance. In 1920 the Los Angeles Chamber of Commerce supported Japanese exclusion, which was "an economic [question] entirely. . . . America needs every tillable acre for her own people, and particularly is this so in California."[39] "A Japanese born of a Japanese father is always a citizen of Japan," argued Dr. George P. Clements, energetic head of the Chamber's agricultural department. Since this ancestral tie linked the Japanese in America with intensive farming, the basis had been laid for tragedy in California. "The question can he be assimilated is beside the mark. We do not want to assimilate him"[40]—California was white man's country. But the Chamber of Commerce gave no open support to the Anti-Asiatic Society. Instead, the ideal was reflected in the growing cry of businessmen for temporary Chinese agricultural labor. Such labor, according to the *Times,* "would replace none of the white workers in California industries," but "would break the Japanese corner on the food market."[41]

As ultimately constituted, the component units of the Los Angeles County Anti-Asiatic Society included the Native Sons and Daughters, the American Legion, two neighborhood associations, organizations of county and city civil servants, the Heavy Odd Contractors' Association, a law fraternity, one church brotherhood, and token representation from Democratic and Republican county central committees.[42] Aside from these, all the adherents were social

[39]Los Angeles Chamber of Commerce, *Members' Annual, 1913,* p. 50; *1914,* p. 31; *1917,* pp. 53–55; *1920,* p. 63; *1921,* p. 29; House Committee on Immigration and Naturalization, *Hearings, Japanese Immigration,* pt. 3, p. 1008. See also Better America Federation of California, *Weekly Newsletter,* 1920, esp. Dec. 15; *Los Angeles Saturday Night,* Sept. 11, 1920.

[40]Los Angeles Chamber of Commerce, *Members' Annual, 1927,* p. 147; George L. Clements, "Dr. Clements Tells Realtors Why Southern California Needs Diversified Farmer," Los Angeles *Examiner,* Dec. 16, 1923; "Survey Interviews Southern California No. 2," SSR Papers; Clements, typescript draft of address "The Japanese Problem" (n.d.), and typescript draft of address "A Practical and Peaceful Solution of the Japanese Problem," Mar. 21, 1921, both folded in Clements's copy of *California and the Oriental,* folder 63, George P. Clements Papers.

[41]Los Angeles *Times,* Jan. 11, Mar. 14, 1920.

[42]An invitation to Meyer Lissner by C. K. McClatchy, highly influential in Progressive circles and an exceedingly devoted anti-Japanese spokesman, noted that "a big play could be made down in certain quarters in your district . . . in reference to the Japanese menace." The remark was unheeded however, and the Japanese question remained peripheral to all but Phelan's politics. McClatchy to Lissner, Apr. 24, 1920, folder 643, Meyer Lissner Papers, Stanford University.

organizations: women's groups, lodges, clubs, and state societies.[43] The Anti-Asiatic Society was in composition as in ideology simply a nativist fraternity.

The Society guarded the racial frontier ("the political, economic, social, moral and religious standards that are the precious heritage of our fathers") with utmost seriousness. Recognizing "no higher obligation to our State, our nation, our descendants and to ourselves" than to stop the Japanese menace, they supported the alien land initiative, urging abrogation of the Gentlemen's Agreement and an end to treaties which fettered the power of Congress to limit immigration. The Society further argued for a constitutional amendment to repeal *jus soli* for children of aliens ineligible to citizenship.[44] Their purpose was not to alter the relationships among groups, but to underline in law the existing caste structure, which they believed was threatened by the success of the Japanese in America and of Japan as a nation, and to perpetuate that structure unto the second generation.

Conspicuously absent from the anti-Japanese crusade in Los Angeles were several types of people, whose absence helps define the ultimate weakness of the movement. First, there was no racial theorist of the Madison Grant school of patrician eugenicism; racial dominance, not racial purity, was fundamentally at issue in Los Angeles. The only arguable exception to this generalization was Montaville Flowers, a member of the press committee of the Los Angeles County Anti-Asiatic Society and a one-time candidate for Congress. His career and notions were, however, somewhat erratic. A native of Cincinnati who had resided in semirural Los Angeles County since his thirties, Flowers was a lecturer and educational entrepreneur (Flowers' Academy of Music and Dramatic Arts). He dated the "new immigration" from 1850, after which America's shores began to receive "another breed of men . . . a large proportion of them . . . weak individuals from the weaker mixed people of lower-standard countries. These filled and overflowed the melting pot." Self-delusion prevented Flowers's contemporaries from recognizing that after this dilution "by other ideas, motives and racial genius . . . the transforming forces in the crucible were dead." Such prejudices may have been too much for most of the Native Sons; they

[43]*Grizzly Bear,* Oct., 1920, p. 20; Daniels, *Politics of Prejudice,* p. 144, n. 22. During the eighteen-month campaign against the Japanese that culminated in the election of 1920, several small interest-oriented groups (*e.g.,* the Pasadena Horticultural Association and the Southwestern Grocers' Association) expressed anti-Japanese views but were never successfully incorporated by the County Anti-Asiatic Society. *Los Angeles Citizen,* Oct. 24, 1919; Los Angeles *Times,* Dec. 25, 1919; Pasadena *Post,* June 10, 1920; *Grizzly Bear,* Mar., 1920, p. 23.

[44]Los Angeles County Anti-Asiatic Society, letter to the editor, Los Angeles *Times,* Sept. 26, 1920.

drew the line to include all native-born whites and, accordingly, began to take in increasing proportions of "new immigrants." Flowers seems to have been connected only slightly with the mainstream of Los Angeles anti-Japanism.[45]

Likewise absent were progressives, although important local people of progressive concern like John Randolph Haynes and Katherine Phillips Edson at one time or another publicly expressed unfavorable views of the Japanese immigration. Haynes, whose particular political passions were direct legislation and municipal ownership of utilities, spoke in 1912 of the undesirability of Asiatic immigration "on account of the gulf existing between their modes of life and thought and ours." But in the midst of the 1920 campaign, when Phelan was the embodiment of anti-Japanese fervor, Haynes (who supported him) wrote his reactions to the campaign without so much as mentioning the Japanese issue. Mrs. Edson, whose leading political concern was for the welfare of the laboring man, wrote in 1921 that there would and could be no intermarriage between Japanese and Caucasians, and that therefore "the Japanese must live in colonies apart from the whites." However, her correspondence takes no note of the anti-Japanese agitation of 1920.[46]

The anti-Japanese cause in Los Angeles also lacked a tough labor leader like Olaf Tveitmoe, who led the fight in San Francisco in the early years of the century. John Buzzell, long-time secretary of the Los Angeles Central Labor Council, had leanings of this kind, but his thoroughly pragmatic attitude encouraged him to lead in the mainly abortive attempt to organize the citizen generation of Japanese before World War II, despite the fact that as late as 1930 he had argued that "social reasons" were making the creation of segregated public schools for Japanese a necessity in Los Angeles, since "in many places it is becoming more and more apparent that Japanese are so numerous."[47]

[45]Montaville Flowers, *The Japanese Conquest of American Opinion* (New York: George H. Doran, 1917), p. 204; *Who Was Who in America, 1877–1942* (Chicago: Marquis, n.d.), I, 408.

[46]Haynes, "Address before the Sunset Club, March 29, 1912," typescript, folder "Immigration—United States," John R. Haynes Collection, Haynes Foundation Library, University of California, Los Angeles; Haynes to Phelan, Sept. 1, 1920, folder "Direct Legislation—California—1920 (Correspondence, Sept.)," *ibid.*; Edson, untitled draft for article intended for publication in *The Woman Citizen,* second of two articles (and correspondence there), Box 1, Katherine Phillips Edson Papers, Department of Special Collections, Library of the University of California, Los Angeles.

[47]Richard Norman Baisden, "Labor Unions in Los Angeles Politics" (Ph.D. dissertation, University of Chicago, 1958), pp. 60–61; Los Angeles *Citizen,* May 30, 1930.

Lacking competent theoreticians and knowledgeable or influential agitators, Los Angeles anti-Japanism remained a loose-knit series of complaints and complainants. The most coherent line of attack developed in Los Angeles was little more than a furious indictment of whites who failed to perceive the racial struggle for California. Those who encouraged the Japanese were not just mistaken but were actually race traitors, and likely venal.[48] The ultimate maintenance of the racial frontier would involve a national decision, but the East and the federal government could not or would not understand that "the Japanese question . . . is national and vital to all the people of the United States, [and] is universal wherever white men dwell and Japanese ships may anchor."[49]

The shrillness of the Los Angeles agitators helped render their efforts fruitless. V. S. McClatchy, publisher of the Sacramento *Bee* and leading light in the statewide California Joint Immigration Committee, was struck by this fact after visiting Los Angeles in 1924 to look into the state of the Japanese question there. He reported to the members of his Committee:

> The aloofness which exists in the southern part of the state is undoubtedly partly to blame for the fact that our side of the question is very little understood . . . . [I spoke to leaders on both sides of the issue and] explained to them how we are working in San Francisco, and strongly urged that they follow a similar method [in] in-forming themselves by friendly contact as to the point of view of the other fellow, and as to the facts, and then making their decision, which, of course, would be in accordance with our established principles. . . . Our Los Angeles friends believe in the aggressive methods, and up to this time have declined even to meet with the other side. I suggested that without any sacrifice whatever of principle they might be able to accomplish their ends more quickly and with less friction if they were in closer contact

[48]See for example Hunt, "Los Angeles Bulletin," *Grizzly Bear,* Apr., 1923, p. 6.

[49]Flowers, *Japanese Conquest of American Opinion,* pp. 3, 53. As late as 1927 the secretary of the now moribund Los Angeles County Anti-Asiatic Society asked whether it was "not time for Americans who want our Pacific Coast to remain a white man's country to begin operations for its defense? It will not be safe to trust Washington, for the Federal administration apparently is far more interested in destroying, than in strengthening, national defense. There is considerable sentiment in the East that is anything but friendly to California's racial problems. There is every possibility that China and Japan may find European allies to attack the East coast when they move upon us. The Pacific Coast may have to fight alone against a virtual Pan-Asiatic combination. Ways and means to strengthen ourselves should receive immediate consideration." Arthur Robert Hinton, "California's Very Existence Threatened," *Grizzly Bear,* Apr., 1927, p. 3.

with their opponents. I am inclined to believe they are disposed to favorably consider the suggestion.[50]

McClatchy had been invited to Los Angeles by George Gleason of the YMCA, who was sympathetic to the Japanese and believed that their cause could be aided by conciliation. McClatchy also believed that relations with the resident Japanese could and should be free of conflict, once the exclusion question was settled and once the resident Japanese had accepted their caste position. Although McClatchy and Gleason developed considerable rapport, the former was never able to induce any reconciliation between his Los Angeles allies and the Japanese they intermittently persecuted; nor could he persuade the local anti-Japanese to tone down their attacks, since their victory consisted largely in reemphasizing the caste line—an end accomplished adequately by sound and fury.[51]

The "aggressive methods" of local anti-Japanists brought no new action in Los Angeles, but that was not because racial attitudes there were any different from those elsewhere. The 1920 Alien Land Law initiative measure proves this. Then 74 percent of the voters in Los Angeles approved further hindrances on Japanese American agricultural activity, the same proportion as in California as a whole; if this was the unquestioned pre-1942 peak of Los Angeles anti-Japanism, the results of the initiative also show that widespread racism per se, in the absence of conducive structural arrangements, does not make a movement. For in 1920 the question of race was put as crudely, and as overtly, as possible.

James D. Phelan, of course, epitomized this brand of legitimated racism in his campaign tours in Los Angeles:

> Wherever I went in the beautiful and productive regions about Los Angeles, I could not but feel a shudder at witnessing the disappearance of the white man's family. . . . I am sure that rural Los Angeles county, where for every three births one is a Japanese, will realize before it is too late that there is a duty just before us which we will have to perform. We must stop this yellow tide and regain the soil for our own people. Fortunately we have the remedy at hand—to vote "Yes"

[50]McClatchy, "Progress Report," Oct. 30, 1924, typescript, folder "McClatchy, Valentine Stuart, 1924–26," Box 72, Phelan Papers.

[51]Gleason to McClatchy, July 23, 1923, folder "Los Angeles Hollywood Japanese Presbyterian Church, 1924–65 Reserve, #1," Papers of the United Presbyterian Church in the United States, Southern California Headquarters. The records were made available to me by the Church's director of public relations, Edward A. K. Hackett, to whom I am greatly indebted. California Joint Immigration Committee, Minutes, Jan. 29, 1926, typed copy in folder 2, Box G II, JERS Collection.

on initiative amendment No. 1 and to elect men to defend the interests of the State.[52]

The truck farms and produce markets of Los Angeles had become the great battlefield in which two tendencies of world history, one white and democratic and the other yellow and despotic, confronted one another. The sale of a bunch of celery to a white shopper by a Japanese, or the rental of a couple of acres by a white to a Japanese farmer, were viewed by the scoffing East Coast as domestic acts of little significance. Yet Phelan believed and hoped that Californians would agree that the westward transit of white civilization was in danger of being reversed in California. On these terms the campaign ground on inexorably toward the quasi-military, quasi-moral confrontation which Phelan promised at the polls.

The moral turpitude, produce monopoly,[53] illegal fishing methods, illegal entry, unsanitary farming practices, and national ambition of the Japanese were attacked by Phelan or his local allies. Phelan publicized a nearly incredible tale about a diabolical attempt by a trusted Japanese houseboy to murder a wealthy Los Angeles matron who earlier, knowing the menace of the Japanese to America, had discharged her many families of Japanese tenants.[54] In an anti-Japanese screen epic, "Shadows of the West," one could see "the hardships of Washington and His Continentals, the struggle of Lincoln for unity and freedom . . . contrasted with the Asiatic's en-

---

[52]Los Angeles *Examiner,* Oct. 17, 1920; Los Angeles *Evening Herald,* Oct. 25, 1920. Phelan worked hard but with little success to establish more concrete local relevance for his issue. As early as March, 1919—when he was just beginning his anti-Japanese fulminations—he asked his ally, who served as the collector of the Port of Los Angeles, for confidential information; he hoped to use such information to involve the Japanese consul at Los Angeles in a scandal involving the illegal entry of his countrymen. A month later Phelan was investigating the possibilities of a Japanese menace by way of a large purchase of land in Baja California. Telegram, John B. Elliott to Phelan, Mar. 14, 1919; Elliott to Phelan, Apr. 4, 1919, Box 50, Phelan Papers; Los Angeles *Evening Herald,* Mar. 25, June 15, 18, 1920; Los Angeles *Examiner,* Apr. 16, July 13, 1920.

[53]A small boycott at one point resulted from this attack. Later Phelan told a Los Angeles audience that he had "been told that in Los Angeles a Japanese sits at a telephone and dictates the prices of vegetables through out the district." Los Angeles *Times,* July 16, 1920; Los Angeles *Examiner,* July 20, Oct. 19, 1920.

[54]Death was planned by placing "a dozen small pieces of bamboo—sharp splinters—each inclosed within a binding of sinew" in the matron's food. She was saved by the ministrations of a physician who happened also to be a leader of the Democratic party in Los Angeles. A Japanese spokesman noted wryly about the supposed attempt: "Of course she never masticated her food!" San Francisco *Examiner,* Oct. 7, 1920; K. K. Kawakami, *The Real Japanese Question* (New York: Macmillan, 1921), p. 140.

slavement of women. . . . Constitutional law is placed beside emperor worship; feudal Asiatic tenets, engrained in the Oriental mind for generations, are proved to be non-assimilable with a government founded upon the Christian doctrine and dedicated to liberty and freedom."[55] Those who chose to defend the Japanese, Phelan explained, merely expose the influence "of this alien host within our boundaries." His forces sought not a majority but a landslide—in order, as Sheriff Traeger put it, "to answer eastern criticism."[56]

Despite the defeat of Phelan (who made only small inroads in highly Republican Los Angeles), the returns were presumably satisfying to the Anti-Asiatic Society. The tremendous popularity of the initiative measure showed how nearly the repression of the Japanese Americans represented a consensus in Los Angeles. Although there were variations in the intensity of feeling about the Japanese problem, Angelenos quite clearly had sided with Phelan, and with his opponent, Samuel Shortridge, who was only less vocal about their common attitudes toward the Japanese: California was to be kept white, and harassment of the Japanese Americans was a way to accomplish that goal.

Within some precincts the vote in favor of the new version of the Land Law was as high as 90 percent; in only ten precincts out of more

TABLE 3.1. Vote on Alien Land Initiative and Social Characteristics of Eight Areas in Los Angeles County, 1920

	L.A. City Assembly Districts				L. A. County cities			
	63rd	65th	72nd	73rd	Whittier	Pasadena	San Gabriel	Huntington Park
es on Initiative (%)	73	73	77	78	59	67	73	77
ll 16–20 years school (%)	51	19	46	27	46	49	15	33
ative whites native rentage (%)	60	22	59	44	80	62	36	58
on-whites (%)	2	12	1	—	—	1	6	—

Source: Los Angeles County Board of Supervisors Minutes. Record of General Election 1920 (Book #73-A); *nsus 1920 PI*, pp. 118–22, 125.

[55]*Grizzly Bear*, Oct., 1920, p. 7. The review in the Los Angeles *Examiner* (Oct. 5, 1920) reported that "the scene at the docks when the terrified girls [later rescued by the American Legion] are packed off by an uncouth crowd [of Japanese] and speedily put to exhausting work made a deep impression on the audience."
[56]Los Angeles *Evening Herald*, Oct. 23, 1920.

than 1,250 did as many as two-thirds of the voters oppose the legislation. Yet the breadth of the popular anti-Japanese consensus thus revealed should not obscure the kinds of variations which permit us a glimpse into the social dynamics of popular racism. Table 3.1, exhibiting voting patterns and selected social characteristics for selected areas, gives us our first clues.

The table suggests a certain relationship between the vote and social characteristics, both for independent cities and for assembly districts within Los Angeles City. It also includes striking exceptions.[57] Those expressing the highest degree of dislike for the Japanese on the alien land initiative did tend to be in areas of lower socioeconomic status, as suggested by the small proportion of 16–20-year-olds attending school and the small proportion of the native white population who were of native parentage. Areas less supportive of Proposition 1 tended, conversely, to be better off. The proximity of non-whites, as shown in the social characteristics in the table, does not seem to have been directly relevant to the initiative vote. But the table also highlights the fact that certain poor cities and districts did not vote strongly against the Japanese, and that some well-off districts and cities were not unusually mild in their treatment of them at the polls. Although nothing conclusive can be argued from such data, a mapping of the more than 1,250 precincts of Los Angeles reveals regularities which are understandable in light of what we know about areas and neighborhoods. The materials needed for analyzing the precinct vote are presented in Map 1.[58]

Anti-Japanese concentrations were particularly common within Los Angeles City. Most existed in the relatively industrial areas to the southeast, extending outside the city into neighboring industrial suburbs, although also taking in the middle-class residential area near Exposition Park.[59] Other clusters of high approval appeared in the

[57]The table includes extreme districts in the initiative vote and in the socioeconomic status measures for Los Angeles City and County tabulation.

[58]The map was constructed by drawing curves through the outermost precincts of clusters consisting of at least eight precincts; some were uniformly high (80% or more approval of Initiative Measure 1) or low (60% or less approval). The cluster in Covina was smaller but stood out equally from its surroundings. The exact boundaries of local opinion on the Japanese question are arbitrary as shown on the map, but the general locations of such areas are certain. Note how the clusters overlap political boundaries. The map is based upon Record of General Election 1920 (Book #73-A), manuscript, pp. 833–77, in Minutes, Los Angeles County Board of Supervisors.

[59]Data characterizing localities proved hard to find. My characterization is somewhat impressionistic, depending upon extrapolations from the present appearance of housing and upon photograph books and guidebooks and local histories of all kinds (which, however, generally slight the less impressive areas). Particularly

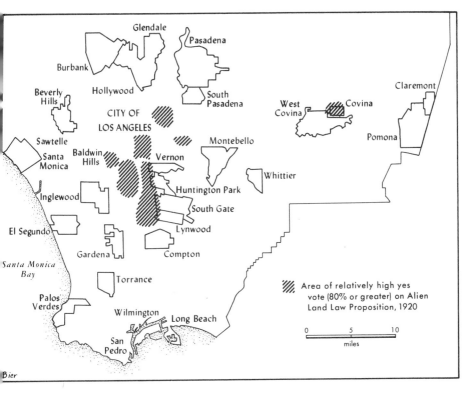

Los Angeles County (excluding San Fernando Valley) and selected minor civil divisions, 1920, showing areas especially opposed to Japanese land ownership.

relatively poor single-family dwelling areas south of Highland Park and East Los Angeles, as well as in Covina, an attractive agricultural area. Areas relatively favorable to the Japanese included one distinctly upper-class residential area within Los Angeles City, but two other somewhat nondescript quarters. The suburban centers of comparatively mild feeling toward the Japanese were found in the upper-middle-class towns, in the oil-and-resort city of Long Beach, and in three widely separated agricultural areas in the eastern portion of the county.

The residents of areas like Pomona, where citrus brought the kind of serenity the Chamber of Commerce liked to boast about and where "the moral atmosphere is just as splendid as the life-giving air that makes the city a health resort," were understandably unconcerned about Phelan's feverish racial fantasies.[60] In Claremont, which as a whole voted *against* the land law (the only town in the county to do so), the response to the anti-Japanese alarms can be attributed to an extremely successful community church encompassing twenty-one denominations, to the colleges located there, and to a citrus-grower population devout and prosperous enough to heed the sentiments of their church on racial issues.[61] In Whittier, moral atmosphere was likewise an important consideration. A fruit-and-nut town with extensive oil deposits, Whittier was named after the Quaker poet. The new First Friends Church had an auditorium capable of holding 1,700 people, and congregants carried out missionary activity in the neighboring towns and among Mexicans and Japanese.[62]

Conversely, lower-middle-class commuting-manufacturing areas like Watts, which boasted of being "distinguished for its seven hundred daily trains" and of being "one of the most successful and

---

useful was Eshref Shevky and Marilyn Williams, *The Social Areas of Los Angeles* (Berkeley and Los Angeles: University of California Press, 1949), analyzing 1940 United States Census tract data, and *Census 1920 P1,* pp. 114, 118–22.

[60]I am unable to explain Covina, which was distinctly "high" when it should have been "low" on the alien land initiative. Traditionally Republican, all white, and moralistic on the Prohibition question, Covina had seemed like any citrus town. Lacking detailed research into its deviance on the Japanese question, one can only point to it as an extreme example of the putative influence of local climate of opinion, perhaps attributable to a local Native Son of great influence, or a crusading newspaperman who shared Phelan's viewpoint. The history of Covina by Donald H. Pfleuger is competent, but reveals nothing that might distinguish its residents from their fellows on the Japanese issue. Pfleuger, *Covina: Sunflowers, Citrus, Subdivisions* (Covina: By the Author, 1964).

[61]*Los Angeles and Southern California Guide Book, 1907-8* (Los Angeles: Los Angeles Home Company, n.d.), pp. 204–5; Philip Smead Boyd, "A Community Church in California," *Missionary Review of the World* 41 (1918): 364–66.

[62]Benjamin F. Arnold and Artilissa Dorland Clark, *History of Whittier* (Whittier: Western Printing Corporation, 1933).

strenuous of suburbs in the world,''[63] seemed to be prime targets for the kind of chiliastic bombast put forth by Phelan and the Native Sons. Although these areas were not objectively threatened by the Japanese, their residents did not want the California which to them held out such promise handed over to an alien race. Yet where Japanese were most immediately undermining the economic basis of white California (in the parlance of the anti's), the areas of the most intense Japanese agricultural cultivation, like Inglewood, Gardena, and Compton (in southwest Los Angeles), Santa Monica, Redondo, and Venice (in the western beach areas), or Van Nuys, Lankershim, and Burbank (in the valleys to the north of the central city), no anti-Japanese concentrations could be found. These areas were slightly above average on the anti-Japanese side, but only slightly. Intangibles, then, appear to have been as important as economic self-interest.

The 1920 campaign against the Japanese was a highly propagandistic effort on the part of a few people to make a quiet social problem into an emotional question of immediate import. The overwhelming support received by the Alien Land Law points to their success. Despite its ostensible agrarian appeal, family-farm areas in Los Angeles were no higher than average on the Japanese issue; the prosperous citrus area was relatively unantagonistic to the Japanese. Especially mild were areas in which moral issues like prohibition had made inroads; these, of course, tended to be upper-income areas. By contrast, the Japanese issue aroused the greatest passion in lower- and lower-middle-income areas where working-class political consciousness and progressivism were at their highest, and where the Democratic party and Phelan in particular did well at the polls.[64]

The alien land initiative brought the Japanese issue into unaccustomed prominence, with an essentially symbolic meaning. The Japanese had repeatedly demonstrated that they knew their place in every realm but the economic. But the growth and increasing prosperity of the Japanese community, and the evidence that neither its resources nor its ambition precluded further growth and prosperity aroused California chauvinists, whose racist rhetoric reflected the common but unspoken beliefs of most white Californians. Although the Japanese had been an economic boon to the white man, when the question was forcefully posed in Los Angeles, most white citizens

[63]Los Angeles Chamber of Commerce, *Los Angeles County, California* (Los Angeles: By the Chamber, 1925), p. 18.
[64]Rogin's analysis of California voting—mainly by counties—during this period has shown a relationship among progressivism, the labor vote, and support for Woodrow Wilson. Michael Rogin, ''Progressivism and the California Electorate,'' *Journal of American History* 55 (1968): 297–314.

(especially those least attuned to the Protestant morality) chose symbolically to interdict their progress. A "Yes" vote, desperately contradicting the experience which prompted it, proclaimed the inferiority of the Japanese. Officially recorded, the vote in and of itself was the triumph of its authors.

But although Los Angeles Japanism was not especially active, it was widespread; thus the glory of the anti's was short-lived. Within a month of their electoral success, the Anti-Asiatic Society began to curtail activities. By its own admission it was "about at the end of its financial resources" and was reduced to soliciting small contributions in the Native Sons monthly, the *Grizzly Bear*.[65] With the Yellow Peril again on the defensive, the Society provided an occasional forum for the disgruntled;[66] even the *Grizzly Bear* stopped mentioning the Society after its financial breakdown.[67] Native Sons assumed responsibilities for local anti-Japanese activity, sometimes in conjunction with the other component organizations of the efficient California Joint Immigration Committee: the California Department of the American Legion, the State Grange, and the State Federation of Labor.[68]

The campaign against resident Japanese fishermen originated outside Los Angeles. In 1920 Phelan had attacked the Los Angeles Japanese fleet on grounds of illegal registry as well as superefficiency, maintaining that behind this convincing front the fleet hid its real functions: espionage and the smuggling of Japanese laborers.[69] When anti-alien fishing bills were introduced in the 1921 legislative session, their original architect was a senator from inland Sacramento County. Because of the California Joint Immigration

[65]Traeger and H. C. Lichtenberger to Phelan, Dec. 2, 1920, folder "Lichtenberger, H. C.," Box 20, Phelan Papers; *Grizzly Bear*, Dec., 1920, p. 20; Los Angeles *Examiner*, Oct. 6, 1920. A similar and simultaneous poverty affected the statewide association. Los Angeles labor in early 1921 agreed to open its mailing list for the Asiatic Exclusion League and to raise its share of the $200,000 fund needed by the League. The campaign failed roundly, in part because Los Angeles labor made no effort to fulfill its promise. Daniels, *Politics of Prejudice*, p. 97; *Los Angeles Citizen*, Mar. 4 (minutes of Central Labor Council, Feb. 25), 11, 1921.

[66]For example: *Long Beach Press*, May 19, 1923; Los Angeles County Anti-Asiatic Society to A[lfred] E. Smith, Oct. 1, 1928, folder "McPike, Henry H.," Box 74, Phelan Collection.

[67]Two exceptions are *Grizzly Bear*, Nov., 1922, supplement, p. 3 (which reports an election in the Society), and Hinton, "California's Very Existence Threatened." Officers, presumably as of 1928, are on the letterhead of the Los Angeles Anti-Asiatic Society to A. E. Smith, Oct. 1, 1928.

[68]Daniels, *Politics of Prejudice*, pp. 96–105; Minutes, Jan. 19, 1925, California Joint Immigration Committie (CJIC); Preliminary Report, Jan. 11, 1927, typescript, folder 4, Box G II, JERS Collection.

[69]Los Angeles *Evening Herald*, Mar. 25, June 18, 1920.

Committee's perception that "presentation of the case . . . [should] be made to the Legislature by parties from San Pedro and Monterey familiar with the facts," the 1923 version was sponsored by a Los Angeles assemblyman.[70] The integration of the Japanese fishermen of Los Angeles into the industry there, and especially their close relationship to the large American canneries, made efforts to hinder their fishing activities economically and politically unwise. Clarence Hunt of the *Grizzly Bear* blamed the defeat of the 1923 anti-alien fishing bill on "twenty-five California State Senators, the Los Angeles Chamber of Commerce, the Southern California tuna-packing trust, [and] a number of protestant ministers."[71] The somnolence of the anti-Japanese of Los Angeles continued throughout the 1920's and into the 1930's, despite occasional echoes of Phelanesque claims—such as that of a sharp-eyed seaplane pilot who noticed "imperial Japanese navy sailors in motor boats from Japanese imperial government oil tankers, at anchor in the San Pedro Outer Harbor, making soundings at various places in the inner harbor."[72] This was not to be the last time that Japanese in Los Angeles would be flayed for the tendency of their fellow plotters in the Japanese military to seek out by stealth information which they could readily purchase legitimately.

Anti-Orientalism in Los Angeles seems to have been a kind of essentially open and honorable activity, like that of the volunteer fireman; it attracted joiners at every level of eminence but the highest. Among its more prominent practitioners were the vile-mouthed and furiously energetic Clarence Hunt, whose initial success had been achieved by rescuing the *Grizzly Bear* by cheapening its paper, typography, and tone;[73] the totally genial Eugene Biscailuz, long-time Los Angeles County sheriff and friend of everybody;[74] the

[70]California, Legislature, *Final Calendars of Legislative Business,* published for each session; Ted Cook to Morgan Keaton, Aug. 11, 1923, copy in folder 4, Box G II, JERS Collection; Minutes, Dec. 1, 1924, CJIC; Preliminary Reports, Dec. 20, 1926, Jan. 11, 1927, folder "1924–26," Box 20, Phelan Papers.

[71]Hunt, "Grizzly Growls," *Grizzly Bear,* May, 1923, p. 3.

[72]*Ibid.,* Apr., 1926, p. 1.

[73]In addition to working on the *Grizzly Bear,* Hunt was on the board of directors of the Los Angeles County Anti-Asiatic Society beginning in 1919. He continued his anti-Japanese efforts until his death in 1943, at times in a column called "Japa-graphs." Hunt was not the first to bring up the Asiatic menace in the *Grizzly Bear,* although the magazine did not begin concerted agitation of the issue until 1911 (after several years of his editorship). A native of Placer County, he moved to Los Angeles in 1905. Herman C. Lichtenberger, "The Grizzly Bear Established in the Interest of the N.S.G.W.," *Grizzly Bear,* June, 1910, p. 10; Los Angeles *Times,* Oct. 8, 1943.

[74]Biscailuz, a native of Los Angeles, was in 1919 a deputy sheriff and important enough to be appointed a member of the board of the Los Angeles Anti-Asiatic Society. Biscailuz was a local society president of the Native Sons by the age of

restrained but ambitious William I. Traeger, Stanford football all-American who used business-like methods to advantage in the Los Angeles sheriff's office before turning it over to Biscailuz;[75] and Buron Fitts, a thoroughly self-seeking and successful politician.[76] With the exception of Hunt, none of these men considered their anti-Japanese work important to their careers: in no obituaries or other contemporary accounts was there mention of their anti-Japanese organizational work, except in the context of articles specifically on the subject which appeared at the time of the work. However vital they momentarily considered the Japanese issue to be, even for

---

twenty-four. In the sheriff's office, he served as Traeger's right hand for public relations, riding a white palomino and becoming identified with many ceremonial functions; in 1933 he succeeded Traeger as sheriff. Biscailuz was famed for his propensity for joining all possible organizations, but his interest in the Japanese issue was sufficient that in World War II he again attacked that much maligned group. Lindley Bynum and Idwal Jones, *Biscailuz, Sheriff of the New West* (New York: William Morrow, 1950).

[75]William Isham Traeger was born in 1880 in Tulare County and moved to Los Angeles after graduation from Stanford. After his brief tenure as a football coach, Traeger held a number of political appointments in law enforcement and in the courts, both before and after he earned a law degree from the University of Southern California. His administration of the sheriff's office prided itself on being a "model of efficiency." Traeger remained in office from 1921 until 1933, when he resigned to become a congressman. In Congress he served one term in utter obscurity. Traeger was a Grand Trustee of the Native Sons, and in 1921 was State Grand President. The Sons regarded him as their central figure in Los Angeles on the Japanese question; his services in this cause were manifold and of unusual duration. Clarence Hunt, "Popular Native Son Passes," *Grizzly Bear,* Feb., 1935, p. 19; *Who Was Who,* I, 1250; Peter T. Conmy, "This History of California's Japanese Problem and the Part Played by the Native Sons of the Golden West in Its Solution" (Los Angeles: The Native Sons, 1942); "Orientals Not Wanted," *Grizzly Bear,* May, 1920, p. 4; John D. Costello (Phelan's secretary) to F. Ray Groves, July 19, 1920, folder "1920, July," Box 14, Phelan Papers.

[76]Buron Fitts was director of the campaign committee of the Los Angeles Anti-Asiatic Society in 1920, at which time he was deputy district attorney of Los Angeles County. He later became a member of the executive committee of the Oriental Exclusion League of California. The logic of his selection for the former post later became quite clear, as Fitts moved with skilled steps to the California lieutenant governorship at the age of thirty-one, in the administration of conservative Republican Friend S. Richardson. In his subsequent tenure as district attorney of Los Angeles, he was seldom on the side of the angels. But his reputedly profitable entente with the growing underworld of the city failed to affect his ability to be reelected until he was finally unseated in 1940. Born in Texas, Fitts was prominent in California American Legion activities, serving as the second elected California department commander (1920–21). June Elizabeth Hallberg, "The Fitts-Palmer Campaign for District Attorney in Los Angeles County, 1936" (Master's thesis, University of California, Los Angeles, 1940); Jerry Saul Caplan, "The CIVIC Committee in the Recall of Mayor Frank Shaw" (Master's thesis, University of California, Los Angeles, 1947).

them it was a fleeting concern, a racial frontier which needed only occasional defense.

When V. S. McClatchy inveighed against the Los Angeles anti-Japanese, he had in mind a short-lived publication, *SWAT the JAP,* which appeared in 1923. *SWAT,* whose title was taken from a phrase of Clarence Hunt's, declared itself to be "like a Godsend from a troubled sky, and with the backing of every real American"; it urged a total economic boycott of Japanese Americans by all who were "100 per cent American and believing in the inferiority of all Asiatics."[77] This activity in 1923 had meaning which struck closer to the hearts of white Angelenos than had the several terrors so bravely combatted by anti-Japanese in 1907, 1913, and 1920. The earlier campaigns had been waged to bar Japanese from full participation in American economic life; in contrast, 1923 was to mark the high point of a sporadic agitation in Los Angeles over residential "invasions" by Japanese Americans.

The 1920 vote had shown that the working man was most susceptible to the scare campaign over the Yellow Peril in California agriculture. Apparently the strength of feeling was not all that great, despite the Asiatic Exclusion League's efforts to portray the purchase of a bunch of celery from a Japanese vegetable stand as an act of treason. Far stronger feelings were generated in the minds of those who felt more directly threatened by the advance of the Japanese race, for the arrival of the Japanese foreshadowed the decline of the neighborhood in which one had invested. A neighborhood where Japanese lived was not a "nice" neighborhood, despite the almost universal testimony (even of those who feared the "invasion") that the Japanese themselves were "nice." The neighborhoods threatened were socially not unlike the areas that most strongly opposed the Japanese on the Alien Land Law.

The area from which the Japanese community was spreading was no beauty spot. Adjacent to Skid Row, Little Tokyo offered the Japanese Americans generally cramped and often dilapidated housing. The price was right, however, and toleration was great in a mixed-ethnic part of the city. In the 1920's these virtues continued to

[77]A photograph of the first issue of *SWAT the JAP* is in Uono, "Geographical Aggregation," between pp. 140 and 141. A typed copy of a later issue is in folder, "Los Angeles Hollywood Japanese Presbyterian Church, 1924–64, Reserve, #1" (henceforth "Presbyterian folder"), United Presbyterian Church File. Though *SWAT* was wholly outrageous, the Central Japanese Association become concerned enough not only to discuss the matter with law enforcement officials, whom they understandably mistrusted, but to arrange a $500 payment to the *SWAT* editor by the Japanese Consulate. Central Japanese Association, Minutes, June 8, 1923: Los Angeles Japanese Association, Minutes, Aug. 12, 1923.

appeal to unattached Japanese-American workingmen and to recent arrivals; however, the burgeoning population of Japanese-American families, whether long-term local residents or new arrivals from elsewhere on the coast, began to aspire to more suitable surroundings in which to raise their children. The question was not an "American" as against a "Japanese" setting; being a converted, rundown piece of the Los Angeles downtown, Little Tokyo bore few identifiably Japanese qualities other than commercial signs. Nor were the Japanese Americans seeking to move out of the ethnic context in which they were comfortable and institutionally well-served. The question, from the Japanese point of view, was housing, pure and simple. Not so, from their opponents' point of view.

That genuine and heated contention should prevail in the realm of housing can be understood when one realizes what Los Angeles stood for to its white residents, and had come to mean for its Japanese inhabitants. The Chamber of Commerce, of course, was exaggerating when it stressed Los Angeles as an idyll—and Fogelson is being naive in treating Los Angeles's white immigrants as though they believed such talk in a literal sense.[78] At issue were areas in which workingmen had caught glimmers of prosperity: a "bungalow" that might be described as "charming," with a "Spanish touch" in its design, and a wide, neat street.

At the time of the conflicts both Japanese and white communities were undergoing rapid growth. Japanese business was in its period of most dramatic expansion, with resultant prosperity and corresponding drives for comfort, beauty, and respectability. Residence became, for the Japanese, an aggregate symbol of their status within their own community. Japanese men married as they could afford it; many saved in order to escape the crowded, commercial downtown. Gardeners pioneered new neighborhoods, attracting friends and relatives. Churches and their associated social services followed (and sometimes slightly anticipated) the movement of their members, seeking better and more dignified facilities in newer areas. The intense mobility and speculative outlook of many white residents made possible the initial Japanese advances.[79] Nineteen outbursts stemming from residential invasion are known to have occurred between 1919 and 1926. (See Map 2 for the locations of many of

[78]Robert M. Fogelson, *The Fragmented Metropolis* (Cambridge: Harvard University Press, 1967), ch. 4.

[79]Joyoshi Uono, "The Factors Affecting the Geographical Aggregation and Dispersion of the Japanese Residences [in Los Angeles City]" (Master's thesis, University of Southern California, 1927), pp. 86–140.

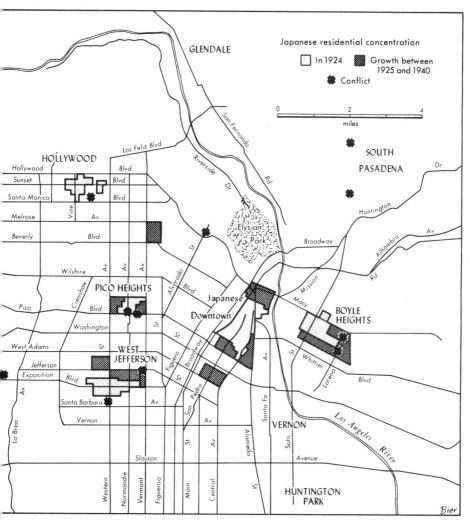

Central Los Angeles, showing areas of Japanese residential concentration, 1924 and 1940, and location of residential conflicts, 1920-40.

these.[80]) In 1919, most areas outside Little Tokyo were fairly new to the Japanese; the further expansion of their growing community brought them up against white homeowners. Already many high-class developments, like Glendale and Beverly Hills, had proscribed Japanese and other non-whites by deed restrictions or restrictive covenants.[81] The practice was encouraged by realtors, whose code stressed "careful consideration for land values when introducing members of less well-appreciated groups into neighborhoods."[82] The city of Montebello refused to accept new subdivisions unless deed restrictions were written in.[83] A similar practice was carried out less formally in Azusa, an area which had been relatively favorable to the Japanese in the 1920 vote. Even Whittier realtors agreed "not [to] sell [to] Mexicans or Japanese outside certain sections where it is agreed by community custom they shall reside." But in the variegated city of Los Angeles, the Realty Board could only "recommend that Realtors should not sell property to other than Caucasians in territories occupied by them."[84] Unified public pressure could not be brought to bear. This was particularly true in the housing of inter-

[80]Besides references which will be cited elsewhere in this chapter, see SRR Papers; Uono, "Geographical Aggregation"; Chotoku Toyama, "The Japanese Community in Los Angeles" (Master's thesis, Columbia University, 1926); John Anson Ford, *Thirty Explosive Years in Los Angeles County* (San Marino, Calif.: The Huntington Library, 1961), pp. 150–54; Los Angeles City Council, Petitions, Volumes 2538, 2539, 2542, files numbered 2890, 2920, 3318, typescript, Los Angeles City Archives; *Rafu Shimpo,* Oct. 4, Nov. 26, 1933, Aug. 10, 1934, June 9, 1941; *Kashu Mainichi,* Sept. 4, 1938. Marks indicate only general neighborhood, not precise location.

[81]A Los Angeles deed restriction dating from before 1919 denied the owner, on pain of the reversion of the property, to "lease or sell any portion of said premises to any person of African, Chinese or Japanese descent." Cited in *Title Guarantee & Trust Company* v. *Garrott,* 42 Cal App 152, p. 153 (1919). Forest Lawn Cemetery, perhaps the most famous if not the most desirable real estate in Los Angeles, included among its rules (legally construed as part of the deed by which a plot was transmitted) that "no interment of any body other than that of a human being of the Caucasian race should be permitted in the said Forest Lawn Memorial Park." *Forest Lawn M. P. Association* v. *De Jarnette,* 79 Cal App 601, p. 603 (1926).

[82]*The Real Estate Hand Book of California* (Los Angeles: Real Estate Publishing Company, 1929), p. 297; John F. Keogh and M. L. White, *Building and Race Restrictions* (Los Angeles: Title Guarantee and Trust Co., 1931).

[83]Such a practice was probably unconstitutional, even under the then-current interpretation of the Fourteenth Amendment, as an illegal discrimination by a government.

[84]Serena B. Preusser, "Color Question in California Reveals Many Problems," *California Real Estate* 7 (July, 1927): 35, 61. Some of the questionnaires on which this article was based are found in folder "Segregated Housing," Box 1, SRR Papers.

mediate age and quality. Such residences were occupied by whites of modest income, and their organization in defense of racial standards was often too late and too weak to prevent the first break in the neighborhood armor.

The Japanese were not the only group whose aspirations for better housing threatened the Anglo homogeneity that was part of most of middle-class life in Los Angeles. Negroes, "foreigners," and even renters (too unstable for local tastes) moved as did the Japanese, often into the same neighborhoods. The university area was reasonably new and quite comfortably built-up, though in rather flat and dull terrain about a mile south and two miles west of the central city; in the early 1920's it was threatened simultaneously by blacks and Japanese. Typically, white residents admired the Japanese at a distance.[85]

> There are a large number of Japs and Negroes down the street and I hope they never get up here. I think the world of Japanese people and would rather have colored help to white any day, but I certainly do not want to live in their midst. Where we lived before we had a Jap servant. They are the nicest people to have around. . . . But I would not want to live in a district surrounded by any foreign race.

> Personally, I really prefer Japs. They keep their places neater. They are very fond of gardening and plants in a yard add much to its looks. They also keep their houses painted better. The Japs won't buy a house if there is a feeling of antagonism among the neighbors. One Jap came to me and said quite frankly that he would like to buy the house but would not consider it if the neighbors had a feeling against his moving in. I assured him that there was a feeling and I wouldn't sell either to the Japanese or to the colored people.[86]

Despite the obvious success of the Japanese accommodationists in projecting the desired image of their group, most whites did not want them as neighbors. Petitions against the colored invasion followed

[85]Bessie A. McClenahan, "The Changing Nature of an Urban Residential Area" (Ph.D. dissertation, University of Southern California, 1928). Bogardus discusses the neighborhood incidents as episodes in the "race relations cycle." Emory S. Bogardus, *The New Social Research* (Los Angeles: Jesse Ray Miller, 1926), pp. 256–62. Frequently Japanese and Negroes lived adjacent to one another, the Negroes having somewhat superior accommodations on the whole. Uono, "Geographical Aggregation," pp. 105–6; Housing Authority of the City of Los Angeles, California, *Housing Survey Covering Portions of the City of Los Angeles, California* (Report of the Works Progress Administration), II: Statistical Tables and Graphic Charts (mimeographed, 1940), Table DS-66.

[86]Quotations from neighborhood respondents in McClenahan, "Changing Nature of Urban Residential Area," pp. 203–4, 198.

informal discussions by neighbors of their common distaste for the newcomers.

A neighborhood association was next formed, progressing from generalized negrophobia to a more clearly defined goal: a restrictive covenant which would shut out non-Caucasians. The University District Property Owners Association succeeded in gaining at least verbal cooperation from most residents, in framing their covenant legally, and in making it "a part of the mores in certain sections in the area."[87] The confrontation between the University District whites and the invading colored people was a mild one, relatively well organized and nondemagogic. Analogous circumstances slightly to the north (where Negroes were not involved) occasioned a far more explosive outburst.[88]

By 1919, about a hundred Japanese families dwelled in the Pico Heights neighborhood, an unimpressive, aging subdivision mainly occupied by working-class whites. The Japanese families frequently paid high rents for the least desirable housing in the neighborhood. In that year or the next, an undetermined number of white residents, assisted by an official of the Los Angeles County Anti-Asiatic Society, decided to rid their environs of the Japanese. They formed the Electric Home Protective Association to serve, in effect, as the poor man's restrictive covenant.[89] From the beginning, Association leaders hoped to use their neighborhood agitation as the foundation for an anti-Japanese constituency of larger scope.[90] Their immediate technique, however, was to visit Japanese residents, asking them in terms more pointed than polite to leave the neighborhood in deference to property values. This policy continued on a small scale for several years.[91] Only two years later, when a more dramatic invasion

---

[87]*Ibid.*, p. 218. The Association later sought to have a segregated neighborhood school built, and a Negro janitor at the existing school fired. It succeeded in the latter but failed in the former.

[88]The only violence engendered by neighborhood conflict with Japanese occurred in 1923, when a Japanese home in the Evergreen-Belvedere district, thought to be the highest quality among Japanese areas, was set on fire. Even Clarence Hunt repeatedly opposed violence and was embarrassed by the incident. Los Angeles Japanese Association, Minutes, June 19, 1923; Hunt, "Los Angeles Bulletin," *Grizzly Bear,* July, 1924, p. 37, Aug., 1924, p. 37.

[89]Chloe Holt, comp., "Pico Heights, Los Angeles Conflict," a collection of documents and interviews, July, 1924, Major Document 111, SRR Papers; Uono, "Geographical Aggregation," pp. 129–32; Los Angeles *Times,* Feb. 6, 1920.

[90]Los Angeles *Times,* Mar. 21, 1920; Los Angeles *Evening Herald,* Mar. 25, 1920; Clarence Hunt, "Los Angeles Bulletin," *Grizzly Bear,* Mar., 1920, p. 23; Holt, comp., "Pico Heights."

[91]The instigator of this policy in the Pico Heights area claimed to have vacated 110 families in a little over a year. Chloe Holt, "Interview with Mr. Duffy," July 28, 1924, in Holt, comp., "Pico Heights."

threatened, did the Protective Association achieve any prominence.

Their broader appeal was achieved in opposition to the Board of Home Missions of the Methodist Episcopal Church, then taking up "the challenge to make the democracy of America safe for the world" by "a program of evangelization, religious education and social uplift." The Board's "main Centenary project" for Japanese was to be "a beautiful modern church" in Pico Heights, which would replace two smaller edifices more nearly downtown. The Pico Heights site would serve Japanese from outside the district, for it was near a streetcar line.[92] The Methodists had asked the support of the Church Federation of Los Angeles—composed of the major Protestant denominations—which devised the move, reasoning that "the promotion of Christian Churches will do much to cultivate the spirit of fraternity and righteousness between the American and Japanese people."[93] But nearby whites were alarmed when the Board purchased a Pico Heights lot, and racism rose to epidemic proportions throughout the city. "I was in hope," wrote Leon Mirp of the *Los Angeles Citizen,* "that the attempt of the Japs to build their church or temple in the Pico Heights district was an invasion of the fashionable part of the city. Until the influential part of the citizenship is menaced close to home it will look with equanimity upon a Jap invasion of working-class districts." Racism combined with class resentment and with anti-clericalism: the "white Japs" were becoming personified in churchmen, "high moguls who live elsewhere who don't care about other people's property being ruined," too blinded by self-righteousness to recognize the "immorality, disbelief, and cunning hypocrisy" of the Japanese, "particularly in the case of those professedly 'converted.' "[94] Under local pressure, the city council let it be known that a building permit would be denied the Methodists, because "practically 100 percent of the property owners in the affected district are opposed to the granting of this permit."[95] The very special outlook of the home missionary had struck no sympathet-

[92]Ralph Welles Keeler, "Making America Safe for the World," *Missionary Review of the World* 42 (1919): 171–82; Herbert B. Johnson, "The Crisis in Los Angeles," report to Los Angeles Methodist Headquarters, n.d. [1922], typed copy in Holt, comp., "Pico Heights."

[93]Johnson, "Crisis in Los Angeles"; J. A. Stevenson to Herbert B. Johnson, July 24, 1923, in file #4365, Vol. 1404 (1923), Los Angeles City Council Petitions, Los Angeles City Archive.

[94]*Los Angeles Citizen,* Jan. 27, 1922; Letter of Mrs. J. G. Fitzpatrick to editor of *Los Angeles Ledger,* a neighborhood newspaper, Oct. 1, 1923, copy in Holt, comp., "Pico Heights"; Clarence Hunt, "Grizzly Growls," *Grizzly Bear,* Feb. 1, 1922, p. 4; Holt, "Interview with Mr. Duffy."

[95]Minutes, Sept. 27, 1923, file #4365, Los Angeles City Council, Los Angeles City Archive. See also the correspondence from Herbert B. Johnson in this file.

ic chord; the council chose to listen to the Pico Heights resident who "looked about at those people . . . who were so anxious to build this church, and where did they live? They all lived in the Wilshire district where they knew there wasn't a chance in the world for them to have a Japanese living next door to them." Though by 1927 the defeated church had been established elsewhere, gradual Japanese residential entry into Pico Heights resumed.[96]

The Hollywood incident was to end far more boisterously than its counterpart in Pico Heights. In late 1922 Hollywood was attracting even greater numbers to its less impressive residential districts. Of the newcomers, Japanese gardeners and tradesmen were a minor component. When a group of Japanese residents proposed to build a bungalow court, white neighbors petitioned the city council. Although the council condemned enough of the property for park purposes to foil the building plans,[97] Japanese continued to move to Hollywood.

In early 1923 Japanese residents, with the approval of the Los Angeles Presbytery, organized a Japanese Presbyterian Church of Hollywood and purchased for it a house and lot.[98] At the same time, another "Japanese" apartment was proposed on land which had belonged to Japanese residents for over a decade. A month later, a nearby white resident called a "mass meeting" and began an ad hoc residents' committee to protest the Japanese encroachment to the Hollywood Chamber of Commerce.[99] Prominent during the early weeks of the resistance was a local realtor, whose views and motives probably typified those of most Hollywood residents and certainly of local realtors.[100] Granting that the Japanese "keep their places up as well as the white men they live next to," he maintained that Japanese

[96]Holt, "Interview with Mrs. Spang," in Holt, comp., "Pico Heights"; Uono, "Geographical Aggregation," pp. 86, 129.

[97]Hollywood *Citizen,* Jan. 4, 1923.

[98]A non-denominational Independent Japanese Church of Hollywood had been established in an older section nearby six years earlier, without conflict.

[99]Hollywood *Citizen,* Apr. 17, 19, 23, 27, 1923; William C. Smith, "Anti-Japanese Agitation in Hollywood," n.d. [1924], Major Document 64, SRR Papers; Guy W. Wadsworth to Herbert B. Johnson, "Los Angeles Hollywood Japanese Presbyterian Church, 1924–64" folder; Minutes, Mar. 6, Apr. 3, 1923, Church Extension Board, United Presbyterian Church.

[100]Of twelve Hollywood realtors interviewed for the Survey of Race Relations in late 1924 (after the agitation had calmed), a heavy majority agreed that Japanese had depreciated or would depreciate property values in Hollywood, but none otherwise expressed strong anti-Japanese feelings. Reasoning along these lines was considered unquestionably sufficient for urging exclusion, and the Hollywood Chamber of Commerce and the nearby Santa Monica Boulevard Board of Trade did just that. Chloe Holt, "Interviews with Real Estate Dealers of Hollywood," Oct. 20, 1924, Minor Document B-323, SRR Papers; Hollywood *Citizen,* Apr. 17, May 2, 1923.

in the neighborhood threatened property values: "No one wants to live near them. . . . They are alright in their places, but they should be segregated. . . . The trouble with them is they worm their way into the best residential districts."

When more strident voices in the newly created Hollywood Protective Association sought what the realtor considered unnecessary and ungenteel publicity, he resigned from the Association,[101] leaving a clear field for men with wide ambitions as agitators. At the initial meeting, advice was tendered by veterans of the Pico Heights and Belvedere anti-Japanese agitations, and by three prominent members of the Los Angeles County Anti-Asiatic Society.[102] A member of the Society made it clear why a patriot not resident in Hollywood should be concerned:

> You people here on the Pacific coast are facing the greatest battle that has ever threatened the white man. It is to be the fight against the yellow man. . . . When it comes to a test between a superior race like our own and the lower standard race like the yellow, the superior race is always the one to go to the wall. . . . The Japanese consider us inferior, and they sneer at us in their complacency [sic]. They call us rabbits, and rabbit-hearted, always filled with terror. They believe we are a race of ape-men, and dream their dreams of yellow domination, when they shall be slave drivers and we the cringing slaves.[103]

A Native Son was less extreme in his rhetoric but slightly more concrete:

> It takes dynamite to stir up Americans when the country is in danger. But when we get aroused watch out. This is not a question of racial equality. It is simply the incompatability of the white and the yellow races. We cannot mingle, socially, industrially, economically, or politically. Once a Jap always a Jap. All their dreams and aspirations are of and for the Mikado. The churches have been our biggest obstacle in the fight against the Japanese. We have had to fight propaganda of the golden rule, the brotherhood of man, live and let live philosophy

[101]Hollywood *Citizen,* Apr. 23, May 2, 1923.

[102]Clarence Hunt was again cheerleader for the Hollywood neighborhood agitators—although reluctantly, because he thought of Hollywood (quite inaccurately, as regards the neighborhood being invaded) as the home of the "Hollywood 500." Hunt believed that these residents had Japanese chauffeurs and gardeners, and that therefore they really deserved to suffer at the hands of the Japanese. "Were we not firm in the belief that, for the good of California, the Japs should be forced out of every section of Los Angeles and the whole state, we would advocate that the City Council set apart Hollywood as a Jap-zone." Hunt, "Los Angeles Report," *Grizzly Bear,* Jan., 1923, p. 24; "Los Angeles Monrovia Bulletin," *Grizzly Bear,* May, 1923, supplement, p. 21.

[103]Hollywood *Citizen,* Apr. 24, 1923.

and all the other countless unthinking sentimental arguments that our religious dictators would have us follow.[104]

A local resident who took the meeting to task for paying little attention to the facts of the case was shouted down with cries of "White Jap, white Jap!"[105]

Yet within a month the momentum of the agitation failed, and tactics shifted. Residents petitioned the city council, stating that the Japanese Presbyterian Church would "have a tendency to further the invasion and colonization of the Japanese in that section." "The natural depreciation" of property values which would follow would be "unjust and unfair" to the white owners in the neighborhood, "a loss they can ill afford to take." The council rescinded the building permit previously granted to the church, citing technical grounds.[106] A Protective Association officer began to warn those considering selling to Japanese—and the prospective purchasers as well—of generally unstated risks in the transaction. A student interviewing the officer recorded that "he said the Japanese are so 'doggoned' well educated that they heed the advice."[107] By late 1923 the Presbytery had become cautious. The Christianizing of the Hollywood Japanese went on during the whole affair, but the construction of better facilities was delayed until three years later and then at a new, larger, and uncontested site. Nothing was ever built on the original property by the Presbyterians.[108]

[104]*Ibid.*

[105]This same nonconformist subsequently chided Hollywood residents for being "inconsistent not to say ridiculous" for simultaneously attacking Japanese for having low standards and for building a new dwelling. He later claimed that this reminder—along with the dynamics of the "white Jap" argument—may have taken the heat off the Japanese residential invasion and placed it mostly upon the church. Bickford, letter to editor of Hollywood *Citizen,* Apr. 25, 1923; Chloe Holt, "Interview with Dr. Bickford," Nov. 3, 1924, Minor Document B-316, SRR Papers.

[106]Mrs. J. O. Poole to City Council, n.d. [mid-July, 1923]; City Clerk to Chief Inspector of Buildings, July 26, 1923, quoting resolution of Public Welfare Committee, both in file #4131, Vol. 1402 (1923), Los Angeles City Council Petitions.

[107]Smith, "Hollywood"; Smith, "Interview of William C. Smith with L. R. Bowles," Apr. 8, 1924, Major Document 340, SRR Papers; Claude Williams, "Interview with R. Kado," undated, Major Document 302, *ibid.*

[108]In Hollywood the Japanese were more aggressive than their clerical sponsors. In 1924 a mimeographed letter went out to all members of the board under the name of the minister of the Japanese church. It argued that "a policy of postponement was deemed to be justified in the hope that Anti-Japanese agitation might die out in time, but the crisis can not be avoided and the Japanese Church in Hollywood must either be allowed to go forward or be broken in courage and finance." The Church Extension Board was not receptive to this line of argument, or to the congregation's desire to purchase a larger lot in a new location. The Home Missions Board was far

Overall, little but mischief was accomplished for either side. Though the Brotherhood of the Hollywood Congregational Church passed a formal resolution in January, 1924, condemning as "un-Christian and un-American" the anti-Japanese activities, which were "productive of race hatred and subversive of their American ideals of equal rights and fair play," other local ministers held that the Presbyterians had been imprudent.[109] Their missionary zeal and excellent intentions must also be weighed against the incongruousness of building a racially segregated church. The agitation reached an absurdity in *SWAT the JAP,* a newspaper so unsophisticated in its expression of racial hatred that McClatchy condemned it "because it would be a detriment to . . . the cause of those who honestly believe that Japanese immigration should be excluded, absolutely, hereafter."[110] Local government revealed its accessibility to even the nastiest of white neighborhood agitation when, under pressure of Hollywood petitions, it requested that the chief inspector of buildings issue no permits to Japanese owners of lots across from Le Conte Junior High; yet when the inspector reported that no grounds existed for him to deny such permits, the council let the matter pass, despite the petitioners' expressed fears of "a very densely populated Japanese colony" menacing the Junior High.[111]

Other minor battles would take place in other years, over residential matters particularly. Small humiliations of Japanese Americans would be continued, even written into the law; in Los Angeles, Jim Crow legislation—symbolic as ever in its pettiness—was directed against the Yellow Peril rather than the black. Such legislation was initially a by-product of the Alien Land Law agitation.

In September, 1920, one such piece of legislation was passed prior to the November statewide referendum. With splendid illogic, it

more so, and eventually the Presbytery backed the more aggressive policy. Rev. Horikoshi to Members of Church Extension Board, mimeographed, n.d. [early or mid-1924], Presbyterian Folder. "Hollywood Japanese Church—March 4, 1932, Amounts Paid by Church Extension Board," Minutes, April 3, 7, June 11, Oct. 6, 1924, Nov. 16, 1926, Apr. 5, 1927, Church Extension Board, United Presbyterian Church.

[109]K. Ogawa, "Christian Treatment of Japanese in America," *Missionary Review of the World* 37 (1924): 525; Smith, "Hollywood."

[110]McClatchy to George Gleason, July 19, 1923, folder 6, Box G II, JERS Collection.

[111]L. R. Bowles to City Council, Sept. 18, 1923, and Secretary of Playground Commission to City Council, Feb. 1, 1927, in file #5031, Vol. 1413 (1923) Los Angeles City Council Petitions; Charles M. Easton to City Council, n.d. [ca. Jan. 20, 1924], file #475, Vol. 1489 (1924), *ibid.;* Chief Inspector of Buildings to City Council Committee on Public Safety, Jan. 28, 1924, Vol. 144, p. 411 (Apr. 10, 1924), City Council Minutes.

barred aliens ineligible to citizenship from the municipal golf links. "Weary American citizens" eager for recreation, having been freed of the Yellow Peril on the golf course, were gratified by a 1921 amendment which added municipal tennis courts to the law's purview.[112] In practice, unlegislated discriminatory treatment at swimming pools troubled many more Japanese, perhaps because of the outrageous implications of bodily uncleanliness.[113]

Discrimination, enforced racial congregation, and legal disabilities enhanced the tendencies to look to one another for social life and for trust; understandable in any group of newcomers, such behavior was reinforced among the Japanese Americans by their home culture. The disjunction between Japanese economic success and their pariah social status grew unabated through the era of the first generation's dominance. For all the accomplishments of their parents—and for all their own accomplishments in the wider world of school—Nisei youngsters grew up in neighborhoods where they were themselves congregated in large numbers, and segregated together with groups which they learned to consider less than desirable. In this setting they grew to understand their parents' advice, designed to teach their community to make as few demands as possible on the obviously uncomprehending white society. "I advise the Japanese not to demand their rights," explained the secretary of the Los Angeles Japanese Association in 1925, "or to expect to be treated on a fifty-fifty basis with white men. It is the psychology of the American common people that they give more if you beg for it than if you demand it. The educated and cultured classes may be different. The Japanese question is very quiet now, though public spirit is easily aroused against us. As long as we keep quiet and make no move the public forgets us."[114]

[112]Ray L. Chesebro, comp. and ed., *Municipal Code of the City of Los Angeles* (Los Angeles: Parker, Stone & Baird Co. and Los Angeles Daily Journal, 1936), section 63.59; Bruce B. Wallace, "Recreation for the Japanese in Los Angeles," Mar. 25, 1924, Minor Document B-189, SRR Papers; Los Angeles *Times,* Jan. 21, 1921.

[113]The religious press considered it an experiment and a small breakthrough when the Los Angeles YMCA became the first on the Pacific Coast to establish a separate Japanese Department in 1926. Through membership, Japanese could participate in nonsegregated branches of the Y. Even this experiment seems not to have affected the fact that Japanese, like Negroes, could use facilities in nonsegregated Y's only in groups and apparently with special permission. Separate branches of the Y continued in sections of the city with heavy concentrations of Japanese population. "Japanese in Los Angeles 'Y'," *Missionary Review of the World* 49 (1926): 474; *Japanese Directory of Young Peoples' Groups* (San Francisco: Japanese American News, 1935), pp. 12–14.

[114]J. Kasai, quoted in "Survey Interviews Southern California No. 2," SRR Papers.

4
Japanese-American Community Organization

Minor "successes" in the residential "invasions" of the early 1920's did little to relieve a tendency for the several Japanese neighborhoods to grow more dense and more extensive. Although Japanese gave more than adequate proof that they wished to move away from their cramped areas, residential segregation was in fact crucial to the support of an ethnic isolation that made the Los Angeles Japanese-American community such a "success" in parochial economic terms. This chapter will look first at the growth of Little Tokyo and several other Japanese neighborhoods, and then at some of the varieties of organized ethnic life they supported.

Before the Japanese claimed it for their own, the Little Tokyo area was one of mixed occupancy and business. Abutting Chinatown and a Negro district, the area enjoyed a high density of second-hand shops, boardinghouses, saloons, and whorehouses. An unembarrassed observer described a corner of what was becoming Little Tokyo as containing "a well-patronized saloon on each of four of the five corners" as well as "eleven saloons within a block of this crossing, besides several 'social clubs' of several nationalities and varying degrees of 'cussedness.' There are several houses of questionable morality, within the block, four or five employment agencies, and two religious missions."[1] Japanese did not concentrate in any of these activities (except for boardinghouses), but the composition of the neighborhood was such that there was little opposition to the entry of the Japanese, and the newcomers followed the path of least resistance.[2] Japanese boardinghouses gradually forced out the American ones; businesses offering distinctive Japanese products and serving other Japanese economic interests proved better located and more profitable than their non-Japanese neighboring establishments.

[1] *Los Angeles Socialist,* Aug. 8, 1903.

[2] At this point overt white resistance was seldom necessary to encourage the strangers to congregate, but as early as 1906 a candidate for the Los Angeles City Council "scored the Japanese for invading the ward, and pledged himself, if elected, to purge the ward of the presence of the little brown men." Los Angeles *Examiner,* Oct. 20, 1906.

Little Tokyo came into its own. The Japanese by and large welcomed this economically rational development, the more so as they felt a distaste for the lower-class ethnic neighbors with whom they were originally thrown. A sympathetic Caucasian observer noted that this process of ethnic succession was followed by a general brightening of the neighborhood.[3]

Brightening—at least at first—could only have been by comparison with the extraordinarily drab condition in which the Japanese first found Little Tokyo. A community survey dating from as late as 1918 declared that the general area including Little Tokyo was characterized by "all the evils of a foreign quarter," and noted the virtual absence of "any American influence [in] this neighborhood. . . . It includes the largest Japanese colony, and everywhere there is bad housing, frightful overcrowding, congestion of people in houses and houses on lots."[4] To judge from photos surviving from its heyday in the 1920's and 1930's, the area developed a highly businesslike aura, reminding one of the central area of a small town. But for the first settlers of Little Tokyo it was a haven, a foothold in America. At first it served as a place in which to organize the activities that attached the participants to their homes in Japan, but later it led to a more nearly middle-class American form of "success."

The first Japanese dwellers flocked to Little Tokyo from the railroads and similar tasks at which they were seasonally employed. These jobs soon proved uncongenial to the Japanese, who began to seek more fixed situations where they could better exert control for the purpose of saving money. The citrus groves and sugar beet fields around Los Angeles seemed to offer such openings. Quickly a primitive "bunk-house farm organization," much akin to the Italian-American *padrone* system though apparently lacking many of its exploitive aspects, arose to meet the need for contract-labor bargaining in an unfamiliar language. The go-betweens, originally nominated from among the workers (and rewarded with a proportion of the earnings of their fellows), later were supplanted by an arrangement in which work orders were handled by the proprietors of Little Tokyo

[3]Chotoku Toyama, "The Japanese Community in Los Angeles" (Master's thesis, Columbia University, 1926), p. 10; H. A. Millis, *The Japanese Problem in the United States* (New York: Macmillan, 1915), pp. 73–74. I am greatly indebted to William Mason, associate curator, department of history, Los Angeles County Museum of Natural History, who has shared with me many insights gained in his study of the early development of Little Tokyo. The museum's exhibition of captioned photographs of early Japanese life in Los Angeles, on view in early 1968, incorporated some of his work.

[4]California, Commission of Immigration and Housing, *Community Survey of Los Angeles* (Sacramento, 1918), p. 15.

boardinghouses.[5] It is unclear whether or not the early boardinghouse proprietors were the same people as the workers who had managed the earliest negotiations with the Caucasian farm mangers, thus earning capital to invest in their boardinghouses. But that phase, too, was temporary, for soon some of these men abandoned the boarding- houses and became labor contractors—and, as such, leading figures in the Japanese community. A temporary tightening of the labor market around 1902 permitted labor contractors to make shrewd bargains for their charges, compensating for their earlier wage cutting in a way that often was characterized by Caucasians as cunning. The hand of the labor contractor was correspondingly strengthened in his own community.

Their places of business, naturally, were in Little Tokyo. For Japanese immigrants in the days before they had any economic strength other than their own labor, organization was their strongest advantage. The degree of organization shown in some of the labor- contractor groups quite amazed the Immigration Commission agents, one of whom reported meeting ''several gangs of about 50 Japanese, all riding bicycles, in process of transfer from one place to another a mile or more away. Very few white pickers own bicycles.''[6] To achieve such organization, as for recruitment and outfitting, the close proximity and clear communications offered by Little Tokyo were crucial. A similar interrelation between economic necessity, white hostility, and ethnic solidarity characterized such other early clusters of Japanese-American population as the fishing villages of East San Pedro and Santa Monica, and the farming center of Moneta-Gardena.

The initial years of the farming communities are largely undocu- mented, save for the rapid growth of proprietorship by the Japanese, and the hostile notice taken of such developments by white neigh- bors. The fishing communities, however, illustrate yet again the

---

[5]Tsuyoshi Matsumoto, ''History of Resident Japanese,'' p. 5, in Togo Tanaka, ''Journal,'' folder A 17.06, JERS Collection; U.S. Immigration Commission, Re- ports: XXIV: *Japanese and Other Immigrant Races on the Pacific Coast and Rocky Mountain States: I, City Trades,* Senate Doc. 635, 61st Cong., 2nd sess. (1911), pp. 236–37.

[6]Immigration Commission, *Reports,* XXIV, pp. 227–28; Varden Fuller, ''The Supply of Agricultural Labor as a Factor in the Evolution of Farm Organization in California'' (Ph.D. dissertation, University of California, Berkeley, 1940), pp. 19, 830; published as Exhibit 8762-A in U.S. Senate, Committee on Education and Labor, *Hearings: Violation of Free Speech and Rights of Labor* (henceforth La Follette Hearings), pt. 54, pp. 19, 777–898; Stuart Marshall Jamieson, ''Labor Unionism in Agriculture'' (Ph.D. dissertation, University of California, Berkeley, 1943), I, 136; Chloe Holt, ''Interview with Mr. George W. Moore,'' Feb. 16, 1925, Major Document 274, pt. 34, SRR Papers.

applicability of the notion of the occupational "niche" to Japanese Los Angeles. These clusters show what the growth and accommodation of the Japanese community of Los Angeles generally demonstrates: that the hard-working strangers were alert, not to the main thrust of the American dream, but to its leavings—leavings by white Americans of exploitable but peripheral resources.

East San Pedro in Los Angeles harbor is a good example. A Japanese fishing village planted here persisted from the early years of the century until it was uprooted as a potential menace shortly after Pearl Harbor. As in other settlements established early in the group's history in Los Angeles, the Japanese discovered at East San Pedro a service which could be sold to the general community but which no one else had yet exploited. The chance which originally attracted Japanese to the area was the discovery by a Japanese fisherman of abalone at White's Point, San Pedro, in 1901. Although Americans then had no taste for the mollusk, dried abalone was of known value in Japan. A group of enterprising young Japanese fishermen, united through common prefectural origin, bought a shed, moved it to White's Point, and began a regular business of catching and drying abalone. Despite the suspicion of their Caucasian neighbors, the men obtained financial backing, a regular contract, and out-of-season employment from a white firm. Hostility at White's Point shortly forced the Japanese entrepreneurs to move a short distance to the nearly vacant Terminal Island; there they drove permanent piles to support docks, correctly anticipating the addition of other species of fish to their commercial catch. Despite growing competition from Italians and Slavs, the head start of the Japanese, together with their ability to bargain as a group with white-owned canneries, permitted expansion of the Japanese preeminence in Los Angeles commercial fishing. Even as the colony outgrew its pioneering period, the internal cohesion requisite for its early advantage—reinforced by a nearly total geographical segregation—continued profitably.[7]

"Segregation" does not accurately describe the residential situation of such a relatively small group as the Los Angeles Japanese.

[7]It is more than coincidental that another Japanese fishing village in Los Angeles County, at Santa Monica, followed exactly the same pattern. Founded in 1906, the town displayed Japanese cooperative initiative, followed by Caucasian financial backing. Rapid expansion then occurred, with close interdependent relations between the Japanese and the whites who shared financial interests in the colony. Los Angeles *Times,* Feb. 16, 1920. See also Kanichi Kawasaki, "The Japanese Community of East San Pedro, Terminal Island, California" (Master's thesis, University of Southern California, 1931), pp. 31–44 and *passim;* Tsuyoshi Matsumoto, "History of Resident Japanese in Southern California," trans. Togo Tanaka, entry for Aug. 25, 1941, in Togo Tanaka, "Journal."

Although several streets in Little Tokyo had few, if any, non-Japanese residents, even in the periods of greatest residential pressure, there were few living in all-Japanese surroundings. Precise data are not available for the period before 1940,[8] but the testimony of the 1940 data are unequivocal on that score. In only one tract, the Terminal Island fishing community, were Japanese in a majority. Even in this very atypical area only about 60 percent of all inhabitants were "other races," almost all Japanese.

Little Tokyo was more nearly typical. Eight contiguous census tracts, each with 10 percent or more "other races," made up Little Tokyo and its fringes; the area contained 20 percent of all the Japanese in Los Angeles County. But only 18 percent of the total population of this area was "other races," providing a maximum estimate for Japanese. The most nearly "segregated" tract in Little Tokyo was no more than 36 percent Japanese; the next, less than 29 percent. Even in its most "Japanese" parts Little Tokyo had, in one instance, a native-white majority and, in the other, very substantial representations of Negroes and Mexicans.

Segregation was not the problem for Japanese Americans in Little Tokyo: after all, census tracts were small areas, traversed in a few minutes' walk. Rather, the difficulty was that Little Tokyo was (at least by 1940) among the poorest places in town. Most units lacked flush toilets. The extended area had a median rent which was less than half the average for the city as a whole; old by Los Angeles standards and dilapidated by any, the neighborhood had filled up with rooming houses and a large non-Japanese population, with whom Japanese would come into frequent contact. Earlier figures show that, for the city as a whole, Japanese were far more likely than the average Los Angeles resident to rent; when renting, to live in cheaper quarters; to have larger families in those cheap rented quarters; and to take in appreciably more lodgers and boarders than other groups.[9]

Outside Little Tokyo, matters were only slightly better than in the ghetto. In 1940 roughly half of all city Japanese lived in houses

[8]At this date the Census Bureau began to publish Los Angeles data on census tracts, "small areas, having a population usually between 3,000 and 6,000 . . . designed to include an area fairly homogeneous in population characteristics." Japanese are not recorded separately from "other races," but virtually all areas of important concentration of either Chinese or Filipinos in Los Angeles were also areas of Japanese concentration. Japanese, Chinese, and Filipinos are mapped separately by tracts (based upon unpublished data) for Los Angeles City in Earl Hanson and Paul Beckett, *Los Angeles: Its People and Its Homes* (Los Angeles: Haynes Foundation, 1944), pp. 39, 41, 42. The tract data are in *Census 1940 P7,* from which (p. 1) the definition of the tract comes.

[9]*Census 1930 P3,* pp. 212–17; *Census 1930 P6,* pp. 158ff.

defined as substandard—twice the proportion as among Negroes, although somewhat below the proportion of Mexicans so housed. And the unhappy situation did not stem from poverty: one in five Oriental families living in high-rent units ($50/month or more) lived nevertheless in substandard housing. Only 3 percent of the white population at this economic level lived in substandard units.[10]

Even as late as 1940, Tract 186, which included Little Tokyo's downtown, had more than twice as many men as women, and virtually no families or owner occupancy. With 64 percent of "families" consisting of one person, most commonly living twenty or more per building, the area retained some of the flavor of the early Little Tokyo, centering then on the boardinghouses. Despite a median gross rent which was considerably less than half that for the city as a whole, the Japanese population was slightly better able to find work in the private sector. (The fact is especially impressive in view of the *white* unemployment rate in this tract—a rate three times the city average.) In this unimposing area lived Japanese whose median education was only half a year below that for all Los Angelenos; yet only 60 percent of the Japanese had radios, while in the city as a whole 95 percent maintained this form of cultural contact with America.

Tract 189, still in Little Tokyo but outside its central business district, had a greater admixture of family living. The sex ratio still favored men, 1.77:1, but the ratio of children to women reflected family-building. Three-fourths of the Japanese families had radios. One in twenty Japanese owned their own homes, though 40 percent of the "families" consisted of one person. Yet here, too, multi-family dwelling units predominated; the median rent was cheap (half the city average) and conditions were mean.

These figures take on added meaning when seen in comparison to the residential areas into which the Japanese emerged as they extended their communities beyond Little Tokyo. Tract 129, which the Japanese shared with white ethnics, was in the Exposition Park area of southwestern Los Angeles; Tract 214, where most residents were Negroes, was in the Evergreen section of East Los Angeles. Here was family territory, for the Japanese Americans as for others. The Evergreen tract had 1.38 Japanese men per woman, while the Exposition Park tract had fewer than 1.1 per woman. About one in ten Japanese owned their own homes in each area, and the typical dwelling unit was single-family detached. Family sizes were above

[10]*Census 1940,* p. 7; Hanson and Beckett, *Los Angeles;* Housing Authority of Los Angeles, *Housing Survey* (1940), III (Maps and Graphs), *passim:* II, Tables DS-66, DS-67, 14, 31.

TABLE 4.1.   Characteristics of the 19 Tracts in Los Angeles City in Which "Other Races" Account for 10 Percent of the Population or More, Compared with Characteristics of the Entire City, 1940

	19 "Japanese" tracts	Los Angeles City
Dwelling units in need of major repairs (%)	8	4
Dwelling units with more than one person per room (%)	22	12
Residents employed in white-collar occupations (%)	34	49
Median years of school for residents 25 or older	8.2	10.7
Foreign-born whites who are naturalized (%)	38	61

Source: *Census 1940 P7.*

the city average; rentals and radio ownership achieved the city norms. From Little Tokyo, Japanese families emerged into a material typicality. Little Tokyo had moneyed residents, it is true, and the zones of emergence were hardly luxurious. But Little Tokyo lacked what these zones most significantly offered: the possibility of achieving an appropriately "American" style of life, centering upon the home, consumption, and family living.

In understanding the discomforts suggested by the Little Tokyo figures, we must not lose sight of the ambitions implied by the immigrants' decision to remain in America. In its first two rows Table 4.1 shows a quantitative measure of such discomfort, but the remaining three rows point to some social implications of residential segregation.

Here 1940 tract data are again referred to; the nineteen tracts with at least 10 percent "other races" are combined for comparison with Los Angeles as a whole. The Japanese areas had appreciably lower proportions of white-collar workers than did the city as a whole. (By way of comparison, the comparable figure for all Los Angeles Japanese Americans was 47 percent.) In a crude sense, many white-collar Japanese had neighbors occupationally "beneath them."[11]

[11]An alternate plausible explanation is that the Japanese were distinctly segregated within their group along class lines, with lower-class Japanese living in the densely Japanese areas.

Japanese neighborhoods also threw Japanese into contact with relatively ill-educated people; this fact was frequently and ruefully noted by the Japanese in explaining their avoidance of social contact with their non-Japanese neighbors. [12] These neighbors were also the farthest from fulfilling the ideal of Americanization which Japanese shared with respectable whites. As the bottom row of Table 4.1 demonstrates, the foreign-born white neighbors of the Japanese were less likely to be naturalized than those elsewhere. [13] For a group with the ambitions of the Los Angeles Japanese, self-segregation would be preferable to the bitter irony of being segregated in a group with the very type of person they least wished to emulate.

Japanese could easily avoid neighbors whose occupations, education, or attitudes they did not approve of; but their children would unquestionably meet the neighbor children in school. [14] However well the Issei were satisfied with their own society, that society surely seemed inadequate for raising children who were American citizens. Though most neighbors of the "segregated" Japanese were native whites, the average Mexican (whose residential patterns were by far the saddest in Los Angeles at the time) was nearly five times as likely to live in a Japanese neighborhood as the average white. Blacks occupied somewhat better residential areas than did the Mexicans or the Japanese, but they were three times more likely to live in Japanese neighborhoods than were native whites. [15] Foreign-born whites were

[12]For example, Gretchen Tuthill, "A Study of the Japanese in the CIty of Los Angeles" (Master's thesis, University of Southern California, 1924), p. 31; Edward K. Strong, Jr., *The Second-Generation Japanese Problem* (Stanford: Stanford University Press, 1934), p. 23.

[13]The low rate of naturalization may have been simply a result of disinterest or inability on the part of low-status people, or of certain ethnic groups. The phenomenon may also have been related to the more recent American arrival of foreign-born white neighbors of the Japanese.

[14]Another social cost was school segregation. Japanese attended more and more explicitly "colored" schools as residential patterns hardened in the 1930's. See the list of public elementary schools showing ratio of Japanese to other students, based on a Board of Education survey taken in 1929, in Tamiko Tanaka, "The Japanese Language School in Relation to Assimilation" (Master's thesis, University of Southern California, 1933), p. 67. See also Federal Housing Administration, Division of Economics and Statistics, "Map of Los Angeles, California, Showing . . . Percentage of Total Enrollment . . . Comprised in the Five Leading Non-English Language or Racial Background Groups, School Year 1935–36," and "Map of Los Angeles, California, Showing . . . Trend in Language or Racial Characteristics of School Enrollment over the Period 1929–30 to 1935–36."

[15]Housing Authority of Los Angeles, *Housing Survey,* II, Tables DS-66, DS-67; Charles B. Spaulding, "Housing Problems of Minority Groups in Los Angeles County," *Annals of the American Academy of Political and Social Science* 248 (1946): 220–25.

nearly twice as likely as their native counterparts to be living near Japanese.

The situation, if distasteful, was far from intolerable. In the 1920's the outward-pushing Japanese were hardly militant, even when led by white churchmen, and Jefferson Park proved their offspring only slightly more assertive in 1939. The Japanese found that the compensations for living together were plentiful: on the basis of residential proximity, they built a complex and rewarding social and organizational structure, of which Little Tokyo was the focus though by no means the sole seat.[16] Only for a new generation, and in a new postwar world, would Japanese-American *organizations* argue that residential dispersal was the appropriate American ethnic-group dwelling pattern. That view was neatly expressed by the Japanese American Citizens League in an *amicus curiae* brief of 1948, directed against the operation of restrictive covenants: "Were the Japanese not forced," the League's brief now maintained, "by reason of race restrictive covenants, to live in definite areas, they would probably have lived normal lives throughout the area and consequently the 'clannishness' which General De Witt found so inimical to national safety would not have existed."[17] The volunteered phrase "normal lives" may well be pondered.

Religion played an important part in the early history of organized Japanese life in Los Angeles, as it has for so many immigrant groups. Yet here the story is somewhat unusual, for the first steps toward organizing the religious life of the Japanese Americans in Los Angeles came from white missionaries. Protestant "home" missionaries were infused not only with the spirit that Asia could be Christianized in America, but also with a broadly humanitarian outlook that made them ready to welcome the "tendency" among their Japanese American clients "to become permanent residents." These missionaries were the first and ultimately the most faithful white friends the Japanese Americans had.[18]

Long before Buddhists took the trouble to establish a congregation or place of worship in Los Angeles, Caucasian Christians sought to win the immigrants over. In 1889 the YMCA established a Japanese

[16]My account will emphasize Little Tokyo, both because centralized activity was directed from there and because documentation for that area is greatly superior to that for peripheral areas.

[17]"Brief of the JACL as *Amicus Curiae,*" in *Hurd et al.* v. *Hodge et al.,* 334 U.S. 24, decided by the Supreme Court on May 3, 1948. The complainant was a Negro.

[18]*A Glimpse of the Institutional Japanese Church, Los Angeles City, California, U.S.A., 1905* (Los Angeles: n.p., 1905).

mission, which was shortly transferred to the Methodist Episcopal church. In 1895 the first regular Christian Japanese assembly (a segregated Methodist Episcopal church with a Japanese pastor) was established. A Japanese Presbyterian congregation was formed in the middle of the next decade. By 1910 five Christian missions served the Los Angeles Japanese, in competition with the first Buddhist mission, which had finally been established six years earlier.[19] Christians (and even Buddhists, though less enthusiastically) argued for Americanization.[20]

Japanese religious organizations in Los Angeles were typically "American" in their voluntary, competitive, and somewhat ad hoc quality. Competition among religious groups was itself a novelty to most Japanese; it encouraged the assumption of many new functions by the churches, and led to new forms of organization. Both Buddhism and Christianity were considered legitimate in the Los Angeles Japanese community, and affiliations were readily shifted from one to the other. Shintoism also changed to a more Americanized form, even to the point of "a beautiful California-style Spanish-style building that has all the dignity of a Shinto shrine."[21] Both Christian and Buddhist organizations took on social-welfare functions, the former more often than the latter. Both participated in the usual variety of American church-community activities—baseball leagues, Boy Scouts, and the like.[22] As early as 1914 the Southern California (Christian Japanese) Church Federation established a department of

[19]Norio Osaki, "A Survey of Interdenominational Cooperation with Each of Three Japanese Religions in Los Angeles, Shinto, Buddhism, and Christianity" (Master's thesis, University of Southern California, 1941), pp. 27, 47, 75; Donald J. Fujiyoshi, "A Study of the Educational Program of the Church School of the Japanese Christian Church and Institute of Los Angeles" (Master's thesis, University of Southern California, 1942), p. 24; Immigration Commission, *Reports,* XXIII, pp. 240–47; *A Glimpse.*

[20]Edmund de S. and Mary V. Brunner, *Irrigation and Religion* (New York: George H. Doran, 1922), p. 91; Dendo-Dan, *Fourth Annual Report* (1915), pp. 6, 12; *Fifth Annual Report* (1916), p. 11.

[21]Osaki, "Interdenominational Cooperation," p. 22; Kyojiro Takahashi, "A Social Study of the Japanese Shinto and Buddhism in Los Angeles" (Master's thesis, University of Southern California, 1937), p. 88.

[22]Although I have seen no local evidence of formal Buddhist social welfare work, their national federation encouraged community service through interpreting, finding jobs, and legal advice. Reading the *Rafu Shimpo* English section, I finally realized that the very successful "Wanjies" baseball team was sponsored by the Hongwanji Buddhist Temple, from which it irreverently took its name. Takahashi, "Shinto and Buddhism in Los Angeles," pp. 92–93; Kosei Ogura, "A Sociological Study of the Buddhist Churches in North America with a Case Study of Gardena, California, Congregation" (Master's thesis, University of Southern California, 1932), p. 85.

social work with a full-time employee. From tasks like teaching English, sewing, and "Americanization," and attacking (in 1915) the rise of organized gambling in Little Tokyo, they progressed to serving those members who, without families to support them, were hard hit by the Depression.[23]

Both religions displayed a tendency toward federation, Christianity again more so than Buddhism. The Buddhist Temple Association, founded only in 1925, was concerned mainly with enforcing a degree of orthodoxy in doctrinal matters, for several unorthodox sects had begun to spring up in the American environment. In contrast, Christian interdenominational cooperation was more concerned with proselytizing and social service.[24] The Southern California Church Federation, founded through the mutual efforts of four denominations in 1906, included thirty of the forty-six Japanese Christian churches within its territory by 1941. The Buddhist temples (three of which were recognized as official "direct branches" of temples in Japan) were more centralized, set in densely Japanese areas; seldom-frequented branches served outlying areas. The Christian churches, on the other hand, had a mutual understanding that they were to disperse widely, in order better to attract new members. As of 1923 this arrangement encompassed twelve Protestant denominations, and, by way of the Japanese Association, even attempted to take in Buddhists, at least to the point of requesting them not to build competing religious edifices in the neighborhoods already served by Christian churches. The denominational church most significant to the communal life of the Japanese in Los Angeles was an ad hoc one called the "Union Church," formed by compact (including formal constitution) of existing Japanese Congregational and Presbyterian congregations. Considered quite a showplace in central Little Tokyo, the Union Church became the core of a number of community activities, including many of the "social church" variety. The edifice

[23]The Federation social worker was for a period sponsored jointly by the Japanese Chamber of Commerce. Osaki, "Interdenominational Cooperation," p. 95; Fumiko Fukuoka, "Mutual Life and Aid Among the Japanese in Southern California" (Master's thesis, University of Southern California, 1937), p. 44, n. 4; Y. Y. Sacon, "A Study of the Religious Organizations in Japanese Communities in America" (manuscript [1932] in General Library, University of Southern California), pp. 65, 68; *Rafu Shimpo*. July 21, 1933.

[24]Osaki, "Interdenominational Cooperation," pp. 86–87. For a description in considerable detail of the falling away from strict Japanese religious practices in the San Francisco area in the mid-1930's, see Paul Radin, ed., "Japanese Ceremonies and Festivals in California," *Southwestern Journal of Anthropology* 2 (1946): 152–79.

itself included a kitchen, library, auditorium, and "an electric cross surmounting the roof."[25]

First in missionary and subsequently in advisory capacities, Caucasians played an important part in the development of Protestantism among the Los Angeles Japanese. Almost all were unabashed admirers of the Japanese nation. Their contact, though having a patron-and-client tone, typically was intense and favorable; Protestant churchmen can well be called the sponsors of the Japanese people in America. Among these men was Herbert B. Johnson of Berkeley, longtime leader of the (Methodist) Pacific Japanese Mission and advisor to the Southern California Japanese Church Federation. Johnson wrote on behalf of the Japanese in the San Francisco school controversy and later took their part in a residential segregation contest in Los Angeles.[26] Another, Harvey H. Guy, first supervisor of the Japanese Christian Institute, went so far as to perform investigations and lobbying on assignment from the Japanese consulate on behalf of the welfare of local Japanese, noting hopefully that the outlook for interracial amity was happier in Southern California than to the north. "I found that the people of this section of the State [were] quite favorably inclined to Japanese," Guy wrote to the Japanese consul in 1914. "I heard no reports of friction or misunderstanding between the races. I noticed Japanese customers in the stores and saw that they were treated with courtesy and kindness. . . . [But] those who are connected with the labor unions may be expected to do their best to create prejudice," a goal they had accomplished up north. Guy's hopes were shared by many Japanese Christian leaders, who lost few opportunities "to lead the Japanese into a more Americanized way of loving [*sic*] from the standpoint of Christianity. This work is very important for the solution of the California problem, as well as for the evangelization of the Japanese." A Japanese Christian laymen's picnic held in a Los

[25]George F. Kennegott (Superintendent, Southern California Congregational Conference) to [Central] Japanese Association of Southern California, May 25, 1923, Minor Document B-194, SRR Papers; Osaki, "Interdenominational Cooperation"; Sacon, "Religious Organizations"; Takahashi, "Japanese Shinto and Buddhism"; Tuthill, "Study of the Japanese in Los Angeles," pp. 66–67; United States, Works Progress Administration, Historical Records Survey Project, Southern California, *Directory of Churches and Religious Organizations in Los Angeles County* (Los Angeles: By the Project, 1940); "Union Japanese Church," *Missionary Review of the World* 44 (1923): 871; *The Eighty-fifth Anniversary of Protestant Work among Japanese in North America* (Los Angeles: [Union Church], 1964), p. 129 and *passim*.

[26]Herbert B. Johnson, *Discrimination against the Japanese in California* (Berkeley: Press of the Courier Publishing Co., 1907).

Angeles park in 1920 resolved that "Americanization can only be realized through Christianity," and proclaimed that "we who are in the United States are to be, first of all, loyal to our land of adoption."[27]

Guy was also the first president of the Los Angeles Japan America Society, a secular group dating from 1909 whose leaders were prominent Christians, both Japanese and American.[28] The Society, stressing activities designed "to acquaint each race with the culture and history of the other and to emphasize every common ground of their life," seemed to believe that the caste line could be crossed by a combination of prosperity and propriety. Dominated by polite religionists and professional men of both races, the Society overlooked sources of conflict while emphasizing culture and uplift—and appreciation of the "beautiful gardens, which were practically barren land until the Japanese came." The founder of this group was the Reverend Charles C. Pierce, who was later to assault the sensibilities of a House committee by talking favorably of the four children of the marriage of a prominent Los Angeles Japanese to a white woman.[29]

It was not friendly relations with whites that concerned most Japanese immigrants, however. The conflict that began in San Francisco in 1900, and especially the continuation of that conflict into the second half of the decade, made most Japanese in Los Angeles despair of brotherly love as a solvent of racial antagonism. Rather, a defense organization was needed. The Japanese consulate concurred; the idea may even have been theirs. In this context the Japanese Association of Los Angeles was established in 1906, six years after its counterpart in San Francisco. The Los Angeles group immediately offered "all possible support" to their embattled fellows to the north (although this probably meant little in concrete terms), and promised

[27]Guy to Acting Consul General Y. Numano, Dec. 24, Nov. 28, 1914, Reel 19, Consular Papers, Japanese American Research Project Archives; Dendo-Dan, Fourth Annual Report, p. 6; Los Angeles *Times,* June 1, 1920.

[28]Their allegiance with the white upper class even as the Society was being born was applauded by the Los Angeles *Times* and by reflex attacked by the *Union Labor News.* "AN ENEMY OF THE STATE[,] THE LOS ANGELES TIMES Heads a Great Conspiracy to Flood the Pacific Coast with Asiatics. 'The Japan Society'." Headline in *Union Labor News,* Jan. 25, 1907, reacting to neutral article in Los Angeles *Times,* Jan. 15, 1907, about the possibilities of starting a Japan America Society in Los Angeles, on the model of the Society in New York.

[29]House Committee on Immigration and Naturalization, *Hearings, Japanese Immigration,* pt. 3, pp. 932–35; [Mary Montoya Jones, comp.], *Silver Anniversary Book. Japan America Society of Los Angeles 1909 to 1934* (n.p., n.d.), p. 27 and *passim;* Neeta Marquis, "Inter-Racial Amity in California: Personal Observations on the Life of the Japanese in Los Angeles," *Independent* 75 (1913): 138–42.

to "fight to the bitter end" to protect the "general interests" of the Japanese people in America.[30] Four major Japanese agricultural districts in Los Angeles County and the San Pedro fishing area formed local Japanese Associations before 1907. Another group was added before 1915, and another before 1921, with one more founded after that date.[31]

As the question of defense grew more pressing, local units seemed insufficient for problems of wider scope. In 1915 the Central Japanese Association of Southern California was formed, with headquarters in Los Angeles. The relationship of this federal organization to its largest component, the Los Angeles Japanese Association, throws light on the complexity of the Japanese community even at this early date, and on the functions of Japanese Associations generally.

The new Central Japanese Association was an amalgam of the locals, with its officers chosen from among officers of the constituent local Associations; more than half of these were selected by the local Los Angeles Japanese Association, which also was assessed for half of the Central's costs. Yet the executives of the Central had a good deal of leeway, partly because of infrequent general meetings, but partly because of the relatively distinct sphere of action it maintained. The Central Japanese Association was organized and maintained as a quasi-government to oversee the condition of the Japanese in its jurisdiction, while the locals had grown more spontaneously as expressions of solidary communal and neighborly resistance to white hostility.[32]

Although constituted of local Japanese Associations, the guidance and influence exercised by the Central Japanese Association was to a

[30]Johnson, *Discrimination Against the Japanese,* quoting the Los Angeles Japanese Association in the *Japanese American* (San Francisco), Oct. 26, 1906.

[31]Michinari Fujita, "The History of the Japanese Associations in America" (Master's thesis, Northwestern University, 1928), pp. 54, 57; E. Manchester Boddy, *The Japanese in America* (Los Angeles: By the Author, 1921), pp. 166–67; U.S. House of Representatives, Special Committee on Un-American Activities, *Hearings, Investigation of Un-American Propaganda Activities in the United States,* 78th Cong., 1st sess. (1943), pt. 15, pp. 9285–86 (henceforth HUAC, *Investigation),* Appendix, pt. 6, pp. 1908–12.

[32]Constitution of the Los Angeles Japanese Association: "The objectives of the Association are to guarantee the rights of the Japanese, to promote their welfare, maintain their dignity, and also to promote friendship betwen Japanese and Americans. This Association consists of Japanese residing in the area under the jurisdiction of the Association." ("Regulations of the Los Angeles Japanese Association [as revised December 20, 1920]," Articles 3 and 4, in Los Angeles Japanese Association, Minutes, Dec. 20, 1920. Friendship clause added, Minutes, Jan. 8, 1919.) Constitution of the Central Japanese Association: "The purpose of the Associa-

great extent that of the government of Japan, through its local consulate.[33] The Los Angeles consulate and the Central Japanese Association were both established in 1915, and one of the Association's first actions was to investigate, for the consul, a conflict that had broken out in one of the local Associations. The consul, who urged that "all" Japanese "should automatically" belong to their local Japanese Association, sat in on key Association meetings, arbitrated internal disputes, and emphasized his position through participation in a variety of Association ceremonies, such as greeting Japanese naval training squadrons.[34] But his main source of authority was his ability to empower the Association to issue (at a fee) the various papers and certificates necessary to resident aliens if they wished to travel to Japan, to bring in relatives, and to remain in the good graces of the Japanese military authorities.[35]

The Central Japanese Association and the Los Angeles Japanese Association were not infrequently at odds with one another, despite essential agreement. In 1918 and then in 1920 the local threatened first to withhold its assessment and later to withdraw from the Central Association, in the former year obviously hoping to exercise more

tion is to unify all the Japanese Associations which are affiliated with the Association and to promote the welfare of the Japanese. The Association consists of all the Japanese Associations in the various jurisdictional districts." ("Constitution and By-Laws of the Central Japanese Association," in Central Japanese Association, Minutes, Aug. 21, 1915. These and other Japanese-language sources in the JARP Archive were intelligently scanned and translated for me by Young K. Hahn.)

[33]The pressure for nation-wide coordination of Japanese Associations, though urged by the Central Japanese Association as late as 1917 (a by-product of such an amalgamation was to be a paid representative in Tokyo, to bypass the Consul-General), never came to fruition. Central Japanese Association Minutes, Aug. 21, 1915, July 16, 1917.

[34]Central Japanese Association Minutes, Sept. 17, Dec. 11, 1915 (quoting Vice-Consul Oyama), Mar. 22, 1918; *Rafu Shimpo,* July 11, 1927; Southern California Japanese Chamber of Commerce, Reports of Committees, July 23, 1929, JARP Archive; HUAC, *Investigation,* Appendix, pt. 6, p. 1906.

[35]"If those between twenty and thirty-six years of age who are in foreign countries wish to postpone their [army] enrollment they must send certificates every year issued by Japanese consuls showing that they are residing in a foreign country. The certificate fee for same is one dollar. . . . The total sum is allowed as a subsidy to all central [Japanese] Associations. . . . The subsidy is not, however, an official one and the associations do not put it in their regular accounts." The large Los Angeles Japanese Association, in turn, was granted the certification boon, and seems for a time to have farmed out some of these duties to the prefectural associations to which most of their members belonged. Fujita, "History of the Japanese Association," p. 87, n. 3; Central Japanese Association Minutes, Apr. 24, 1916, Jan. 15, 18, 1917; Los Angeles Japanese Association Minutes, Feb. 2, 17, 1919.

control over the Central. When the consul mediated this conflict in favor of the local, he was tacitly recognizing limits to his own power over the Japanese population of Los Angeles.[36]

In 1919 the Los Angeles Japanese Association had some 2,500 full members, out of fewer than 5,500 adult males in Los Angeles City. This strikingly high rate of membership must, however, be seen in the context of a relatively low rate of member participation: less than 20 percent voted in a dull election, and less than 40 percent participated even in a hotly contested one.[37] The annual budget of $15,000 included a $1,270 subvention of the Central Japanese Association; $2,040 was devoted to education of the Nisei. Most of the balance (including $4,260 for salaries) was expended for maintaining and furthering the organization's programs. The Central Japanese Association that year had a slightly smaller budget, half of it from a consular grant. Most of the money was spent on agricultural, educational, and other programs[38] administered by the three active departments of the Association: education, fishery, and agriculture.

The finances of the Japanese Associations in their heyday are most impressive, as is the range of activities with which the group concerned itself. Rent control in Little Tokyo, hygiene, and good scholarship (the last rewarded by small sums of money) were urged upon constituents. When the Los Angeles Japanese Association Moral Reform Committee boycotted Little Tokyo gambling houses, the good offices of the consul and the local police were both called upon, bringing about the deportation of certain men who had blackened the name of the race by becoming involved in an internecine gunfight. At another point, the authorities were convinced by the Los Angeles Japanese Association to give a Japanese-language driving test. The translations were to be performed by the Association; this service alone was said to have benefited more than 700 Japanese in the first four days the test was given.[39]

[36]Los Angeles Japanese Association Minutes, July 9, 20, 22, 1918; Central Japanese Association Minutes, Apr. 8, 1920. In 1919 the Central Japanese Association discussed with the consul their power to withhold from breakaway local Associations the right to issue certificates, which may indicate that by 1920 the Los Angeles Japanese Association's threat to withdraw was somewhat empty. Central Japanese Association Minutes, Feb. 5, 1919.

[37]*Aochi* v. *Japanese Association of Los Angeles,* Superior Court, Los Angeles County, Docket Number B79661 (1920), Stipulation as to Facts, p. 8.

[38]Los Angeles Japanese Association Minutes, Jan. 8, 1919; Central Japanese Association Minutes, Feb. 5, 1919.

[39]Central Japanese Association Minutes, Sept. 17, 1915, Feb. 6, 1918, Feb. 5, 1919, Feb. 23, Mar. 24, 1924; Los Angeles Japanese Association Committee

The Japanese Association and other community organizations strove continuously to emphasize internal harmony and cooperation, and to show unity and fortitude in the face of hardship. The Immigration Act of 1924 incorporated a Japanese exclusion clause; while the measure was still before Congress, the Central Japanese Association resolved:

(1) We expect to be sincere and serious lawabiding residents of the United States.
(2) We expect the United States to rightly execute all the rights endowed upon us.
(3) We expect to foster the unyielding spirit under adversity to overcome all difficulties.
(4) We expect to enhance our spirit of cooperation among us and work for friendly relationships between us and Americans.[40]

The Association placed good citizenship first, holding to the principle that while legal and political action against official discrimination was necessary, respect had to be won from white American individuals, and could be won by proper behavior.

The Japanese actively courted such respect and adapted their ways to American standards, even when such standards were apparently irrational. In an elaborate letter of self-justification, the Japanese Association of America in 1919 recited at considerable length their great achievements in opening up new areas of California agriculture. But the organization reported that it was now advising constituents to relax their efforts somewhat, ''and to create some leisure for self-development. At the same time, it appears even to us rather strange that the Americans should complain of Japanese industry.''[41] In support of this policy the Los Angeles Japanese Association moved in November, 1919, to reduce what was to many Caucasians the most

Reports (1919); Southern California Japanese Chamber of Commerce Committee Reports, July, 1930, Jan., 1931.

[40]Central Japanese Association Minutes, Feb. 7, 1924. Although the third part of the Association resolution could be read as a call to strengthened resistance, in the value system of the group ''unyielding spirit'' clearly meant the acceptance of discomfort rather than resistance.

[41]This very interesting document is reproduced in California State Board of Control, *California and the Oriental,* pp. 203–15. Park and Miller, who quote a portion, find ''these opportunistic concessions . . . not to be praised. . . . Whether we like them or not, no other foreign-language group has so completely and intelligently organized to control its members, and no other group has at all equalled them in the work of accommodating themselves to alien conditions.'' Robert E. Park and Herbert A. Miller (nominal authors; actual author William I. Thomas), *Old World Traits Transplanted* (New York: Harper, 1921), p. 180.

striking manifestation of their tendency to work too hard: "woman's labor on Sundays in the outdoors."[42] In the following year the Central Japanese Association convened several Japanese agricultural associations to hear interested white Americans express their thoughts on Japanese labor practices. Convinced of the wisdom of accommodation, the Association ratified a decree ending *all* Sunday field labor, except at critical harvest times. The decree also halted Sunday field labor by women without exception, and reduced daily field labor by women.[43]

Japanese leaders warmly embraced the concept of "Americanization," an enthusiasm documented in both Japanese and Anglo sources. Americanization activities permitted Japanese to associate with white Americans on a client basis, freely and without dishonor: Americanism was a subject that could be learned. Japanese attended such classes in numbers which greatly gratified the authorities, with the sponsors of the 1917 pilot project exclaiming that "their demands often outstripped the knowledge of their teachers." The Japanese "clamored for classes in first aid, embroidery, tatting, crocheting and knitting, and in spite of these many requests, their interest in English was paramount. . . . [In one class] as soon as the men had learned to read a few words in English, they demanded the words of 'America' and were soon putting the words to a rather perverted form of the tune of our national anthem."[44] Americanizing Californians apparently saw no irony in their most eager pupils' ineligibility, by federal law, to translate their Americanization into citizenship, or in the legal disadvantages placed upon them by California law because of this fact. Similarly eschewing the irony, the Japanese Chamber of Commerce explained in 1919 that "the anti-Japanese feeling among Americans is irrelevant to the [war] bonds" which Japanese had purchased and continued to purchase in profusion. The purchase of

[42]Los Angeles Japanese Association Minutes, Nov. 10, 1919. A perplexed white Los Angeles man had previously exemplified the reaction of whites to Japanese labor practices in a letter to a friend: "To-day, Sunday, I passed a truck farm . . . and saw three Japanese and their wives hoeing a large tract industriously. How can a white farmer compete with them and at the same time inform himself sufficiently to make a good and efficient citizen, and how could his wife rear good citizens?" Quoted in James A. B. Scherer, *The Japanese Crisis* (New York: Frederick A. Stokes, 1916), p. 89.

[43]Central Japanese Association Minutes, July 15, 1920.

[44]California State Commission of Immigration and Housing, *Report of an Experiment Made in Los Angeles in the Summer of 1917 for the Americanization of Foreign-Born Women* (1917), pp. 16–18; *A Community Survey Made in Los Angeles City*, p. 28; Central Japanese Association Minutes, Mar. 27, 1918, Mar. 1, 1919.

the bonds was a visibly Americanized activity in which Japanese could comfortably partake.[45] California Japanese bought a total of $2,648,800 in five liberty loans, or an average of over $75 per Japanese male fifteen years or older. Los Angeles Japanese accounted for about $750,000 of this total. The war-bond effort formed a pathetic note in the protests of the Japanese at the ill treatment they would soon receive.

Part of Americanism involved staying out of trouble, and in this the Japanese community of Los Angeles was remarkably successful. The full range of group sanctions was employed, from gossip (made more potent by residential segregation) to the publication of disgraced names[46] to ostracism.[47] Those who could not cope with the economic system were sometimes helped to return to Japan, as were particularly egregious moral offenders. The Japanese Association, church, and lay groups worked to reduce crime and discourage undesirable elements, in emulation of an idealized crimeless Japan.[48] Both arrest and incarceration rates for Los Angeles Japanese were very low. Most violations were minor, and even the slight propensity to liquor-law, traffic, and drunk-and-disorderly violations declined.[49]

[45]Central Japanese Association Minutes, Mar. 5, 1918; Southern California Japanese Chamber of Commerce Reports, Apr. 16, 1919. K. K. Kawakami, *The Real Japanese Question* (New York: Macmillan, 1921), p. 267; testimony of Junzo Sasamori, Los Angeles Japanese Chamber of Commerce, in House Committee on Immigration and Naturalization, *Hearings, Japanese Immigration,* pt. 3, p. 1046.

[46]Even before this technique was formally instituted with the addition of a "police blotter" feature in the English section of *Rafu Shimpo,* it was not uncommon. A very interesting meeting of the Board of Editors of *Rafu Shimpo,* discussing the question of publication of names, is recorded in Togo Tanaka, "Journal," July 14, 1941; an earlier example is in *Rafu Shimpo,* Mar. 9, 1930.

[47]Toyama, "Japanese Community," p. 30, reports such a case concerning a libidinous minister; *Rafu Shimpo,* Jan. 11, 1931, relates the case of an ostracized extortionist who declared himself generously treated; Hidesaburo Yokoyama, "The Japanese Association in America" (Master's thesis, University of Chicago, 1921), pp. 19–21.

[48]Emory S. Bogardus, *The Survey of Race Relations on the Pacific Coast* (Los Angeles: Council on International Relations, 1926), p. 6; *Rafu Shimpo,* Oct. 26, 1930, Jan. 11, 25, 1931, Sept. 9, 1936; *Kashu Mainichi,* May 27, 1937. The Japanese of Los Angeles were not without the systematic occupational specializations outside the law typical of urban immigrant groups in America—in this case narcotics traffic, prostitution, and (despite strong efforts within the group to suppress it) gambling. From all indications, however, those few who prospered in these lines were never accorded respect or influence within the Japanese community. On the elaboration of the gambling and narcotics industry in Little Tokyo, see *Rafu Shimpo,* Apr. 20, 1935; Los Angeles *Times,* Jan. 11, 28, 1939.

[49]Walter G. Beach, *Oriental Crime in California* (Stanford: Stanford University Press, 1932), pp. 29, 56–61, 84–85; Sidney R. Garfield, "Los Angeles County Jail

The Japanese community was deeply concerned with caring for its own social problems, and on the whole it succeeded quite well in keeping needy Japanese from white charity and correction authorities. In 1923 only seven Japanese received state home relief in Los Angeles (out of 7,429 recipients), and only two of 4,877 Christmas baskets went to Japanese from the city. Fewer than twenty-five Japanese applied for job placement through a free city bureau in 1914, preferring to get jobs through their own boardinghouses and prefectural connections. Even at the depth of the Depression, when underemployment faced many Japanese, only eleven families were on the county, and another fifty on unemployment relief. Occasional formal and more frequent informal help had long been available to the needy from the Japanese Association or the prefectural associations; Los Angeles Japanese established a society to direct Japanese to proper medical care, as well as a clinic and an orphanage. In those rare instances when the needs of sick or indigent Japanese exceeded the facilities of their community and they were forced to take advantage of outside assistance, they often made a point of eventually compensating their benefactor.[50]

That the general outlook of the Japanese Associations was far from militant is unquestionable. The authorities were ultimately thought to be more easily mollified than bullied: by the suppression of "undesirable" aspects of Japanese American behavior, by settling problems within the Japanese community, by the exhortation to "Americanism" in its various forms.[51] Pressure could be brought where discrimination was costly to the Japanese but of little symbolic

---

Records of Mexicans, Japanese, Chinese, 1923," manuscript (1924?), in folder 3273–57, Governor Young's Mexican Study Commission File, California State Archives, Sacramento. On a few occasions Japanese expressed the belief that Caucasian law in Los Angeles gave them insufficient protection, proposing either self-policing or more patience. See, for example, an interview with Consul Ujiro Oyama, ca. 1925, "Survey Interviews Southern California No. 2," folder "Interesting Material," Box 2, SRR Papers; *Kashu Mainichi,* Apr. 8, 21, 1938.

[50]Joyoshi Uono, "The Factors Affecting the Geographical Aggregation and Dispersion of the Japanese Residences [in Los Angeles City]" (Master's thesis, University of Southern California, 1927), p. 73; Fukuoka, "Mutual Life and Aid," pp. 26–27, 44–46; Los Angeles Social Service Commission, *Annual Reports, 1916–17,* pp. 34, 42, *1917–18,* p. 9; Los Angeles Municipal Charities Commission, *Third Annual Report, 1915–16,* p. 53; Lydia Siemens, "A Study of Poverty as Found among Racial Groups in Los Angeles," manuscript (1924?), in folder 3273–57, Governor Young's Mexican Study Commission File; California Commission on Immigration and Housing, *A Community Survey Made in Los Angeles City,* pp. 31–32.

[51]Undoubtedly, such community control was fully congruent with tradition in the homeland.

value to Caucasians. In 1925, the white Chamber of Commerce was brought into play to convince the state legislature to excise an offensive passage from a bill; the proposal would have denied licenses for the brokerage of farm products to anyone who was not a citizen of the United States *or had not declared his intention to become such.*[52]

One basis for such conservatism was the interest of the consulate, which was always well represented in the Japanese Associations and concerned that local Japanese not embarrass larger foreign-policy goals. The consul himself seems to have entered internal disputes only when invited, and to have acted more as a conciliator than as dictator, although sometimes as a court of last resort. Yet the Associations were occasionally able to take a stand in conflict with that of the Japanese government when interests obviously clashed. A particularly clear example occurred when the Japanese government, to mollify the internationally dangerous anti-Japanese agitation in California, voluntarily terminated the migration of the so-called picture brides. Without waiting for the official announcement of suspension of picture-bride migration, the Central Japanese Association defended the custom, resolving that they were "absolutely" opposed to its suspension. The Los Angeles Japanese Association, one step further removed from Japanese officialdom, was more outspoken. The suspension, they declared, was "a premature and unilateral action, which ignores public opinion." They resolved to join the Central Japanese Association in efforts to head off the proclamation.[53]

Inner cleavages were sometimes based on prefectural loyalties, such as the successful revolt of a "reform" faction in the 1921 Japanese Association election against a "staff" faction representing only three prefectures among its leaders.[54] Despite these cleavages,

[52]Southern California Japanese Chamber of Commerce Reports, Feb. 10, Mar. 25, 1925; A.B. 225, 46th sess., 1925; California, *Journal of the Assembly,* 46th sess. (1925), pp. 754–57 (emphasis mine).

[53]Central Japanese Association Minutes, Oct. 4, 1919; Los Angeles Japanese Association Minutes, Dec. 10, 1919. It is interesting that both Central and Los Angeles Associations made their attack only indirectly upon the consul, placing the blame directly upon the Japanese Association of America, in San Francisco. The latter group, representing a different population and more under the influence of the consul general, had declared picture marriage to be "not only in contravention to the accepted American conception of marriage, but . . . also out of harmony with the growing ideals of the Japanese themselves." Quoted in Fujita, "History of the Japanese Associations," pp. 98–99.

[54]The previous election had been challenged vigorously but unsuccessfully in court by a purported private party who said he had been fraudulently misled about the place of the voting. Caucasian lawyers of considerable repute had to be employed by the Association, the case going its route without compromise. Los Angeles Japanese

the Japanese Associations continued well into the 1920's to define and coordinate the Japanese community. Ultimately, as "defense" became less salient, as the ethnic economy expanded, and as the Los Angeles Issei accepted the fate of being permanently on the wrong side of the caste line, a united front seemed less imperative. Community centralization was reversed, and the basis of the power of the Japanese Associations began to disappear. The Central Japanese Association gave way in real significance to the local Associations,[55] which in turn lost prominence to commercial groupings and to nascent second-generation groupings.

The Japanese Chamber of Commerce of Los Angeles had been founded in 1916 to coordinate the many commercial and occupational groups already operating. Merger with the Los Angeles Japanese Association was contemplated in 1924, with the Chamber as the junior partner. But the Japanese Association backed out, and did so again two years later. In 1929 the merger was completed, with the Chamber apparently now the full equal of the Association; the old Association constitution remained, with new clauses treating the promotion of commerce and industry. The new organization was to have the English name "Chamber of Commerce," but its Japanese title remained *Rafu Nihonjin Kai* (Los Angeles Japanese Association).[56] Although the merged Chamber carried on the old solidarity programs like social welfare, much of its attention shifted to commercial problems: encouraging the sale of goods made in Japan and cooperation with the National Recovery Administration, and redesigning Little Tokyo for greater commercial appeal. The latter was a pet project of the Chamber from its inception. The plans for the refurbishment of the Japanese quarter became more and more ambitious, starting with a quest for street lamps and a movie theater for the Little Tokyo shopping area, proceeding to the search for a clinic, post office, and an athletic field, and culminating in support for a mid-1930's plan to tear the area down and rebuild it along clean and synthetically Oriental lines (as was subsequently done in New

---

Association Minutes, Jan. 15, 1920, Jan. 18, 21, 31, 1921, Jan. 17, 1922; *Aochi v. Japanese Association*.

[55]The Immigration Act of 1924, ending all Japanese immigration, reduced occasions for consular paperwork, and thereby many of the fees which might accrue to the Japanese Associations. Such Associations, however, continued to collect those fees which remained. Central Japanese Association Minutes, Feb. 5, 6, 1925; Southern California Japanese Chamber of Commerce, Minutes of Committee Meetings, Dec. 19, 1921; Fujita, "The Japanese Associations in America."

[56]Southern California Japanese Chamber of Commerce Reports, May 17, 1922, Feb. 7, June 3, 1924, Jan. 19, Mar. 10, 23, Apr. 2, 9, 1926; Minutes and revised regulations, Apr. 16, 1929.

Chinatown in Los Angeles).[57] With consular encouragement, the Chamber actively sought to form a cordial relationship with the white Chamber of Commerce, explicitly enschewing political purposes but hoping to achieve a commercial entente.[58]

Organized as a ''defense'' organization above the other groupings in the Japanese American community, the Japanese Association had commanded more respect than affection. In Japan voluntary organization was a lively affair, but the village itself regularly performed a large number of vital functions. At the same time, the hierarchy of which the emperor was the apex was based—and in mythology supported—in familial analogy. The type of influence exercised by the consulate and by the consul's quasi-agents in the Japanese Associations could never be expected to have the kind of hold upon the emotional life of the Japanese Americans that the integrated social and symbolic structures in Japan had.[59] Substituting for the kind of social life they had known in Japan were the *kenjin-kai*—the regionally based groupings that had brought about the revolt in the Los Angeles Japanese Association in 1921.

In Japan the *ken,* or prefecture, constituted the largest political subdivision of the nation as a whole. Like American states, *ken* had certain traditions and cultural and economic emphases with which all Japanese would be familiar. Yet in Japan the *ken* was too large a unit to engage much affection: the village was the real political and social context within which the average person lived.

Nevertheless, by 1940 Los Angeles had no fewer than forty *kenjin-kai* (there were 46 *ken*), amorphous and varied associations based upon common prefectural origin, which served to re-create in

[57]Southern California Japanese Chamber of Commerce Reports, Dec. 27, 1918, Mar. 25, 1919, May 15, 31, 1922, May 16, 1923, May 14, 1925; Japanese Chamber of Commerce, Minutes of Committee Meetings, Feb. 21, 1930, Jan., 1931; *Rafu Shimpo,* June 14, 1931, July 20, 23, 1933; Los Angeles *Times,* Aug. 4, 1935; *Kashu Mainichi,* June 11, 1938.

[58]Southern California Japanese Chamber of Commerce Reports, June 18, Sept. 23, Oct. 6, Nov. 19, 1924, Jan. 27, Sept. 24, 1925.

[59]The *buraku,* or rural hamlet, made decisions in irrigation planning, road maintenance, proper observation of the agricultural and sacred calendars, and liaison with the legal authorities. On the other hand, the village itself took its authority from the fact that it was the amalgam of a number of stable families. Richard K. Beardsley, John W. Hall, and Robert E. Ward, *Village Japan* (Chicago: University of Chicago Press, 1958), pp. 248–59 and 349–58; Chie Nakane, *Kinship and Economic Organization in Rural Japan* (London: Athlone, 1967), pp. 26, 82, 172 and *passim;* Masao Maruyama, *Thought and Behaviour in Modern Japanese Politics* (London: Oxford University Press, 1963), pp. 9, 16; John F. Embree, ''Acculturation among the Japanese of Kona, Hawaii,'' *Memoirs of the American Anthropological Association* 59 (1941: Supplement to *American Anthropologist* 43): 1–162.

America some of the conviviality associated with life at home. Initially the *kenjin-kai* filled an especially vital need for human warmth, as the immigrants were cut off not only from their home villages but also from their families and from almost all hope of immediately establishing a family in America. The first *kenjin-kai* was undoubtedly founded quite early. Twelve were operating in Los Angeles in 1909; more than double that number were found in 1924. *Kenjin* lacking enough fellows to form a *kai* were often granted honorary membership in existing *kai*. That many new *kenjin-kai* were formed even in the fifteen years after immigration was cut off provides strong evidence of how satisfying this form of association was, even in the years after the Japanese Association entered its decline, and as the immigrant generation itself began to look more toward its progeny as their investment in America. Since residential patterns within Los Angeles as well as other areas within California were based substantially on prefecture of origin, *ken* fellowship remained a valued basis of group solidarity and solace.[60]

Besides being building blocks for other, more differentiated institutions within the Japanese community, the *kenjin-kai* functioned as employment agencies, provided legal advice, published newspapers, and performed notable deeds of charity for their members and even (when no other *kenjin-kai* could step in) for other Japanese. Especially are the *kenjin-kai* remembered for their lavish annual picnics. The *kai*, in one sense, presented the opposite pole to the Japanese Association with respect to "Americanization": while the Associations were exhorting the Japanese population to act toward the norms of the majority community with greater and greater propriety, the *kenjin-kai*, while adaptive, provided an effective link with Japan.[61]

Yet in another sense this is not so. Although the strength of the *kai* would seem to point to a devolution away from the group solidarity indicated by the first brave statements of the Japanese Association in its "defense" period, and away from the united front accommodationist position the Association later stressed, the *kai* and the Japanese Association (and its successors) were in fact complementary. Take, for example, the field of social welfare. As we have

[60]Strong, *Japanese in California,* p. 53, for survey data bearing on residence by prefecture. Immigration Commission, *Reports,* XXIII, p. 247; "Classified Japanese Institutions in Los Angeles, California," Minor Document B-348, SRR Papers; HUAC, *Investigation,* Appendix, pt. 6, p. 1924.

[61]Fukuoka, "Mutual Life and Aid," pp. 17–23, 47–53; Robert E. Park, *The Immigrant Press and Its Control* (New York: Harper, 1922), p. 151; Los Angeles Japanese Association Minutes, Feb. 2, May 17, 1919, Jan. 18, 1921, JARP Archive.

noted, Japanese Americans prided themselves on their very infrequent reliance upon white charity and upon state welfare. In this matter, *kenjin-kai* and Japanese Association neatly though informally cooperated; the former was recognized as the appropriate organization to be called in first, with the latter at hand if needs should exceed the resources of the *kai*. It was, presumably, the same with legal advice and employment.

Although questions of economic organization within the Japanese community have been reserved for the succeeding chapter, room must be made here for a most unusual sociological argument that demonstrates the complementary effect of the *kenjin-kai* and more formal and less diffuse community institutions like the Japanese Associations. This is Ivan Light's argument, which hinges upon a comparison of the economic and social welfare associations of Chinese, Japanese, and Negro Americans in the pre-1940 period.[62] Among the Japanese and Chinese, Light discovered "lower order moral communities"—groups smaller than the ethnic community as a whole, to which members were bound by ascriptive ties depending upon tradition rather than individual choice. Such ties enforced right behavior, also defined traditionally. Although Light somewhat overemphasizes the traditionalness of *kenjin* solidarity, he is distinctly correct in his perception of the *kenjin-kai* as a moral community. In contrast, he maintains that the black American lacked the "unchosen, automatic moral community in which one's membership is simply ascribed," and had thus to depend upon voluntary associations in which individual self-interest was preeminent over common morality.[63] Basically, Light derives two of the persistent differences among the Oriental-American and the Negro communities in the prewar North from this difference. One difference we have already touched upon: community welfare.

Here Light is drawn to the contrast between the ultimate failure of the small Negro fraternal groups in providing mutual insurance to their members, and the continued success of informal Oriental groups like the *kenjin-kai* in providing succor to the needy. Light correctly notes the traditional nature of the aid provided to the Japanese immigrant in need, and the sense of mutual support that accompanied it—although he does not discuss the degree to which such mutually supportive behavior was enforced by the nature of the white-dominated society in which they were living. His comparative

[62]Ivan H. Light, *Ethnic Enterprise in America: Business and Welfare among Chinese, Japanese, and Blacks* (Berkeley and Los Angeles: University of California Press, 1972).
[63]*Ibid.*, p. 170.

discussion is brilliant: he points out that the failure of the informal groups in the black community to see adequately to the needs of its members gave rise to formally rational actuarial procedures; these, in turn, led to competition among insurers to enlarge their risk pools, rational in "Western-style" insuring practice. Such competition, in turn, broke down the internal solidarity still remaining in the more strictly fraternal organizations, leaving the black fraternal insurance companies in the position of being generally inferior (because smaller) copies of white insurance companies.

Because the black man was poor and his insurer shaky, his policy would be cancelled if his account fell into arrears. By contrast, mutual aid associations like *kenjin-kai* provided benefits that were diffuse. "If sick, a member could expect friends to operate his store or get him into a hospital for treatment. . . . If he were unemployed, a member's friends would help him to find a job. . . . Friends could provide goods in kind and services for free."[64] In a community like the Japanese of Los Angeles, the Japanese Association or any formally organized group would have needed immense resources to handle such functions for all. The presence of the lower-level moral solidarities permitted the Japanese Association to operate in extraordinary situations with dispatch, to coordinate activities going on elsewhere within the community, and to deal with that type of activity that small moral solidarities were insufficient to handle—especially designing a group position vis-à-vis the white community.

Light's other major contribution is in his understanding of the *tanomoshi-ko,* a traditional Japanese grouping brought over in many cases intact. The *ko* (which has a Chinese counterpart) is a "rotating credit" institution, bringing together a group of individuals sharing similar (but not common) economic interests, and held together by moral bonds of social solidarity—often *kenjin-kai* membership. *Ko* members contribute a certain amount to a pool on a regular basis and distribute this pool according to prearranged formula, usually by bidding or by chance, until each member receives the pool once. At this point the *ko* dissolves. *Ko* meetings were sociable affairs, with the convivial atmosphere forming an integral part of the whole, just like the solidarity upon which mutual trust was based. *Ko*'s, of course, paid no interest; but neither did they charge it. And they did provide a lump sum of money to a large number of individuals— quite apart from the flexibility which they could show in case of death or distress, benefits which no rational banking institution could offer. Light concludes that "rotating credit associations filled a role in the

[64]*Ibid.,* p. 161.

Oriental economies which Western banking was chronically unable to do for Negroes, . . . [to break] the cycle of underdevelopment which mutually inhibited Negro business and finance."[65]

In Los Angeles, where perhaps as many as half the Issei were involved in *ko*'s, the *tanomoshi-ko* itself developed from its fully traditional expression to the point where in 1921 the Japanese Chamber of Commerce organized a committee to oversee the conduct of the *ko*'s, to see that individual *ko* members were treated fairly, and that money was properly managed.[66] The "cycle of underdevelopment" seemed to have been broken, and Los Angeles *ko*'s began to emphasize capitalistic rationality at the expense of ritual and expressions of social solidarity. By this time the burgeoning ethnic economy had quite clearly generated demands for capital which were too great for the *ko*—at least as traditionally organized. In 1919 the Japanese Chamber of Commerce organized a mutual savings bank in Little Tokyo, but by the end of the 1920's the group's economy was on such a sound footing that, within the limits imposed by the caste line, credit shortage was not a pressing problem. Japanese-run enterprise in Los Angeles had the same credit ratings as white-run enterprise for all but the largest sums. Conventional banking had entered Little Tokyo from two directions, as a branch of the Yokohama Specie Bank competed with branches of two Caucasian-run California banks.[67]

In the economic realm the *ko* had served its original function early, and it lost economic meaning as the Japanese community gained in size and enterprise. In like manner, the Japanese Association within a generation had outlived its usefulness, giving way to organizations that were functionally more specific.

---

[65]*Ibid.*, p. 57.

[66]*Ibid.*; John F. Embree, *Suye Mura: A Japanese Village* (Chicago: University of Chicago Press, 1939), pp. 138–47; Southern California Japanese Chamber of Commerce Reports, June 8, 1921, JARP Archive.

[67]Owing to the limited nature of many Japanese enterprises, however, relatively fewer received the highest levels of credit rating. Edward K. Strong, Jr., *et al.*, *Vocational Aptitudes of Second-Generation Japanese in the United States* (Stanford: Stanford University Press, 1933), pp. 141–43; "Classified Japanese Institutions in Los Angeles"; Southern California Japanese Chamber of Commerce Reports, Mar. 25, Apr. 16, 1916, Aug. 25, 1920, Jan. 21, Aug. 20, 1925.

5

The Ethnic Economy

Agriculture was the foundation of much of the enterprise and prosperity of the Los Angeles Japanese-American community. This base was explored early, developed vigorously, and exploited and enjoyed with a marked degree of community co-operation—a kind of ethnic-based welfare capitalism. The peculiar economic specialization in food production, processing, and distribution constituted the economic health of the Japanese community of Los Angeles—a health, however, which was quite compatible with (and indeed, sustained by) racial separation.

In describing the growth of the all-Japanese fishing villages in Los Angeles County, we pointed to a characteristic of Japanese-American enterprise that was visible in their agricultural expansion: the tendency toward group exploitation of resources that whites had largely overlooked. The fabulous productivity of Los Angeles County climate and soil, when irrigated and farmed intensively, was such a resource, and a disproportionate number of farmers from Japan were attracted to the county.[1] By the first decade of the twentieth century,

[1] Data on the backgrounds of Issei farmers of three areas in California with markedly different agricultural concentrations suggest that, in each, about four in five Issei farmers had farm backgrounds in Japan. But in Los Angeles County there were more Japanese agriculturalists than there were jobs in farming; hence, almost half of Los Angeles Japanese *not* farming shortly before World War II had had farm backgrounds in Japan. This figure was far above the 13% for the less agricultural San Francisco Bay area, though a bit below the 60% in the highly agricultural central valley of California. These observations, in turn, are linked by the fact that in Los Angeles 88% of all Issei males who had worked in Japan had been in agriculture, whereas of all Issei males in the Bay Area only 53% had been agriculturalists in Japan. For Issei males in the Central Valley the comparable figure was 81%. Despite Los Angeles's clearly metropolitan tendencies, it was, from the perspective of a Japanese, almost a farm area. These figures are based on War Relocation Authority's inquiries of all Nisei relocatees about their parents. Place of residence in 1942 (before relocation) actually refers to the Nisei respondent, but both U.S. and Japanese occupation refer to the Issei parents. Punchcards for these data are in the JERS Collection. The Japanese American Research Project, UCLA, placed the cards on magnetic tape with the file name PRISON.

clusters of Japanese farmers were working on their own account in many farming areas of the county, taking advantage of the short supply of agricultural labor and of whites' tendency to produce less labor-intensive (but also less profitable) crops than the land could support.

Quite soon after Japanese laborers entered an area—in one case, as early as 1901—some began to enter leases in their own names. (In that same year the president and general manager of the Southern California Fruit Exchange told the Industrial Commission that "the Japanese want the light jobs, and the house places, and things like that."[2]) In the case of the first known Japanese farm proprietor, two years as labor boss had provided him with the stake he needed to start his farm. The Japanese were adventurous in a peculiar sense of the word; they settled in some areas considered relatively marginal as farmland, where they paid high rents and practiced intensive interplanting, gambling upon spectacularly high productivity. For maximal exploitation, techniques and familiarity with the soil and other conditions had to be shared—hence the oft-remarked tendency of the Japanese to "colonize."

The internal economic integration of the Japanese agricultural colonies increased with their size. Before long, Japanese operated facilities for peddling, and then developed more elaborate approaches to the distribution of their goods. They shifted crops and areas of concentration to keep ahead of the market and land exhaustion. Once risen from the cramped quarters allotted to agricultural laborers, the Japanese farmers maintained their spartan existence, in pursuit of a larger economic stake.[3] From these areas the previous occupants— most often Chinese or whites—departed in the face of Japanese competition. Largest was the Moneta-Gardena area, where 31 leased Japanese farms were found in 1905, and 101 (four of which were

[2]A. H. Naftzger, in U.S. Industrial Commission, *Report,* X: *Agriculture and Agricultural Labor* (Washington: Government Printing Office, 1901), p. 957. Naftzger went on to note that "the Japanese dress exactly like the Americans, and their habits are about the same. . . . They want to live in a little better style [than the Chinese laborers] and are more particular about the class of work they do." Yet "they are classed much the same as the Chinese."

[3]Nichibei Shimbunsha, *Nichibei nenkan* [*Japanese American Yearbook*], no. 1 (San Francisco: Nichibei Shimbun, 1905), pp. 169–70; U.S. Immigration Commission, *Reports,* XXIV: *Japanese and Other Immigrant Races on the Pacific Coast and Rocky Mountain States:* II, *Agriculture,* Senate Doc. 633, 61st Cong., 2nd sess. (1911), pp. 383–92; Kaizo Naka, "Social and Economic Conditions among Japanese Farmers in California" (Master's thesis, University of California, 1913), p. 78; Japanese American Citizens' League, "History of the Japanese People in the San Gabriel Valley and Pomona," typescript, Folder T 6.13, JERS Collection; California State Board of Control, *California and the Oriental,* p. 111.

owned outright) in 1909.[4] Although the Japanese operated less than 1 percent of all land farmed in Los Angeles in 1910, this represented a twofold growth in five years. Moreover, because of the intensiveness of the Japanese nurture, their proportion of the *value* of the farm produce was a good deal higher. By 1910 the Japanese had a virtual monopoly of berry production in the county; in fact, about half the Japanese farmers in the county were raising berries—a specialty within a specialization. Even more propitious, they had made important strides toward dominance in local truck farming; they already farmed no less than one-fifth of the Los Angeles County acreage devoted to these products.[5] The growth of the city of Los Angeles had created a demand for fresh fruits and vegetables which few local people were trained and willing to supply. Distant sources of these crops were uneconomical, given the current technology of food distribution. When the more aggressive and younger Japanese arrived, Chinese and Caucasian competition retired from the backbreaking work.[6]

Once he had learned the techniques involved in the work (often from his employer), the Japanese farmer was ready to work unusually hard, and in a more cooperative and innovative fashion. Strawberries, a crop which demanded intensive care and in which competition was slight, proved an ideal point of entry for the Japanese. The average Japanese berry farm of six acres (in 1909) could produce a very valuable crop, averaging $1,500 worth of strawberries alone— and in fact a small area was virtually an indispensable element of Japanese farming success. Small size limited capital outlay and obviated costly tools and improvements; moreover, a small farm made possible the most detailed application of labor. The average improved acreage of Japanese-run farms in Los Angeles County in 1909 was only 11.6 acres, as compared with 52.9 acres for all farms in the county. Japanese farms in this year produced 18 percent of the value of Los Angeles farm products, employing 1.5 percent of the improved farmland.[7]

The Japanese entry into Los Angeles agriculture violated the cautions usually thought appropriate to American farming. Driven by a

[4]Immigration Commission, *Reports,* XXIV, pp. 382–96. The 1905 figures cited by the Commission are from a Japanese yearbook and might be underestimates.

[5]*Ibid.,* pp. 381, 384–85; *Census 1910 P2,* p. 43; *Census 1910 P1,* p. 652.

[6]Immigration Commission, *Reports,* XXIV, pp. 385–86 and *passim.*

[7]*Ibid.,* pp. 381, 785, 789. U.S. House of Representatives, Select Committee Investigating National Defense Migration, *Fourth Interim Report* (H.R. 2124), 77th Cong., 2nd sess., p. 123 (henceforth cited as Tolan Committee, *Fourth Interim Report); Census 1910 A1,* pp. 150, 156; *Census 1910 P2,* pp. 49–50.

distinctly speculative urge for large earnings which would permit an early, triumphal return to Japan, Los Angeles Japanese rented small parcels of close-in lands held by white absentees who anticipated future subdivision. For such land they often paid unusually high rents. Japanese tenants were even more attractive to speculative absentee landlords because they demanded ''little or no outlay on the part of the landowner for their housing. In some cases the Japanese tenants occupy the [old] Chinese bunkhouses . . . in other cases, they occupy boarded-up, unceiled, and unpainted structures. Frequently the tenant erects the cheap structure himself.''[8] Such close-in land made simple the distribution of unusually fresh produce. Even before the Alien Land Law of 1913 forbade alien Japanese in California to own farmland, Los Angeles Japanese had by choice moved toward land operation rather than land ownership as a route to success. This fact in itself indicates the extent to which their farming in Los Angeles was a nontraditional and economically rational pursuit: owning was simply not as profitable as renting. Acreage owned by Japanese for farming purposes in the county started to decrease even before 1909 and declined further thereafter; by 1912 it amounted to only 459 acres. As late as 1940 Los Angeles had the smallest proportion of owners among its Japanese farmers of any California county.

The philosophy of farming in Japan was also an important ingredient in the striking success of the Japanese in Los Angeles, despite the obvious contrast in crops, soil conditions, and legal relationship to the land. Japanese agriculture stressed a high evaluation of the land's potential, a close relationship of the family to the land's products which sustained it, and the cooperative working of the land by family and community. The aim of Oriental agriculture was always the maximization of long-run yield. As an early twentieth-century agricultural traveler in Asia explained, the Orientals ''have adapted conditions to crops and crops to conditions.'' The same approach also worked in Los Angeles.[9]

[8]H. A. Millis, *The Japanese Problem in the United States* (New York: Macmillan, 1915), pp. 187–88.

[9]Immigration Commission, *Reports*, XXIV, pp. 382, 385, 392; California, Bureau of Labor Statistics, *Fifteenth Biennial Report*, (1910–12), p. 634; Tolan Committee, *Fourth Interim Report*, p. 124. While Japanese agriculture was, in the late nineteenth century, highly traditional, it nevertheless in practice was highly rational, given the assumption of abundant labor. Crops were staggered, interplanting was practiced, and each stalk was treated by hand. Land was terraced and canalized; water was diverted, held back, and utilized at the optimal moment. Hoes, drills, and spades were widely used, but plows were not. Franklin H. King, *Farmers of Forty Centuries*, ed. J. P. Bruce, 2nd ed. (New York: Harcourt, Brace, n.d.

Explanations of the marked economic success of the Japanese in America have often held that these immigrants brought certain skills—or cultural traits, or attitudes—which were particularly adaptable to American economic conditions. In one sense, Los Angeles agriculture bears out this line of argument; but in another, it indicates some of the argument's limitations.

White Californians, first with admiration but later with scorn, told of the Japanese ability to perform "squat labor." This prowess explained their value as agricultural laborers, and their subsequent success in growing small fruits and vegetables. True, many operations of Japanese agriculture in Japan required squatting, as did truck farming. But rice and strawberries are quite distinct crops, and Japan and Southern California have widely different climates. Skills were only transferable in a highly generalized sense. It helped to be able to squat, but the posture was less critical than the willingness to assume it; experience in intensive farming was less important than the fact that American factors of land and labor could be varied to benefit the Japanese. The *notion* of cooperation in economic enterprise was carried to America, more than the specific forms of cooperation.

The "Japanese" frame of mind, while distinctly facilitating economic "success," does not explain it. We must look to structural considerations. Of these, none is more central than the initial rather single-minded focus of the immigrants on making money and returning to Japan. Working hard was characteristic of Japanese culture, but it was a trait considerably emphasized when amplified by the commitment of immigrant Japanese to return home with enough money to start a family. In the early years especially, hard work, frugality, and cooperation were widely practiced. That entrepreneurship (agricultural or other) and not labor was the way to return home enriched was clear enough to those in the underdeveloped western states. Through the consuls and the Japanese Associations, an interested home government reinforced the message. Thus the immigrant generation intentionally moved into proprietorship.[10]

Once established in business, the same proven traits of hard work, frugality, and cooperation led to a continuing pattern of acquisition and the application of hard work and self-denial, broken only by triumphant return. The ideal labor force, widely used by Japanese

---

[1927]); Johann J. Rein, *The Industries of Japan* (London: Hodder and Stoughton, 1889), pp. 3–54.

    [10]This paragraph and the next draw heavily upon the theoretical framework advanced in Edna Bonacich and John Modell, *The Economic Basis of Ethnic Solidarity* (forthcoming).

entrepreneurs, was of younger relatives or prefectural fellows, the former especially bound to the business by a sense of their possible future interest. On the whole, such businesses looked inward, not outward, or to more of the same. And why should they do otherwise, when discrimination or the threat of it indicated that acquisitiveness—and the plowing back into the business of profits and of spare time—was the most prudent course for an uncertain future, whether or not return to Japan was still contemplated as the Nisei came of age?

In Southern California, this combination of motivation and capabilities was explosive, especially in contrast to the rather lackadaisical way in which the resources of the place had up to then been employed.

The subsequent expansion of this promising start is displayed in Table 5.1. The growth of Japanese farming in Los Angeles between 1910 and 1920 was fully as spectacular as the group's opponents would have wished to portray it in arguing for the Alien Land Law; it is unclear how long this progress might have continued if that law had not interfered. Already in 1920 there was in Los Angeles County one Japanese farm per thirteen Japanese men, women, and children. Especially considering that Los Angeles was even in 1920 primarily an urban area, this high ratio indicates that the Japanese had already gone far in the direction of being a farm caste, surely a more radical form of racial segregation than external influences forced upon them. Since immigration had stopped and relatively few children were coming of economically productive age during most of the 1920's, continued growth of Japanese farm proprietorship would soon force Japanese farmers into dependence upon the labor of other groups—

TABLE 5.1. Development of Japanese[a] Agriculture in Los Angeles, 1910–40

	1910	1920	1930	1935	1940
Number of acres farmed by Japanese	6,173	44,503	24,815	28,135	30,820
Percentage of all farmland farmed by Japanese	0.8	5.1	4.7	4.5	5.2
Number of Japanese farms	531	1,567	1,278	1,634	1,592
Mean number of acres per Japanese farm	12	29	19	17	19

[a]All figures after 1910 are for farms operated by non-whites; with very few exceptions, these were Japanese. (For example, in 1940, 1,523 of the 1,592 non-white farms were run by Japanese.)

Source: *Census 1920 AI*, p. 346; *Census 1930 AI*, p. 519; *Census 1940 AI*, p. 691.

the same type of dependence that whites had earlier experienced, and that had given the Japanese their initial opportunity.

Masakazu Iwata maintains that the Alien Land Law of 1920 and the exclusionary Immigration Act of 1924 "did much to discourage the Japanese from entering farming or expanding their operation" in California, a view consistent with that of the contemporary leaders of the Los Angeles Japanese community. Roger Daniels, to the contrary, holds that the Alien Land Law was "an empty gesture, an ineffective irritant," because so many devices permitted the Japanese to circumvent it, notably leasing in the name of an American citizen, especially minor offspring. T. Scott Miyakawa helpfully mediates between these two positions, holding that the Japanese were inhibited in their usual creatively entrepreneurial application to farming by the insecurity induced by being consistently on the shady side of the law, even though the law could with some ease be evaded.[11]

What is certainly true is that the Alien Land Law was tenaciously opposed by the Japanese Americans. The Japanese Associations displayed their continued willingness to function as "defense" organizations when they saw crucial economic structures at risk. As early as 1915 the Central Japanese Association had consulted with the local Associations about court action to frustrate the Alien Land Law of 1913. When the State of California challenged the purchase of farmland by Jukichi Harada in the name of his citizen children in 1914, the Central Japanese Association established a committee to gather legal opinion and to assist the Haradas. Their efforts at first were encouraging: Harada won his case. The court praised his motive of providing a better life for his family, while maintaining that the interest of the citizen children was unassailable.[12] The Central Japanese Association was soon talking of launching a new campaign to abolish the Alien Land Law, apparently by influencing public opinion.[13] But this optimism was quickly shattered by the anti-Japanese campaign which began in 1919 and gained momentum

[11]Masakazu Iwata, "The Japanese Immigrants in California Agriculture," *Agricultural History* 36 (1962): 25–37; Roger Daniels, *The Politics of Prejudice* (Berkeley and Los Angeles: University of California Press, 1962), p. 88; T. Scott Miyakawa, review of *The Politics of Prejudice* by Roger Daniels, *Southern California Quarterly* 66 (1964): 105–8. For a reflection of the contemporary Japanese-American assessment of the damage, see Chotoku Toyama, "The Life History as a Social Document," May 27, 1924, Major Document 69, SRR Collection.

[12]Central Japanese Association Minutes, Dec. 11, 1915, Oct. 16, 1916: *California v. Harada*, opinion and relevant documents, in Consulate General of Japan, comp., *Documental History of Law Cases Affecting Japanese in the United States 1916–1924* (San Francisco: By the Consulate General, 1925), II, 700–736.

[13]Central Japanese Association Minutes, Feb. 6, 1918.

during the 1920 election, with its Alien Land Law initiative measure. The courts provided a forum in which the Association felt competent, but contesting public opinion against the likes of James Phelan seemed impossible. A feeble "Keep California Green" campaign fared poorly. Defeated at the polls, the Japanese Associations explained the law to their people, looked into the possibilities of migration to Mexico, and planned a legal attack upon the new legislation. In conjunction with the Japanese Association of America, a fund of $20,000 was established for jointly sponsored legal action to be carried, if necessary, to the U.S. Supreme Court.[14]

The leading tests of the California Alien Land Law were decided by the Supreme Court in November, 1923. All were unfavorable to the Japanese.[15] Although months earlier the Central Japanese Association had formulated contingency plans in case of defeat, hoping in that case for a revision of the Japan–U.S. treaty of 1911 to permit Japanese to hold farmland, the Court's quick work resulted in "a situation of instability and bewilderment" in that association and in the Japanese community at large.[16] Only vigilance could keep the legal implications of the judgment within reasonably narrow bounds.[17]

Meanwhile, until the practical effects of the rulings were determined, the Japanese Association had to work out plans for coping with the new situation. The most radical proposals called for the relocation of the unwanted Japanese farmers in Mexico, elsewhere in

[14]Michinari Fujita, "The History of the Japanese Associations in America" (Master's thesis, Northwestern University, 1928), p. 49; Japanese Chamber of Commerce Reports, Feb. 23, 1921; Central Japanese Association Minutes, Aug. 27, Oct. 8, 11, 14, 15, 1921.

[15]*Webb* v. *O'Brien,* and *Frick* v. *Webb,* 263 U.S. 326 (1923) reprinted with briefs and lower court decisions in Consulate General, *Documental History,* II, 1-179, 213-499. See also Thomas Reed Powell, "Alien Land Cases in the United States Supreme Court," *California Law Review* 12 (1924): 259-82.

[16]Central Japanese Association Minutes, Mar. 12, Nov. 24, 1923. The California Alien Land Law formally guaranteed to all aliens ineligible for citizenship the rights already guaranteed them by treaty.

[17]In the "White's Point Case," *California* v. *Tagami,* 195 Cal 522 (1925), for which the Central Japanese Association helped to defray costs, the California Supreme Court ruled that (contrary to the arguments of the state) the Alien Land Law did not affect the rights of ineligible aliens under the Treaty of 1911 to buy land for even such questionably "commerical" (the wording of the Treaty) purposes as a sanitarium. A later case, *Tashiro* v. *Jordan,* 201 Cal 236 (1927), saw white Californians defeated in their attempt to use the Alien Land Law to harass Japanese—in this case, the incorporators of a proposed Japanese Hospital of Los Angeles. The White's Point case is discussed in Central Japanese Association Minutes, Oct. 3, 18, 24, 1922, and documented in Consulate General, *Documental History,* II, 625-99.

the West, or even in the South.[18] Less drastic were plans to alter the characteristic tenure of the Japanese farmers to wage or contract farming, with urban entrepreneurs being counted upon to provide an investment outlet in place of the farm proprietorship.[19] To the extent possible, the Central Japanese Association encouraged reassignment or purchase of agricultural lands in the names of citizen offspring, and asked that the Japanese government give financial assistance to effect such purchases.[20] Anticipating opposition to a plan they had devised for citizen-owned, immigrant-operated agricultural cooperatives, the Central Japanese Association resolved as early as April, 1923, that a change in the treaty was desirable. Copies of their resolution were sent to the Japanese government (a copy went by hand to the Japanese ambassador to Washington), to congressmen, and to Japanese newspapers with the idea of affecting public opinion. Treaty revision, however, was far beyond their power. Even two years later, when California began to challenge Japanese agricultural corporations, the Japanese Association could only get the assurance of the Japanese government that a narrow American interpretation of the treaty as applied to agricultural incorporation would be applied reciprocally in Japan.[21]

Despite all the contemporary passion, it would seem that as far as Los Angeles agriculture is concerned, Iwata's argument about the crippling of Japanese farming — even with Miyakawa's modification — does not fare well. In February, 1925, Chloe Holt conducted a series of interviews to examine the effects of the Alien Land Law upon the wholesale produce business of Los Angeles. Her informants agreed that little effect had been felt, although they disagreed in both diagnosis and prognosis. Holt herself concluded that ''it is too soon to tell just what the effect of the law is going to be because it is not yet in full working force.''

A less conservative assessment of her evidence would suggest that there was never going to be a serious enforcement of the Alien Land Law, given the lack of passion immediately after its passage, and also taking into consideration the continuing financial interest in Japanese

[18]From time to time the American press carried stories of such mass migrations, but no migration ever substantially depleted the Japanese farming group in Los Angeles. Central Japanese Association Minutes, Apr. 4, 1924; San Francisco *Chronicle*, Dec. 30, 1922; Los Angeles *Times,* July 19, 1924.

[19]Central Japanese Association Minutes, Nov. 27, 1923; Japanese Chamber of Commerce Reports, Nov. 21, Dec. 13, 1923. Both groups worked closely with the Central Agricultural Association during the crisis.

[20]Central Japanese Association Minutes, Jan. 26, 1924.

[21]*Ibid.,* Oct. 25, 1922, April 2, Dec. 15, 1923, Dec. 4, 1925; remarks of Consul Ohashi in *Rafu Shimpo,* Aug. 1, 1926.

agriculture by many white businessmen. By the time of Holt's study, despairing reports had already appeared in the press. "The expected has happened. A group of American-born Japanese, who are just as much citizens of the United States as you or I, have formed a syndicate under the laws of California for the acquiring of land by lease or purchase. That just about 'settles the hash,' to use the old familiar slang phrase, of the anti-alien land law."[22] By 1935 Carey McWilliams, classic interpreter of Los Angeles culture and society and long-time champion of the underdog in California, noted that the land act "is a dead letter. It is no longer enforced, nor is there any sentiment for its enforcement. . . . To strike at the Japanese [farmer] today means to strike at American capital," so virile had Japanese agricultural enterprise grown. The truth of McWilliams's observation is amply borne out in the evidence from a darker day. A conference was called by California Attorney General Earl Warren shortly after Pearl Harbor, to look into ways of harassing the local Japanese-American community; its "Proceedings," with very different tones, agreed that the law was indeed a "dead letter," and not just in Los Angeles.[23]

A close examination of Table 5.1 indicates that even the 1920's figures do not suggest a dropoff of Japanese farming in Los Angeles. Though the very substantial decline in total acres farmed by Japanese from 1920 to 1930 would seem to confirm Iwata's argument, other rows of the table greatly modify it. The 1920–30 drop scarcely

[22]Chloe Holt, untitled study, Feb. 27, 1925, Major Document 297, SRR Papers; Los Angeles *Express,* Nov. 14, 1924.

[23]Carey McWilliams, "Once Again the Yellow Peril," *Nation* 140 (1935): 735–36; "Proceedings, Conference of Sheriffs and District Attorneys Called by Attorney General Warren on the Subject of Alien Land Law Enforcement," Feb. 2, 1942, typescript verbatim minutes, folder A15.02, JERS Collection. For legal cases describing the operation of such conspiracies to defeat the operation of the Alien Land Law (cases in which, unusually, the conspiracy had come to grief), see *Mori Saiki* v. *Hammock,* 207 Cal 90 (1929; the case, however, dates from 1920) and *Takeuchi* v. *Schmuck,* 206 Cal 782 (1929, the conspiracy dating from 1923–24). The report in *Takeuchi* notes: "Schmuck testified upon cross-examination that he was dealing directly with the father and knew it was against the law for the father to buy the property; that the girl did not have the money; that he knew the title was being taken in the girl's name 'to get around the law,' and that the plaintiff and her father were violating the law, but that he did not know it was a violation of the law for him to participate in an unlawful transaction. . . . They [Schmuck and his wife] were conspirators in an attempt to violate the statute in the same sense as were the Japanese father and daughter with whom they dealt, and their conduct, because of their citizenship, was more culpable than was the conduct of the ineligible alien or his daughter, who was of alien blood." Griffith Jones, "Who May Own Property in California?" *Los Angeles Realtor* 7 (Sept. 1928): 11–12, is splendidly coy about the practical nullity of the law.

affected the Japanese proportions of all lands farmed in the county. The Japanese decline was largely a function of the decline of total land farmed in the county, probably due to urban encroachments. Overall, average farm size declined sharply during the first half of the decade, while the total number of farms in the county was about constant: Los Angeles agriculture appears to have moved toward the Japanese model during this decade. During the 1920's the *value* of Japanese farmland and buildings increased no less than fourfold. Increasingly intensive farming evidently explains the declines in total farm acreage and in Japanese farm acreage.[24]

Although the total number of Japanese farms in Los Angeles continued to be roughly the same from 1920 to 1940, indications are that 1930 was the peak year for Japanese farm value, and that the Depression rather than the Alien Land Law set back Japanese farming.[25] An unanticipated consequence of the Alien Land Law may have been the migration to the city of Los Angeles of Japanese from farms elsewhere in the state—a migration which materially aided the vertical integration of the fruit-and-vegetable industry of the Japanese.[26] Yet even in 1940 the Japanese farming position was a most substantial one. In southeast Los Angeles their hold on the available farmland was tenacious and general, as Map 3 clearly shows. The special favorability of the area's soil and climate for raising truck crops permitted the Japanese to grow no less than 99 percent of the county's berries and cauliflower.

In 1940 Japanese tenancy in Los Angeles, as noted, exceeded that in any other county in the state. It also exceeded the rate for white farmers *in comparable types of farming* in Los Angeles. If the latter comparison can be explained by uncertainties introduced by the Alien Land Laws, the former is largely attributable to the outlook of the Japanese truck farmers in Los Angeles. Clarke Chambers's description of the modern California farmer applies a fortiori to the Japanese

[24]The crucial 1925 Census of Agriculture data are not truly comparable to the data from any previous or subsequent censuses. It is clear from them, however, that there was indeed a very abrupt shift of Los Angeles Japanese out of farm tenancy between 1920 and 1925, although there was a slight compensatory shift into ownership. With natural increase taken into account, the 1925 Japanese farm population in Los Angeles was more or less maintained for at least the next decade, and probably until World War II. In addition to the sources for Table 5.1, see *Census 1925 A1*, pp. 449, 457, 482; *Census 1935 A1*, p. 945; consular census, enclosed in response of George C. Clements to SRR, Mar. 19, 1925, folder "Historical Background," Box 4, SRR Papers; U.S. Wartime Civil Control Administration, *Bulletin No. 10* (1942), p. 5.

[25]*Census 1940 A1*, p. 691.

[26]This was the conclusion of the 1925 "Findings Conference" of the Survey of Race Relations, reported in their pamphlet entitled *Tentative Findings of the Survey of Race Relations* (n.p., n.d.), p. 10.

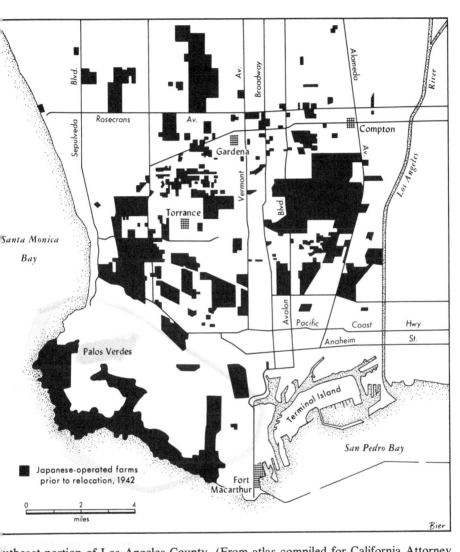

Japanese-operated farms
prior to relocation, 1942

0   2   4
miles

Bier

...utheast portion of Los Angeles County. (From atlas compiled for California Attorney
...neral.)

agriculturalists of Los Angeles: "to be successful, [he] must be a skillful agronomist, a careful manager of labor, an astute businessman, a speculator, and certainly an optimist."

This was nowhere more true than in truck farming. Characteristically undramatic, but displaying uncompromisingly businesslike attitudes toward land, capital, and production, and talking in "the very vernacular of the gambler," produce led the powerful surge of California agriculture in the first three decades of the century.[27] Japanese tenancy in Los Angeles was characterized by cash rents, frequent moves, and a tendency toward quick exploitation of the farm's market potential. Japanese fitted themselves into whatever land was temporarily open for lease, sometimes among oil refinery tanks or below power cables. Japanese resented the charge that their farming depleted the soil; but this could not have presented a major problem, since white owners, with their interests in industrial uses or in residential real estate speculation, seldom cared.[28]

A high profit-to-capitalization ratio was the condition of success in Los Angeles truck farm enterprises, and this fact was continually before the Japanese. Accordingly, their movement was toward those endeavors in which their forte, intensive care, could most completely be transformed into cash. Their typical operation, small even in the early years, became smaller. Their initial emphasis on berries declined, for berries, though valuable, did not offer the speculative opportunities of vegetables. The Japanese berry monopoly in 1941 was grown on the same acreage devoted to the crop in 1909. Simi-

[27]Clarke A. Chambers, *California Farm Organizations* (Berkeley and Los Angeles: University of California Press, 1952), p. 1 and the balance of ch. 1, which is an excellent introduction to the unique qualities of California agriculture; Adon Poli, "Japanese Farm Holdings on the Pacific Coast," U.S. Department of Agriculture, Bureau of Agricultural Economics (Berkeley, 1944), map facing p. 14; Paul S. Taylor and Tom Vasey, "Historical Background of California Farm Labor," *Rural Sociology* 1 (1936): 401–19; George M. Peterson, *Composition and Characteristics of the Agricultural Population in California,* University of California College of Agriculture, Agricultural Experiment Station, Berkeley, Bulletin No. 630 (1939); William Michael Gilmartin, "Truck Farming in the United States: A Study of the Industrialization of Agriculture" (Ph.D. dissertation, University of California, Berkeley, 1942): *Census 1930 Al,* p. 519; *Census 1940 Al,* p. 697.

[28]R. L. Adams and William H. Smith, Jr., *Farm Tenancy in California and Methods of Leasing,* University of California College of Agriculture, Agricultural Experiment Station, Berkeley, Bulletin no. 655 (1941), pp. 8–15; untitled study by Commonwealth Club of California on farm tenancy in Los Angeles County and statement of Los Angeles Chamber of Commerce, "Oriental and Agriculture," 1921, both in folder "California County Reports," Box 1, SRR Papers; Lloyd H. Fisher and Ralph L. Nielsen, "The Japanese in California Agriculture," printed in Tolan Committee, *Hearings,* pt. 31, p. 11822; Japanese Agricultural Association, *The Japanese Farmers in California* (San Francisco: By the Association, 1918[?]), p. iv.

larly, though consignment sales to large sugar companies had almost guaranteed the Japanese a safe profit on sugar beets, the product offered neither speculative possibilities nor further profits from its distribution, since beets required large investments to translate into a consumer product. Over 6,000 acres of sugar beets were raised in the county by Japanese in 1919, but none in 1940. Even within the category of truck crops, the Japanese increasingly specialized in the most intensive crops. Celery replaced lettuce in the favor of Japanese growers in response to a statewide drop in lettuce prices during the Depression. In the 1930's the average crop value per acre in Los Angeles was $68 for sugar beets, $155 for lettuce, and $715 for celery.[29] The move into truck farming coincided with their move into the southwest area, and typifies the odd relationship between Japanese-American prosperity and Caucasian land use in Los Angeles.

Early in the twentieth century, most Anglo farmers believed that the hilly Palos Verdes Peninsula (at the extreme southwest of Map 3) was too arid to be fertile. Convinced of the efficacy of irrigation and intensive care, Japanese-American farmers disagreed. By 1919 the peninsula, its piedmont, and the low-lying areas in a semicircle around it were recognized as the best soil for growing truck crops, and these were soon to command the highest rent of any truck-lands in the state. Already the Japanese were concentrated there, to become more so by 1942.[30] After 1920 several of the areas where Japanese farmers had initially centered their berry production passed into the hands of

[29]Immigration Commission, *Reports*, XXIV, p. 381; U.S. House of Representatives, Committee on Immigration and Naturalization, *Hearings, Japanese Immigration*, 66th Cong., 2nd sess. (1920), pt. 3, p. 1056; Tolan Committee, *Fourth Interim Report*, pp. 129–30; Los Angeles County Chamber of Commerce, Agricultural Department, *Southern California Crops, Annual Statistical Reports* (1931–34), and *Los Angeles County, Southern California Crops, Annual Statistical Supplements* (1935–40); H. Fukuoka, "Economic and Social Conditions of the Japanese in Southern California," p. 78, typewritten manuscript (1917) in General Library, University of Southern California; J. W. Nelson *et al., Soil Survey of the Los Angeles Area*, California, U.S. Department of Agriculture, Bureau of Soils (Washington: U.S. Government Printing Office, 1919), p. 12; L. A. Crawford and Edgar B. Hurd, *Types of Farming in California Analyzed by Enterprises*, University of California College of Agriculture, Agricultural Experiment Station, Berkeley, Bulletin No. 654 (1941), pp. 56, 61–62.

[30]Louis Mesmer, *Soil Survey of the Los Angeles Area, California*, U.S. Department of Agriculture, Department of Soils (Washington: Government Printing Office, 1904), pp. 13 and Map 1; Nelson, *Soil Survey*, pp. 11–12; California State Board of Control, *California and the Oriental*, map, p. 61; Ralph Fletcher Burnight, "The Japanese Problem in the Agricultural Districts of Los Angeles County" (Master's thesis, University of Southern California, 1920), pp. 10 (map), 11; Adams and Smith, *Farm Tenancy in California and Methods of Leasing*, pp. 70, 74; Tolan Committee, *Fourth Interim Report*, p. 130.

suburban developers. Japanese farmers congregated increasingly in the southwest, particularly by filling in higher on the Palos Verdes foothills and by occupying even more solidly the areas to the north.[31]

The continuing centrality of agriculture to the occupational structure of the Los Angeles Japanese community is apparent in Table 5.2, based on 1940 census data. Indeed, outside the city of Los Angeles, Japanese men found more than half of their employment in agriculture, and about a third of Japanese women were also so employed. These figures were quite close to those for the rest of the state. Apart from this direct employment in agriculture, many of the modal employment categories reflect the continuing emphasis on the agriculturally based ethnic economy, with a striking degree of congregation in certain categories.

Most notable—particularly in view of the great contrast between the Los Angeles picture and that for all California Japanese—are the large proportions of Los Angeles Japanese-American males and females, city and county alike, who are gathered in two interrelated categories: "proprietors, managers, and officials," and "clerical and sales." These were the men and women who planned, financed, operated, maintained, and cherished the small retail outlets, and who, in meeting the white public in these roles, most nearly lived the local Japanese stereotype. Nearly half of the non-agricultural Japanese working in Los Angeles were in one of these categories, men more frequently as proprietors than women. The greater complexity of the Los Angeles ethnic economy is reflected in (and was brought home to the Nisei by way of) the relatively high ratio of employees to employers: for California as a whole, the latter outnumbered the former, so small were most Japanese businesses outside Los Angeles.

Table 5.2 also reveals certain other concentrations which suggested difficulties for the Japanese. Although the males had by 1940 generally managed to escape the domestic servant roles of Irwin's Hashimura Togo, their sisters had done so only to a lesser degree—although both were less limited than Japanese Americans elsewhere in the state. Such roles clearly were unacceptable in the long run, yet they persisted, at least for women. The "laborer" category, extremely high for Japanese men in Los Angeles City, needs some explaining. It conceals the two skilled specialties of contract gardening and fishing, as well as the truly unskilled laborers headquartered in Little Tokyo.

[31]Board of Control, *California and the Oriental,* p. 61; California, Attorney General, Atlas and "List of Los Angeles County Farms Reported in January, 1942, as Leased or, Owned by Persons with Japanese Names," California Attorney General's Collection, Bancroft Library, University of California, Berkeley; WCCA, *Bulletin No. 6* (1942), p. 2.

BLE 5.2.   Occupational Distribution of Male and Female Japanese, Not Employed in
riculture, in Los Angeles City, the Rest of the County, and the Rest of California, 1940

	Males			Females		
	L.A. City (%)	Rest of L.A. County (%)	Rest of California (%)	L.A. City (%)	Rest of L.A. County (%)	Rest of California (%)
fessionals, ni-professionals	4	4	6	5	6	5
prietors, nagers, and icials	22	28	23	10	7	7
rical and es workers	23	31	11	27	43	17
ftsmen, foremen, operatives	10	10	23	18	5	14
mestic service	2	6	13	14	28	42
er service	9	6	9	21	9	14
orers	30	15	15	4	1	1
	100%	100%	100%	100%	99%	100%
of all in labor e omitted ause in agriculture	9	58	61	11	31	34

rce: WCCA, *Bulletin No. 12*, pp. 42–44; *Census 1940 P4*, p. 107–9.

Professionals were notably rare in Table 5.2, more so in Los
Angeles than elsewhere. So were craftsmen, foremen, and operatives. The relative absence of Japanese in these categories points to
the refusal of white employers to take on Japanese in areas where their
employees would have to deal either with the general public (as was
the case with professionals) or with large numbers of other employees
(as would be the case with operatives). Exclusion from these ranks
was costly to the Japanese, not only because such exclusion denied
them casual contact with whites, but also because in Los Angeles
both categories were likely areas of growth as the country emerged
from the Depression.

The Japanese thus developed commercial health of a particular
kind. Because the pressures of a caste system limited their entry into
the professions, higher civil service, or managerial positions outside
the ethnic group, the Japanese community was forced to place its
emphasis upon very few lines. In 1940 the most common Japanese

occupations in the county seem to have been agriculture, food retailing, gardening, restaurant work, fishing, food wholesaling, food processing, hotel-keeping, and domestic service.[32] The sum of these, naturally, came to define the economic and even the communal health of the group. Power was distributed accordingly, and these roles even characterized the ethnic community's position in the broader community of which it was a part.

Such detailed data are unfortunately not available for earlier years, but enough can be gathered to show that for at least three decades the Japanese of Los Angeles had been hustling very hard just to maintain their middling position. This interpretation slights the growth and size of the economic base of the community, but the point cannot be overstressed: any Japanese gains in terms of income levels and comforts implied thereby were made without fundamentally altering the group's community standing. We see this stasis within apparent "progress" by examining occupational distributions wihin the Japanese community between 1910 and 1940, and the Japanese share of the population performing these occupations.[33]

Table 5.3 arranges these data in such a way that the general lack of trends for most occupational types becomes clear. Although the data are available only for the city, I suspect that essentially the same story applies in the rest of the county. Their occupational distribution was roughly the same in 1940 as it had been scarcely a decade after the local Japanese community's founding; furthermore, the Japanese retained their initial lopsided position within the city. The major exception to this argument is the striking decline in domestic service, the phasing out of the famous "schoolboys."

A contrary trend is also present in the table, although it is obscured because the census lumped agriculture, fishing, and gardening into the same category in the earlier years. The growth of these three pursuits is the sum of one rapidly growing form of Japanese employment, one moderately declining pursuit, and a third essentially stable one. The case for agriculture's stability has already been made. The decline of fishing, one of the first local Japanese industries, probably began in the mid-1920's because of competition from other ethnic

---

[32] These rankings are somewhat conjectural, since they do not coincide in a uniform manner with the census categories from which they are derived. WCCA, *Bulletin No. 10* (1942), p. 5; *Bulletin No. 12* (1943), pp. 42–44.

[33] Census Bureau occupational categories such as those used in Table 5.2 were not used before 1940. Table 5.3 depends upon somewhat arbitrary combinations of imperfectly equivalent occupational titles for the three censuses treated. Note also that neither women nor agricultural workers are excluded from this table, as they were from Table 5.2; hence some discrepancies.

LE 5.3.   Number and Proportion of "Other Races" in Selected Occupations, Los Angeles
, 1910–40, and Proportion Represented by "Other Races" among All in Those Occupations

upation	Number 1910	1920	1940	Percentage all "other races" jobs 1910	1920	1940	Percentage "other races" of all workers in that occupation 1910	1920	1940
fessionals	37	245	504	1	4	4	1	1	1
ail dealers	551	850	1,031	12	12	8	8	8	6
olesale dealers	9	42	260	—	1	2	2	5	5
rks in stores	151	400	1,223	3	6	10	2	3	7
ing, manufacturing, oad, street rail-l, and common labor	563	1,138	1,720	12	12	13	2	1	1
nestic service	1,010	786	576	21	11	4	38	20	24
i-domestic service	967	968	3,188	20	14	25	17	9	9
iculture, fishing gardening	681	2,061	3,816	14	30	30	24	21	27

ce: *Census 1910 P3*, pp. 560–61; *Census 1920 P2*, pp. 1129–31; *Census 1940 P3*, pp. 244–45.

groups. Even so, the Japanese concentration remained striking
enough in the late 1930's to generate a considerable "spy" threat as
war with Japan approached. The growth industry for the Japanese
was gardening. Since this was almost the only really new line of work
widely exploited by Japanese between 1910 and the war, it is unfortunate that exact figures showing its growth cannot be discovered.
But the meaning of the growth is apparent to anyone who has seen a
Japanese gardener, still a familiar sight in Los Angeles. Gardeners
were not classified as personal service workers, because they hired
out their services (and machinery) rather than working for wages.
Nevertheless, the position was in many ways that of a menial. The
Japanese gardener fulfilled the Japanese stereotype by his hard and
honest performance, and by his patient and quiet demeanor. According to scattered reports, the Depression permitted rapid Japanese
expansion into this line of work, as the less affluent members of Los
Angeles's house-proud middle class took them on in preference to
full-time servants. Japanese gardening, unlike agriculture, saw no
complex economic structures built up, probably because entry into
the trade on one's own was so simple for anyone who could afford a
truck and a few tools, and who was Japanese. Gardening was an
entrepreneurial activity of the low-risk, no-establishment variety
which allowed the translation of human sweat into income, but which
(unlike agriculture) did not lead to new entrepreneurial and occupa-

tional opportunities. By 1940 some 1,500 Japanese gardeners were operating in Los Angeles County.

The balance of Table 5.3 presents a basically straightforward story. Retailers declined, while wholesalers and clerks increased. The growing complexity in the ethnic economy in no sense implied growing diversity: businesses became larger, and the ratio of employees to employers rose. In these lines (except for wholesaling) Japanese started out, and remained, overrepresented.

A series of quantitative inquiries into Japanese business in Los Angeles City during 1909–28 permits us to explore the internal dynamics of the immigrant generation's entrepreneurial evolution. The data are not fully comparable and thus permit only a typological approach to growth. Four distinct patterns are revealed by an analysis of eight typical Japanese-run businesses; those patterns indicate the economic impact of the maturation of the Los Angeles Issei community.

Billiard halls and express and forwarding companies illustrate the first pattern. These two types of services flourished in the earliest years of Japanese settlement, before the immigrants had acquired families, "regular habits," and familiarity with American institutions. Both of these businesses seem to have lost their earlier vitality as early as 1917; the billiard parlors, in fact, were able to hang on largely by appealing to other ethnic groups who were in their own pre-family stage. The business changes associated with the decision to remain in America evidently had occurred by the mid-'teens and were solidified during the next decade.

Tailor and barbershops (combined with baths), the latter at one time a significant Japanese business venture in Los Angeles, represent the second pattern of entrepreneurial development. Tailor and barbershops have often been first entrepreneurial attempts by members of immigrant groups in the United States, since foreign-trained craftsmen could expect the rewards available to good workers without needing much initial capital. Such businesses, moreover, could hope for patronage both within and outside the ethnic group. The data imply that this latter hope failed those Japanese who overpopulated these occupations. The expansion of the Japanese tailoring business was turned back in Los Angeles by 1924, not to expand again—the same number of tailors was listed for the county in 1940 as for the city in 1928. Barbershops and associated services fared slightly better, though their growth was distinctly stunted; the Japanese barbershop, which once seemed about to become part of the Japanese occupational stereotype, never achieved that position. By at least the mid-

1920's it was obvious that these two typical attempts to enter into free competition with whites had failed.

Two enterprises which prospered within clearly set limits illustrate the third type of growth. These were the restaurants serving Japanese food (at that time to an almost exclusively Japanese clientele), and lawyers and various agents. Both of these businesses catered to needs of the Japanese themselves; unlike billiard halls, they could be counted upon to grow at least as fast as the Japanese population. Lawyers and agents served the increasing need for legal and quasi-legal services following from increasing commercial and familial complexity; Japanese restaurants, as centers of community social life, grew more varied and elaborate along with the community.[34] Although the steady growth of these industries undoubtedly enriched certain individuals whose services benefited the Japanese community directly, they brought little income into the community itself.

Two illustrative industries succeeded in wresting increasing amounts of money from the general community: florists-nurseries, and retail food outlets. Though the two differ in exact "take-off" points, they are similar in overall pattern. Each grew constantly from 1909 to 1928; in fact, growth continued until relocation, though at a slower rate because of the Depression. They both took off in the early 1920's, perhaps because of the Alien Land Act. The importance of these industries in defining the community's prewar economy is second only to agriculture's.

Success in these lines made apparent the precise direction of Japanese commercial expansion. The active Japanese entrepreneur no longer sought new fields to conquer; rather, he honed the techniques and gathered the capital necessary to gain even larger proportions of the market in his chosen field. By the 1930's the first-generation business group was essentially defensive, sharing the conventional enemies of white petty businessmen: innovation and labor.

The growth of the Japanese flower and nursery business is emblematic of this pattern. With minute capital, the first Japanese flower-growers brought their own products to market on the street railroad, in baskets, peddling them door-to-door to white customers. After their early competition was outdistanced, Japanese business became more certain and larger; as certain florists became identified

---

[34]This account omits Japanese restaurants serving non-Japanese cuisines. By 1909 several restaurants run by Japanese catered to Negroes, Mexicans, and down-and-out Anglos. California, Bureau of Labor Statistics, *Fifteenth Biennial Report* (1910–12), p. 607; Millis, *Japanese Problem*, pp. 53–54.

with the trade, they established shops. With remarkable rapidity, and what can only be called daring, the Japanese set out in 1912 to rationalize the chaotic floral business, to take better advantage of the possibilities of cooperation between Japanese growers and their outlets. Using for their model a San Francisco floral exchange, the Japanese growers of Los Angeles set up a fifty-member group which incorporated in 1914 as the Southern California Floral Market. The Market constituted a mediating institution between grower and dealer, freeing each to concentrate more directly their time and capital. The business prospered.[35] The key to the floral and nursery business in decorative plants, flowers, and food seedlings alike was efficient propagation and land utilization, uniform growth and rapid turnover; satisfactory results could be best achieved in a calm and coordinated economic setting. By 1931 the per-acre value of nursery products in Los Angeles County was about $7,000, easily the most intensive kind of agricultural activity measured in these terms. The extraordinary pains taken by Japanese businessmen to damp competition within the ethnic industry and to create agreement among the various branches of the trade indicates how well they knew this fact.[36]

The Southern California Floral Market followed the quick profits but ultimate confusion of a violet fad in 1911, at which time the Japanese began to glimpse the benefits of organization. The crowded downtown location of the Floral Market provided a place where Japanese retailers and growers could congregate to do their business under conditions of mutual trust. But observation of Market behavior soon revealed a tendency of the Japanese growers toward overproduction, leading to price-cutting. Voluntary limitation of production was called for by the Floral Market; this was accomplished by the unoriginal strategy of limiting membership to the Market while discouraging the sale of seeds to non-members.[37]

By the mid-1920's, when the Market moved to new quarters of original design, the ethnic organization had already withstood the challenge of the white-run American Florist Exchange, which had been organized to compete with the Japanese in the preceding

[35]Isamu Nodera, "A Survey of the Vocational Activities of the Japanese in the City of Los Angeles" (Master's thesis, University of Southern California, 1936), pp. 75–81; Shiro Fujioka, "History of the Southern California Flower Market," trans. Togo Tanaka, typewritten manuscript in Tanaka, "Journal," at entry of Aug. 12, 1941, folder A 17.06, JERS Collection.

[36]Los Angeles County Chamber of Commerce, Agricultural Department, *Southern California Crops: Annual Statistical Report for 1931* (mimeographed).

[37]Nodera, "Vocational Activities," pp. 80–83; Fujioka, "Flower Market," pp. 9–19.

years.[38] During this same period the Japanese industry developed its division of labor to a high degree, with the Market itself assuming entrepreneurial, protective, and mutual-assistance functions. Individual growers began to specialize, selling either seedlings to truck gardeners, plants to nurserymen, or cut flowers to florists. Each class of customers included large proportions of Japanese. So well did the Japanese succeed that when the flower industry of Los Angeles was organized to comply with the National Industrial Recovery Act, half of the board of directors was Japanese.[39]

Horizontal and vertical integration were likewise characteristic of the Japanese retail produce industry. This line was far more important quantitatively than flowers and nurseries, although proportionately less "Japanese." As in flower-selling, the initial entry of the Japanese was modest. Japanese truck gardeners began early in the century to sell their crops from stands along semi-rural roads; in the city proper, Japanese produce retailing was judged minimal even as late as 1909, in the Immigration Commission survey. Although a number of fairly sizable provision stores had been established by Japanese earlier in the decade, they catered mainly to Japanese work gangs; little produce was carried by Japanese merchandisers at this date. Most Japanese food retailers ran one-man businesses, usually in conjunction with a pool hall or other Japanese business, as often candy stores as groceries.[40]

By this time, however, the Japanese were substantial producers of fruits and vegetables on their farms, and these capitalistic tillers had begun to seek a superior outlet for their enterprise and products. The

[38]Apparently in an attempt to undercut the American Exchange, the Japanese market at this point opened its membership to Caucasians, though no one seems to have taken advantage of the offer. Although the historian of the Japanese Floral Market claims that the two thereafter competed amicably, a lawsuit for $100,000 damages was brought in 1935; a jury awarded the sum to the Caucasian market on the grounds that the Japanese market had fraudulently misrepresented its intentions. A motion for retrial was accepted, and the issue seems to have been settled out of court. *Rafu Shimpo,* Jan. 21, Mar. 23, 1935.

[39]In early 1942 Caucasians in the industry complained that Japanese dominance was even then increasing—a result of "a planned attempt" to squeeze whites out of the trade "through close cooperation of growers and retailers by price control." J. S. Whyte and John Brown, "Report on Japanese Activities in the Cut Flower Industry in Southern California," Feb. 26, 1942, Folder A 16.201, JERS Collection; Fujioka, "Flower Market," pp. 17, 25–28; Fumiko Fukuoka, "Mutual Life and Aid Among the Japanese in Southern California with Special Reference to Los Angeles" (Master's thesis, University of Southern California, 1937), p. 57.

[40]Leonard Bloom and Ruth Riemer, *Removal and Return* (Berkeley and Los Angeles: University of California Press, 1949), pp. 83, 95–96; Immigration Commission, *Reports,* XXIII, pp. 225, 232–35, 362–63.

motor truck, new techniques of refrigeration, distribution centers which were too small and too slow, and vastly increased consumer demand had combined to add middleman upon middleman. Despite repeated efforts to rationalize the industry, distribution never caught up with production and demand. Shady practices were common and inefficiency rife in an industry where a piece of fruit might find its way into the hands of a retailer by way of nine different types of distributing agencies, or a combination thereof. Such general market irrationality persisted at least into the 1930's in Los Angeles, and under these conditions the Japanese prospered.[41]

The City Market of Los Angeles was an early attempt at organizing the turbulent industry. In 1909 94 Japanese growers joined with Caucasians and Chinese of similar inclinations as the original incorporators of the City Market of Los Angeles, a highly structured and (for the time) modern central market, the first of its kind in Los Angeles. Even at that early point in their economic development, the Japanese were able to subscribe stock to a value of $36,000, 18 percent of the total.[42]

As in flowers and fishing, the Japanese were able to operate with comparative efficiency because they were tightly organized as an ethnic group to achieve limited and clearly defined goals. The narrowness of these goals simplified their business: growing perishables for a primarily local market, the Japanese grower had relatively little need for any of the middlemen and transportation agencies to which Caucasian growers consigned their goods. The pioneer Japanese of the City Market were relatively small entrepreneurs not too far removed from the growers; most were stallholders—that is, jobbers—rather than commission merchants. Despite the sizable proportion of the Los Angeles produce business that was carried on by the Japanese, small stallholders continued to predominate among the Japanese at the Market. Although a few large Japanese houses did over $1 million gross business in 1940, eight in ten Japanese businesses there were stalls, as compared with fewer than half of those run by Caucasians and one-third of those owned by Chinese and Koreans. And Japanese, along with other non-Caucasians, were excluded from

[41]William C. Crow, *Wholesale Markets for Fruits and Vegetables in 40 Cities,* U.S. Department of Agriculture Circular no. 463 (1938), pp. 75, 138, and *passim;* U.S. Department of Agriculture, *Yearbook 1925,* pp. 647, 655–59; Walter Kingsbury, "Speaking of Utopias," *California Cultivator* 79 (1932): 325; Richard O. Been, *Price Spreads between Farmers and Consumers,* U.S. Department of Agriculture, Bureau of Agricultural Economics, Agricultural Information Bulletin no. 4 (1949), p. 12.

[42]Tsuyoshi Matsumoto, "History of Resident Japanese," pp. 24–25, in Tanaka, "Journal"; Nodera, "Vocational Activities," pp. 99–102.

the group of incorporators of the larger and more modern Wholesale Terminal Market which opened in 1915 (with immediate railway access). Few Japanese did business there, for the division of labor in produce was expressed along ethnic lines. Caucasians handled almost exclusively the large quantities of produce brought to the markets (particularly the Wholesale Terminal Market) for transshipment to distant consuming areas; Japanese handled most of the fresh green vegetables consumed within Los Angeles. Relations between the races were cordial but cautious.[43]

Organization among the Japanese was provided by their Wholesale Market Operators Association, so that smallness would not cause inefficiency. The ethnic bond in the industry grew tighter as Japanese Market men provided informal crop-loans to growers at the beginning of the season in exchange for future patronage, a function once handled by Caucasian wholesalers. The original economic logic of growers looking for a market and moving thence into retail business was now reversed, and a gap originally left by the shortage of capital in the Japanese community was closed by prospering Japanese merchants. By the time of relocation, the total sales of Japanese wholesale produce dealers were about $25 million.[44] By this time produce was the economic preoccupation of the Japanese community of Los Angeles, and the Japanese fruitstand man was a popular stereotype: polite, a bit strange, and able to sell unusually attractive produce.

The growth of the "breakthrough" industries—flowers and produce—has shown the prevalence of cooperative economic behavior on the part of Japanese Americans. Such behavior was critical to the successes achieved along these lines. The ability to cooperate, of course, was not born out of economic need; it had a traditional base.

[43]Nodera, "Vocational Activities," pp. 102, 110; Associated Produce Dealers and Brokers of Los Angeles to Earl Warren, in Tolan Committee, *Hearings*, pt. 29, pp. 11006–8; Eliot G. Mears, interview with F. M. Hudson, secretary of Produce Exchange of Los Angeles, June 27, 1924, folder "Agriculture," Box 1, SRR Papers; W. L. Jackson, "The Importance of the Los Angeles Market," *California Cultivator* 74 (1930): 22; Fukuoka, "Economic and Social Conditions," pp. 20–22; Bloom and Riemer, *Removal and Return*, pp. 88–89.

[44]Testimony of Taiji Kita in U.S. House of Representatives, Committee on the Judiciary, *Hearings: Japanese-American Evacuation Claims*, 83rd Cong., 2nd sess. (1954), p. 334; statement of Sam Minami, in Tolan Committee, *Hearings*, pt. 31, pp. 11722–23; California State Board of Control, *California and the Oriental*, pp. 79–86; Joyoshi Uono, "The Factors Affecting the Geographical Aggregation and Dispersion of the Japanese Residences [in Los Angeles City]" (Master's thesis, University of Southern California, 1927), pp. 56–57; Nodera, "Vocational Activities," p. 103; Associated Produce Dealers and Brokers to Warren, in Tolan Committee, *Hearings*, pt. 29, pp. 11006–8.

But the extraordinary richness of Japanese economic organization in Los Angeles was more than a mere carryover; in form it was anything but traditional—witness the supplanting of the Japanese Association by the Japanese Chamber of Commerce. Economic organization was in fact both a rational accommodation to legal and informal discriminations, and a reflection of values which set a general goal of launching the youth toward still greater success.

The ability to cooperate had far-reaching ramifications. In agriculture, for example, a coordinating organization was formed as early as 1907, and a second began two years later. Although created exclusively by farmers, these organizations operated as joint efforts of Japanese farmers and merchants who sold farm products. From the beginning, a perceived unity of interest reduced the producer-middleman hostility which was traditional (and costly) to white American farmers. As the industry grew in size and importance, so did the complexity and sophistication of the Japanese organizations, and their interrelationships. Early in its existence the Southern California Central Japanese Association annexed the Southern California Agricultural Association, apparently as a semi-autonomous department, and empowered it to employ a few technicians and to organize and convene a directorate of its own, eventually reforming it as the Central Agricultural Association.[45] By World War II there were regular Japanese-language broadcasts about wholesale market prices, and a daily market sheet was published under the auspices of the Southern California Japanese Farm Federation. Before this, a number of smaller Japanese cooperatives had federated to provide constituent groupings with a daily specialized market-prognosis service, to be passed on to its individual farmer-members in the form of definite allotments for sale.[46]

By the late 1930's there were signs that ethnic solidarities in the agriculture and produce industry were being upset by more narrowly economic concerns, as growers and merchants began to conflict with one another during the Depression. In 1939, for example, the well-

[45]From its early years, the Central Japanese Association took an active interest in the organization of small as well as large Japanese industries. Central Japanese Association Minutes, Sept. 17, 1915, June 24, 1916, Feb. 6, 1918; E. Manchester Boddy, *The Japanese in America* (Los Angeles: By the Author, 1921), p. 168.

[46]The central organization, too, was empowered to order dumping, with compensation for members. Organizations also existed among the smaller Japanese farming specialities. For example, the Federation of Berry Associations of Southern California, founded in 1935, within four years claimed to be prepared to establish its own cooperatively run specialty wholesale market. Fukuoka, "Mutual Life and Aid," pp. 29, 38–39; *Rafu Shimpo,* Mar. 19, 1935, Mar. 26, 1939.

organized farmers prevailed in a commission-rate controversy by threatening to form a cooperative produce market to compete with existing arrangements. Even though this threat brought capitulation from the merchants, the farmers continued to entertain the idea of the cooperative market, for they perceived in it "a method of successful disposal of surplus produce . . . [to] prevent cut-throat prices."[47]

Similar cooperative themes existed in fishing. There the value of cooperation was particularly dramatic, and its practice extended from boat level, where profit-sharing included all hands, to fleet level, where the Japanese Fishermen's Association worked to reduce disruptive competition among boats. The Fishermen's Association also handled negotiations with white cannery proprietors and governmental agencies. A second organization of the same name built "Fishermen Hall," which became the social as well as the economic center of the community. The Association "handled all community affairs and negotiations with other neighboring communities"[48] and harmonized its activities with the goals of the Japanese community through the fishery department of the Central Japanese Association. The department secured expert advice and progressive counsel on the fishing trade from sources in Japan; it also publicized new inventions, techniques, and research, and encouraged local efforts to advance the state of the art and to keep the Japanese a step ahead of their competitors.[49]

From a very early period Japanese cooperated with white capitalists in developing the Los Angeles fishery. Capital initially unavailable in the Japanese community was solicited from whites. Since the growth of the industry demanded ever larger boats and more efficient netting and equipment, the level of Japanese entrepreneurship was considerable even when ventures were guaranteed by the white cannery operators. Japanese often developed equity in the industry by way of gradually amortized mortgages on boats and other equipment; the mortgagor was usually the canning company to whom, in return, the fisherman promised to bring his catch.[50]

[47]*Rafu Shimpo,* Oct. 29, 30, Nov. 27, 28, Dec. 3, 1939.

[48]Kanichi Kawasaki, "The Japanese Community of East San Pedro, Terminal Island, California" (Master's thesis, University of Southern California, 1931), pp. 44–47, 53–54, 130–32; William Kinchelve, "A Study of the Japanese Fishermen at Curtis Packing Company in Long Beach," Major Document 301, SRR Papers.

[49]Central Japanese Association Minutes, Mar. 23, 1918.

[50]Edward F. Bamford, "Social Aspects of the Fishing Industry at Los Angeles Harbor" (Master's thesis, University of Southern California, 1921), pp. 2–3; California State Board of Control, *California and the Oriental,* pp. 91–93; Bloom and Riemer, *Removal and Return,* pp. 169–75, 182–84.

Indeed, by 1923 fourteen different Japanese occupational associations had been established in Los Angeles. These continued to increase spontaneously, eventually including the Japanese Book Store Keepers' Association and the Southern California (Japanese) Chop Suey Operators Association. These groups fixed standard wage scales in American-style restaurants, established cooperative buying in the grocery business, prevented "unnecessary competition" among Japanese dry goods dealers, aided in the enforcement (according to the relevant Association) of NRA codes in the retail fruit and vegetable industry, and, remarkably, were able for a while to circulate a journal for the fewer than fifteen members of the (Southern California) Japanese Physicians' and Surgeons' Association.[51] Even a trade like retail jewelry, in which the Japanese had few units, displayed cooperative efforts. The (Los Angeles) Japanese Jewelers Association Minute Book records an early agreement with a Caucasian jewelry wholesaler to refuse to sell to non-member Japanese retailers. The purpose was to cause the whole industry to sell at markups decided upon by the Jewelers Association. Some years later competition again broke out and was again repressed, this time by the Japanese Chamber of Commerce. At times this kind of consensual pressure was added to white pressure against Japanese, when it was considered to be in the interest of the Japanese as a whole; for instance, there was a Japanese-white move to end the flourishing but scarcely profitable ten-cent-meal houses set up in Japanese downtown during the Depression.[52]

Because the Japanese community was cut off from the larger world by discrimination (and, to some extent, by deliberate policy on the part of its own leadership), and sternly limited in the types of employment its members could enter, it provided for its own by entrepreneurship. Minority capitalism was successfully tried by this colored group well before it became a political catch-phrase. The fact of the group economy was intensified in the consciousness of the Japanese Americans by its cooperative bases, by the growth of a new generation clamoring for jobs, and by the impossibility of broadening its scope in the depth of a depression. Nowhere are the costs of a segregated economy—even a successful one—pointed up more sharply than in the attitude which their own group economy led the

[51]Masao Dodo, untitled study of Japanese and their industries in Los Angeles County, ca. 1923, Major Document 289, SRR Papers; *Rafu Shimpo,* Jan. 18, 25, 1931, July 31, 1933.

[52]Japanese Jewelers Association Minutes, Apr. 2, 3, 1917, Oct. 18, 1918, JARP Archive; Southern California Japanese Chamber of Commerce Reports, July 1, 1925; *Rafu Shimpo,* June 29, Nov. 1, 1933.

Japanese to adopt toward subordinate ethnic groups. By the 1930's, many Japanese felt that they had to preserve what they had.[53]

Some years earlier, the Mexicans had replaced the Japanese as the primary non-white agricultural labor force in Los Angeles County,[54] and they were vital thus to the Japanese economy. Mexican farm labor organizations began in 1928, when the Confederacion de Uniones Obreras Mexicanas was formed in Los Angeles. The following decade was one of change, during which unstable membership, ostensibly radical ideology, and connections with both Mexican and American radicals were constants. For many Mexicans, the Japanese provided a bogeyman useful in holding such an organization together.[55]

Agricultural unrest had long been brewing in Los Angeles. There wage rates for agricultural laborers were the lowest in the state, and during the Depression decade the number of agricultural laborers employed fell by half. In 1933 the unrest surfaced in a major strike in which an estimated 217,000 man-days were lost; nor was the discontent submerged thereafter. Although the unrest can hardly be blamed upon any particular unkindness practiced by the Japanese employers, these employers had, like others, apparently decided to withstand the Depression by squeezing the Mexican workers who stood in the position which the Japanese themselves had occupied a quarter of a century earlier.[56] In vegetable farming during the Depression there *were* no attractive alternatives. The Japanese could

[53]A survey of Los Angeles County vegetable farming conducted during the mid-1930's showed that on a medium-size farm (20–24 acres), a family (usually Japanese) would provide 58% of the labor from its own resources, and hire about eight part-time laborers to perform the balance. The average net return was $4,229. Although the survey was taken at the depth of the Depression, it indicated that fewer than one in five such farms suffered a monetary deficit, thus demonstrating remarkable resiliency. U.S. Works Projects Administration, California, "Los Angeles County Vegetable Growers Survey" (n.p., n.d.).

[54]George P. Clements to SRR, Mar. 19, 1925, folder "Historical Background," Box 4, SRR Papers; California, Governor C. C. Young's Mexican Fact-Finding Committee, *Mexicans in California* (1930), p. 159.

[55]Mexican Fact-Finding Committee, *Mexicans in California,* pp. 123–24, 143–44; Stuart Marshall Jamieson, "Labor Unionism in Agriculture" (Ph.D. dissertation, University of California, Berkeley, 1943), I, 235–40; Charles E. Spaulding, "The Mexican Strike at El Monte, California," *Sociology and Social Research* 18 (1934): 571–80; George P. Clements to [?] Gast, June 27, 1933, Clements to [?] Arnoll, July 13, 1933, in folder "Agricultural Labor," Box 62, George P. Clements Papers.

[56]*Census 1930 P2,* p. 274; *Census 1940 P2,* p. 558; *Census 1935 A1,* p. 945; "Strikes in Los Angeles County, 1933–39," exhibit 10710 in La Follette Hearings, pt. 65, pp. 23990–24000; [?] Yerkes to Clements, memorandum, Sept. 12, 1934, in folder "Agricultural Labor," Box 62, Clements Papers.

accept a reduction in margin of profit, which would place their Depression-threatened farming in even greater difficulty; or they could raise their prices but risk losing their market, thereby endangering the entire structure of their local economy, since they might lose their competitive advantage over large non-local producers. The Depression had a nationwide effect on all aspects of the fruit-and-vegetable industry, but farmers suffered more than distributors, and small distributors proved more vulnerable than large ones.[57] As a group the Japanese farmers, backed by the Japanese community, chose to pass Depression stringencies on to their workers when possible, wistfully hoping that if only "the radical element [were] weeded out of the union movement [,] the farmers [would] have better chance to cooperate with labor." The wages of the Mexican workers were cut a number of times on an industry-wide basis; the reductions were enforced by the strong Japanese farming organizations.[58] The Japanese farmers, however, regularly promised to raise wages when economic conditions permitted.[59]

In June, 1933, Mexican workers went on strike in the middle of the picking season in the El Monte berry-growing area. The leaders of the strike protested "the inhuman, oppressive, un-American and low wage scale of 6, 9, 11 and 15 cents per hour."[60] The strike quickly spread to other heavily Japanese growing districts in the county; ultimately 1,500 Mexican employees of Japanese farms had walked off their jobs, joined by many who worked for whites. The very few Japanese pickers who joined the strikers were ignored by the Japanese community, which vigorously counterattacked the Mexicans and their leaders, stressing the latter's radical connections. Los Angeles was still an anti-labor bastion; white farmers adopted the Japanese side of the conflict, class considerations overriding racial ones. The

[57]U.S. Federal Trade Commission, *Agricultural Income Inquiry* (1937), II, 55–74.

[58]An article in *Rafu Shimpo* in 1930 told its readers of the new wage schedule decided upon by the Venice (Japanese) Growers' Association: "It was only after a lengthy and heated discussion participated in by the entire membership that the new wage scale was adopted. . . . A circular printed in three languages, Japanese, English and Spanish has been distributed to every door of the farming population in Venice. The Association is said to be determined to take appropriate measures whenever there is a violator among its members." *Rafu Shimpo,* Aug. 10, 1930, June 29, 1933; *Kashu Mainichi* (Los Angeles), June 27, 1937; WPA, "Vegetable Growers Survey," p. 9.

[59]WPA, "Vegetable Growers Survey," pp. 6, 12; WPA, "Los Angeles County Vegetable Workers Study" (n.p., n.d.), pp. 1, 17, 22; Spaudling, "Mexican Strike," pp. 572–73.

[60]*Villardie* [sic] *and Flores* v. *Central Japanese Association,* Superior Court, Los Angeles County, Docket #360101 (1933), complaint, p. 2.

intercession of white landowners with the El Monte and Los Angeles Chambers of Commerce brought the Los Angeles Police Department and the sheriff's office to the aid of the Japanese. Shortly after picketing began, the sheriff's farm detail and the notoriously anti-labor police "Red Squad" were "warning" pickets and jailing them for "loitering," though still lacking a much-desired county anti-picketing ordinance. While employing such allies to help break the strike, the Los Angeles chapter of the Japanese American Citizens League was able to convince area high school principals to release Japanese-American children from school to work in the fields for the duration of the strike.[61]

Thus protected, the Japanese were able to harvest their crop with schoolchildren and white strikebreakers from the bread line. Frustrated and weak in organization, the Mexicans terminated their strike against the Japanese by temporary agreement after a month. The agreement between the Mexican union and the Central Japanese Association of Southern California (acting for nine federated Japanese growers' associations) promised a $1.50 daily wage and the reinstatement of as many strikers as economically possible, in exchange for a pledge to finish out the season. Even before the brief term of this agreement expired, however, Japanese and Mexicans again clashed over the wage issue and over the question of supposed Japanese perfidy in not rehiring strikers.[62] During the next three years, as Mexican laborers intermittently threatened new walkouts, Japanese growers perfected their strategy against the inevitable day when the Mexicans would feel strong enough to strike again. In late 1933 Japanese Chamber of Commerce officials proposed jointly with their white counterparts that "Mexican farm labor strikers . . . be deprived of further county relief aid if found participating in any labor agitation. . . . Deportation of foreigners implicated in such action is further recommended."[63]

[61]White Angelenos who had animosity toward both Japanese and Mexicans concluded that "the Federal Government should cure the sore [the strike] by deporting all concerned." Clarence Hunt, "Grizzly Growls," *Grizzly Bear*, Aug., 1933, p. 3; Memoranda: Clements to Gast, June 27, 1933; Gast to Clements, June 28, 1933; Clements to Arnoll, July 26, 1933; Ranger to Clements, Aug. 22, 1933; Gast to Clements, Sept. 7, 1933; Ranger to Arnoll, Sept. 15, 1933; all in folder "Agricultural Labor," Box 62, Clements Papers; R. A. Wellpott *et al.* to Captain William F. Hynes, June 7, 1933, exhibit in La Follette Hearings, pt. 64, pp. 23628–29; *Rafu Shimpo*, June 7, 9, 1933.

[62]*Villardie and Flores* v. *Central Japanese Association*, complaint, p. 5; Jamieson, "Labor Unionism in Agriculture," Appendix D; Central Japanese Association Minutes, July 5, 1933; *Rafu Shimpo*, June 9, July 7, 1933.

[63]*Rafu Shimpo*, Nov. 10, 1933, Feb. 12, June 22, 25, 1935.

The position of the Japanese farmers was tested again in 1936. The Mexicans, in concert with ethnic labor organizations of Filipinos, white Americans, and Japanese, began to pressure growers in Los Angeles and Orange Counties; the union shop and wage increases were the issues. The presence among the strikers of Ann Charloff and Lillian Monroe ("known reds" in the eyes of the Los Angeles *Times*) was too much for the growers; the latter steadfastly refused to negotiate the issue of recognition, although Guillermo Valerdes, president of the striking Mexican union, indicated that "we have nothing whatever to do with the Communists, and have weeded them out of our strike."[64] To extend their influence over the Mexican workers, Japanese employers decided to issue badges to identify "worthy" workers and to create a permanent card-file system which would permit the operation of a blacklist. The secretary of the Southern California (Japanese) Farm Federation explained that while he believed that some "honorable workers" walked out with the strikers, "mostly radicals, Communists, Public Works & Unemployed Union members" were now on the picket lines. The card-file system would serve the best interests of the honorable workers themselves.[65]

The Japanese community as a whole responded "with the greatest enthusiasm" by forming second-generation strikebreaking units. The ethnic press applauded their crusade:

> a definite challenge of the young citizens of America against the shady operation of the Communistic labor agitators. . . . The Southland community rises in respectful salute to those brave young men who have set forth on the battle front to save the farm lands from the tentacles of a group whose aims and objects are at variance with the best interests of the people's welfare. The Citizens League is to be commended for the outspoken stand that it has taken to support this band of nisei strike breakers. . . . SO LONG AS THE GOVERNMENT AND PEOPLE OF THE UNITED STATES DOES NOT ACCEPT COMMUNISM AS IT IS PRACTICED TODAY THE NISEI WHO ARE CITIZENS OF THE UNITED STATES CANNOT AND WILL NOT TOLERATE THEIR INFLUENCES.[66]

The young men marched forth under the combined protection of the sheriff's office, the Los Angeles and Culver City police, and special guards hired by the growers. The Red Squad was again particularly in

[64]*Ibid.*, Apr. 8, 18, May 20, 21, 24, 1936; Los Angeles *Times*, May 19, 26, 1936.

[65]*Rafu Shimpo*, May 12, 1936; *Kashu Mainichi*, May 12, 1936; unidentified newspaper clipping in Carey McWilliams scrapbooks, Haynes Foundation Library, University of California, Los Angeles.

[66]Editorial in *Rafu Shimpo*, Apr. 26, 1936.

evidence, preemptively quelling violence. Its vigilance and that of its allies allowed strikebreakers to work in the fields with but one casualty, despite sporadic violence in which pickets were sometimes injured, and which resulted in the temporary incarceration of Miss Monroe.[67]

The card-file system and the police intercession were, nevertheless, unable to break the resistance of the Mexican unionists in 1936. Putting Japanese schoolchildren to work in the fields was at best a desperate expedient; when it began to look as though such released-time juvenile strikebreaking was to become an annual affair, the growers saw fit to deal with the union. A temporary settlement was made in July, 1936, which gave the workers a wage increase (to 25 cents an hour, with 30 cents for celery) and union recognition (but not union shop). In 1937 the workers won another raise, but they were soon threatening to strike again, and no conclusive settlement was made before the war.[68] The strikes had demonstrated that although the Japanese could no longer be entirely self-sufficient, by now their interests in agriculture were interrelated with those of their white counterparts, and they could call upon the most potent weapons controlled by the white economic power structure of the area—at least when these weapons were to be used against a more disadvantaged group. That the Japanese were ready to employ these weapons is apparent.[69]

More remarkable, perhaps, is their willingness to employ these weapons even against unsympathetic members of their own group. In

[67]Red Squad activity extended to the breaking up of peaceful picket lines, and elicited the unheard protests of the local branch of the American Civil Liberties Union. *Rafu Shimpo,* Apr. 20, 25, 27, 28, 30, May 1, 18, 20, 25–28, June 2, 1936; *Kashu Mainichi,* May 27, 1936; *United Progressive News* (Los Angeles), May 1, 9, 11, 1936.

[68]Los Angeles *Times,* July 10, 1936; *Rafu Shimpo,* Apr. 30, 1937, Sept. 15, 1939; *Kashu Mainichi,* Dec. 20, 1937, Jan. 6, 1938.

[69]The shift from have-not to have is also illustrated by the fishery strikes of 1917 and 1938. In the earlier strike, the Japanese fishermen led the Italians, who were then entering the trade in Los Angeles, and kept the canneries closed during a four-month strike that forced federal intervention. Even the hostile AFL leadership of Los Angeles credited the Japanese fishermen with ''having made this fight for the fishermen of the entire South.'' In the latter strike, the Japanese fishermen happened temporarily to have been aligned with the non-discriminatory CIO local in San Pedro which was striking against the canneries for a more favorable contract. After a point the Japanese workers despaired of making any earnings for the season, and they felt that their position in the industry was threatened by the strike. They disaffiliated en masse, joined the Italians in a newly chartered non-striking AFL local, and broke the strike. *Los Angeles Citizen,* Nov. 9, Dec. 7, 1917, Jan. 11, 1918; *Rafu Shimpo,* June 17, 21, 23, 1938, Apr. 7, 1939; *Kashu Mainichi,* June 30, 1938; testimony of Harry

1936 Japanese-American labor activism was so evident that it could not be ignored, as it had been in 1933. When the secretary of the Japanese Farm Laborers proposed alliance with the other ethnic unions after being frustrated in their separate and more modest "requests" to the growers, their employers inveighed in the vernacular press against the supposed Communist agitators:

> This cooperative act of the various nationality groups which claims to represent the moderate faction [as had the Japanese Farm Laborers Association] is merely following in accordance with the Seventh Communist International congress at which time the first principle of Communism was abandoned and the adoption of a united action with the Second International or the social mass principle. This is quite apparent in that the method is purely in accordance with the dictates of Miss Monroe, the leading head of the strike faction in the California farm agitation.[70]

To repress such activity, the growers employed both community and legal pressure. With the cooperation of Little Tokyo boardinghouse-keepers, who provided job information and what little informal security belonged to Japanese seasonal agricultural laborers in Los Angeles, the Japanese agricultural organizations warned that anyone "connected with such radical groups [as the Japanese Farm Laborers Association] who are known to have Communist connections are to be deprived of all credits as a tenant and boarder." The radical patrol of the sheriff's office was called upon for further assistance. A raid on the labor camp of a Japanese farm labor leader in Orange County netted "several bales" of purported Communist propaganda; only four hours elapsed before federal immigration officials arrived with an order to detain the Japanese pending further investigation.[71]

Although this was an unusual instance, it was entirely characteristic that the Japanese community in Los Angeles perceived with great clarity its economic underpinning and moved with concern and purpose to preserve it, whether against outside attacks or from dissident elements within. Much of the unified face it presented to the rest of society, and much of the hierarchical order which characterized its internal structure, expressed this group's conscious economic motive.

Lundberg (Sailors Union of the Pacific, AFL) in U.S. House of Representatives, Committee on Merchant Marine and Fisheries, *Citizen Ownership and Operation of Certain Vessels: Hearings,* 76th Cong., 3rd sess. (1940), pp. 20–22; testimony of John Buzzell (Los Angeles Central Labor Council, AFL) in HUAC, *Investigation,* pp. 9285–86.

[70]*Rafu Shimpo,* Mar. 31, 1936. The text is reproduced as written.

[71]*Rafu Shimpo,* Mar. 17, 29, 1936; Los Angles *Times,* May 29, 1936.

6

The Nisei Dilemma: A Place in the World

By the late 1930's, unfortunately, the local ethnic economy was failing to accommodate its own, at least at a satisfactory level. Though the Depression could not shake the tenacious Issei from their position in the food growing, processing, and distributing industry of Los Angeles, it did not provide a base large enough to accommodate the Nisei as they came of age. The 1930's saw some 4,200 Nisei males and an equal number of Nisei females attain their majority in Los Angeles City; at the same time, death and departure removed 2,200 males and 700 females from the Issei generation. New jobs had to be found somewhere. The Nisei were desperate, for most had wholeheartedly accepted what their teachers and parents had told them: hard work in school would be suitably rewarded in the job market, and in the occupational world one should expect a major portion of one's satisfaction.

The Nisei had worked hard in school, with many attending college. By 1940 22 percent of the Los Angeles Nisei males twenty-five or over had attended college; the figure for native whites was 21 percent. Unlike many other institutions of the white community, colleges and universities seem to have established no restrictive quotas for Nisei.[1] To aid their attendance, parents and the Japanese community were generous in providing wherewithal for those who showed promise or inclination. At college, Japanese students prepared (and overprepared) themselves for expanded versions of their fathers' small-

[1]Though not discriminated against at admission or overtly thereafter, Japanese students in Los Angeles colleges seem often to have been treated with "some kind of pity" by whites, as a Japanese student at the University of Southern California noted in the 1920's, or with the kind of condescension that shines through uncomfortable professions of racial fellowship. "When he was awarded his letter in the Occidental [College] chapel the student body gave him a veritable ovation, which was a magnificent tribute to Tanake as a baseball player and in which all racial discrimination was absolutely eliminated. . . . One of his team mates voluntarily remarked, 'Tanake may be yellow on the outside but he is white inside.'" Fisk University, *Orientals and Their Cultural Adjustment* (Nashville: Social Science Institute, Fisk University, 1946), p. 96; George M. Day to Eliot G. Mears, May 4, 1927, folder "Personal Contacts," Box 4, SRR Papers.

business careers. Most Japanese students at the University of California at Los Angeles concentrated in business subjects in the decade before Pearl Harbor, with secondary emphasis upon social sciences, especially economics. A Japanese sorority and a "Japanese Bruin Club" helped make Nisei feel at home at the University.[2] The drive to attain the ordinary rewards which society offered to those who had labored well in school was understandably strong in these people.

The Nisei performance in school, their training, citizenship, and profound commitment to the American competitive pattern, ought to have been rewarded suitably in the occupational structure. But when Nisei contemplated their careers, the betrayal of their ambitions increased in direct relation to their academic success. College graduates had more reason than others to feel cheated of the reward for their labors. Their perspective, dominated by thwarted but thoroughly American goals of personal success, became the quasi-official view of a generation. Their disappointment became a serious topic of discussion among Nisei and was early understood by the first generation. With considerable bravery, mixed sometimes with despair but more often with self-delusion, Nisei accommodated themselves to the occupational difficulties that faced them.

> Frankly, the time-worn 'emotion-rouser'—racial discrimination—is very distasteful to me. The word is promiscuously applied to every situation which may seem repugnant to an individual of Japanese ancestry. Too often, it is used to excuse oneself for his own shortcomings. It is almost axiomatic that there is always room for those with the ability to 'produce the goods.' . . . However, the nisei knows that there are a few places difficult to break into. . . . Let the nisei place himself in the place of a Caucasian employer and explanations are needless. . . . In the meantime, the education of the mass is a slow evolutionary process. Constant 'wrong way fur rubbing' isn't going to help. We are not the first nor the only group to suffer racial discrimination.[3]

A ritualistic faith in individual effort was always part of the Nisei credo, as it had been for their parents. A Los Angeles Nisei physician bravely declared that, in his profession and others, "the stigma of being a Japanese can only be overcome by surpassing ability. The

---

[2] *Southern Campus* (U.C.L.A. yearbook), 1930–41.

[3] A Los Angeles Nisei personnel technician, quoted in George Yasukochi, "A Study of the Vocational Experiences of University of California Alumni of Japanese Ancestry" (report for National Youth Administration, 1941), p. 7; Japanese Chamber of Commerce Minutes, Mar. 25, 1925; Edward K. Strong, *Vocational Aptitudes of Second Generation Japanese in the United States* (Stanford: Stanford University Press, 1933), p. 110.

world is full of mediocrity.'' Nisei sometimes said they believed that their generation had more opportunities than their parents had had, along with more difficult problems to face.[4]

It was the Nisei way to insist that these problems must be faced *by individuals*. When a Hawaii CIO organizer complained to authorities in 1940 that Japanese Americans were discriminated against in defense work, a Nisei organization in Los Angeles expressed public disapproval.

> This is typical of a labor leader's tactics to fight any kind of discrimination. Whether it is wise or not is a matter of question. We feel it will probably do no good and was unwise. Out here in Southern California, nisei airplane mechanics cannot get jobs at Lockheed Aircraft. It is just a matter of company policy. To make a big hullaballoo and fuss would be merely to build that wall still higher. While Lockheed's portals have not yet been entered by trained nisei in this promising field, the Douglas Aircraft plant, largest in this area, has two nisei. Harlow in Alhambra has three. We shall probably see the day soon when a deserving and especially capable American citizen of Japanese ancestry will secure employment at Lockheed as well as any airplane plant.[5]

The Nisei occupational structure was notably distinct from that of the Caucasians, although the Nisei's own job preferences were quite similar to those of their white peers.[6] Table 6.1 shows the occupational distribution of Nisei in Los Angeles City and County in 1940. These distributions are then compared to those of employed people in the first generation, and of all employed persons. The figures indicate the ratio of Nisei concentration in a given occupational category to that of the comparison group: a ratio of 2.00, for example, would mean that the Nisei were twice as concentrated in that category.

A simple approach to the very complex Table 6.1 is through its most exaggerated ratios: for "unpaid family laborer," the magnitude

[4]Yasukochi, "Vocational Experiences," pp. 2–3; Charles K. Ferguson, "Political Problems and Activities of Oriental Residents in Los Angeles and Vicinity" (Master's thesis, University of California, Los Angeles, 1942), p. 108. In a nonrepresentative survey of Los Angeles Nisei in the late 1930's, Ross found that nearly all believed that their opportunities were superior to those of their parents, and almost two-thirds believed that their problems were also greater. Robert Howard Ross, "Social Distance as It Exists between First- and Second-Generational Japanese in the City of Los Angeles and Vicinity" (Master's thesis, University of Southern California, 1939), pp. 167, 179–80.

[5]*Rafu Shimpo,* Mar. 19, 1940.

[6]Strong *et al., Vocational Aptitudes,* pp. 94, 101. Strong and his colleagues found a remarkably close correlation between the occupational preferences of Nisei and white high-school students in California, which became only slightly less similar among college students. Nisei showed greater preferences for teaching and chemistry, and lesser preferences for the ministry, law, and personnel management.

TABLE 6.1. Occupational Distribution of Employed Nisei in Los Angeles City and the Rest of the County, Compared with Occupational Distributions of Issei and of All Employed People, by Sex 1940

| | Los Angeles City | | | | | |
| | Males | | | Females | | |
	Nisei (%)	Ratio: Nisei to Issei[a]	Ratio: Nisei to all[a]	Nisei (%)	Ratio: Nisei to Issei[a]	Ratio: Nisei to all[a]
Professional, semi-professionals	3	0.71	0.30	5	1.20	0.38
Proprietors, managers, and officials	12	0.49	0.86	4	0.32	0.77
Clerical, sales	37	3.24	1.73	35	2.48	0.98
Craftsmen, foremen, and operatives	13	1.60	0.38	12	0.57	0.78
Non-farm laborers	20	0.63	2.74	2	0.32	4.56
Domestic service	3	1.43	4.83	19	2.97	1.56
Other service	4	0.38	0.41	15	0.62	1.04
Farmers, farm managers	2	0.33	0.38	*	**	**
Paid farm laborers	3	1.03	0.42	2	0.50	21.10
Unpaid family laborers	3	18.56	78.20	5	0.63	37.90
	100			100		

| | Rest of Los Angeles County | | | | | |
| | Males | | | Females | | |
	Nisei (%)	Ratio: Nisei to Issei	Ratio: Nisei to all	Nisei (%)	Ratio: Nisei to Issei	Ratio: Nisei to all
Professional, semi-professionals	1	0.73	0.20	2	1.32	0.15
Proprietors, managers, and officials	8	0.55	0.58	2	0.72	0.36
Clerical, sales	19	3.62	1.05	22	1.87	0.68
Craftsmen, foremen, and operatives	5	2.28	0.13	2	1.43	0.15
Non-farm laborers	6	0.66	0.95	*	**	**
Domestic service	2	0.52	6.22	16	2.60	1.10
Other service	1	0.40	0.26	3	1.18	0.21
Farmers, farm managers	13	0.31	6.10	1	**	**
Paid farm laborers	18	0.82	5.24	10	0.67	21.67
Unpaid family laborers	27	12.45	99.80	41	0.79	44.50
	100			100		

[a]Ratio of concentration of Nisei in given occupational category to concentration of comparison group in the category.

*Less than 0.5%

**Not computed, fewer than 10 persons.

Source: *Census 1940 P2*, p. 558; *Census 1940 P3*, pp. 244–45; *Census 1940 P4*, p. 108; Leonard Bloom and Ruth Riemer, *Removal and Return* (Berkeley and Los Angeles: University of California Press, 194 p. 13.

of these differences is enormous. So, for that matter, is the proportion of all Nisei working in such capacities outside Los Angeles City: 40 percent of the women who worked, and nearly 30 percent of the men, worked without pay for their parents. What was virtually a norm for Japanese employment was exceedingly rare in the community at large—an interpretation reinforced by the far lower ratios for non-family farm labor. To emphasize the normative character of this employment, one should note that while Nisei men were unpaid family laborers far more often than were Issei men, the reverse was true for females; before the Nisei daughter would be put to work without pay on her father's farm, her mother would work. These farmers were overwhelmingly Issei: only one-third as many Nisei men actually ran farms.

Other than agriculture, where did Nisei concentrate in comparison with the community at large? Table 6.1 points to two categories: non-farm labor (unskilled or pick-up jobs, or contract gardening or fishing) and domestic service. That these concentrations should extend across sex lines indicates that these were ''Japanese'' statuses in Los Angeles, and, for domestic service (except among county males), Nisei statuses in particular. Los Angeles was unusually fruitful as far as clerical and sales jobs for Japanese Americans were concerned. Despite the fact that these employees were quite disproportionately Nisei rather than Issei, by and large such jobs were not much more available to Nisei than to the average Los Angeles worker—somewhat more so for male Nisei, but somewhat less so for females.

When we move from points of Nisei concentration to points of Nisei absence, two weaknesses of the Nisei position appear. First, they were very low relative to the general population in the professions and in craft and factory jobs; second, they were quite low, compared to their parents, in the proprietary category. As the Nisei came of age, they found their progress blocked both by the caste line and by their fathers' successes. Few alternate routes were available, a fact reflected overwhelmingly in Table 6.1. First-generation enterprise had developed the obvious markets for Japanese services where they were permitted. In the Depression, Nisei needed employment by their parents' generation more than the latter needed Nisei employees; however, few independent sources of employment for Nisei were available. Capital and other means to advancement were seldom available to Nisei without parental intervention. Proprietors and farm owners and managers represent the labor-force Nisei who had come to vocational maturity by owning an establishment in their own right. Thus, as of 1940, male Nisei were often dependent directly upon first-generation enterprise, and proprietorship was virtually the only route out of such dependence. In 1940 only about 5 percent of Los Angeles City Nisei were working for Caucasian employers, and then very often in "Japanese" occupations, especially produce. Approximately two-thirds of unpaid Nisei family workers, both farm and non-farm, were over twenty-five.[7]

The overall testimony of the table is clear: Nisei were growing into the occupational structure established by their parents years before. Forced upon the Issei by discrimination and by their own readiness to seek a quickly profitable economic niche, this structure was now forced upon the Nisei by the Depression and the conservative outlook of the aging Issei, as well as by discrimination.[8]

Even though Los Angeles City Nisei possessed a median education 3.6 years greater than that of their parents, the professions offered the new generation surprisingly few opportunities. There were thirty-eight Los Angeles Japanese physicians in 1940, a rather substantial number; but these men depended almost entirely upon the patronage of their own race. Many of the physicians were of the first generation, and their practices probably encompassed much of the available Japanese clientele. Nisei physicians were forced to look outside the race, generally finding patients only among the least prosperous groups.[9] Only thirteen Nisei lawyers were counted in 1940. The first generation still controlled most of the money in the Japanese community, and they preferred to hire conciliators or "court interpreters" from among their own generation to handle all legal matters except courtroom appearances. Thus Nisei monopoly of legal positions (lawyers had to be citizens) was far less valuable than it might seem.

Journalism was attractive to the Nisei, but Japanese employees in responsible positions on white-run newspapers in Los Angeles were unheard of, and the vernacular press paid even less than clerking in one's father's or uncle's store.[10] In the city only 1 percent of male Japanese workers were classified as working in "transportation, communication, and other public utilities." These categories in-

[7]Dorothy Swaine Thomas, with the assistance of Charles Kikuchi and James Sakoda, *The Salvage* (Berkeley and Los Angeles: University of California Press, 1952), p. 605; Leonard Bloom and Ruth Riemer, *Removal and Return* (Berkeley and Los Angeles: University of California Press, 1949), pp. 19–20.

[8]*Census 1940 P4,* p. 105.

[9]WCCA, *Bulletin No. 12,* p. 42; Yasukochi, "Vocational Experiences," p. 2; Bloom and Riemer, *Removal and Return,* pp. 13, 26.

[10]Togo Tanaka, "The Vernacular Newspapers," typewritten manuscript for War Relocation Authority, folder A 1.11, JERS Collection.

cluded a large proportion of all positions subject to political manipulation.[11]

The civil service likewise offered no opening to Nisei, although teaching was the stated ambition of many Nisei college women. No Nisei was a public school teacher in Los Angeles City in 1940–41. Although ninety-five Nisei were listed as city and county employees in 1941, there was not a single Japanese fireman, policeman, or mailman.[12] Rarely could even a highly qualified Nisei muster enough political influence to get a job with the city or county. In 1933 *Rafu Shimpo* rejoiced that the "vocational prospects" of the Nisei had dramatically improved when a "young Japanese-American physician—a veteran of World War I—had 'been practically assured' of a position at the Los Angeles County Hospital. 'The position was made possible through the recommendation of American Legion Post No. 8 of which [he] is an active member. . . . Further weight was carried toward his selection through George W. C. Baker, councilman of the Ninth District, for whom [he] had waged an intensive campaign in Lil' Tokio at his election.' "[13]

Although the labor market was glutted in the Depression, the Japanese ethnic economy succeeded in accommodating its own, on some terms. In 1940 only 3 percent of all Japanese in Los Angeles County were on relief or seeking work, as compared with 12 percent of all workers.[14] This was achieved by spreading work as thin as possible, and by excluding from the labor force those for whom no job could be created. The ethnic economy was greatly strained by this effort, and complaints of distress and underemployment abounded in the vernacular press. In any case, the ethnic economy stood the strain only because the Nisei were willing to emphasize ethnic cohesion and eschew the pursuit of individual mobility.

But Nisei bravely struggled on, in perpetual hope of attaining a higher rung on the white occupational ladder. Humiliation after humiliation must have scarred them far more than they would admit, as when a widely touted white "friend," the principal of a local high

[11]Tolan Committee, *Fourth Interim Report,* pp. 111, 113; Bloom and Riemer, *Removal and Return,* p. 19.

[12]Los Angeles, Board of Education, *Directory of Personnel, 1940–41;* WCCA, *Bulletin No. 12,* pp. 42–44; *Los Angeles Daily Journal* and Los Angeles *Times,* both Jan. 28, 1942.

[13]*Rafu Shimpo,* Sept. 22, 1933.

[14]Jacqueline Rorabeck Kasun, *Some Social Aspects of Business Cycles in the Los Angeles Area, 1920–1950* (Los Angeles: Haynes Foundation, 1954), p. 32; WCCA, *Bulletin No. 12,* p. 26; *Census 1940 P1,* p. 558.

school, addressed a Nisei meeting on how they could break into teaching. He advised them to "learn the Japanese language and train [your]selves for a particular position."[15]

Unlike their now conservative parents, Nisei were constantly striving to find some "new" occupation. Such an occupation had only to be one from which Japanese were not barred by race (hence usually a job which whites had not exploited because of distaste or ignorance), and one in which Japanese Americans had or could develop some special advantages. The first generation had employed the same formula decades before. Foreign trade with the Orient frequently seemed to offer such an opportunity, as did work for a big firm from Japan. According to a 1939 survey, about one-fifth of Los Angeles Nisei and their parents believed this was the "best vocational possibility" for Nisei.[16] Japan never played a large part in the vocational arrangements of the Nisei, however, even through the Central Japanese Association at one time encouraged the Imperial Japanese Government to hire "superior" Nisei for posts in agriculture and fishing in Manchuria.[17]

The Merchants Association, a first-generation group, decided in 1938 that meat-cutting was a craft for Nisei to enter, perhaps as the Issei had developed produce.[18] Chick sexing seemed an opportunity in the 1930's, a delicate (and repetitious) art, perfected in Japan. The Southern California Chick Sexing Association, founded in 1933, was by 1935 using the columns of *Rafu Shimpo* to offer to advance the money needed for Nisei to travel to Japan to study the art. As of 1942, 96 of 138 certified chick sexers in California were Nisei, but even then so many Nisei had entered the occupation that the original demand had been exceeded, and wage-cutting had set in.[19]

More strong and persistent was the first generation's effort to remind their children that their future was on the land. The only apparent hindrances to even more spectacular first-generation farming success had been white opposition and the shortage of capital. As citizens, Nisei were unaffected by the Alien Land Law, and the community's capital resources had grown immensely. For the Nisei,

[15]Paraphrased in *Rafu Shimpo,* Oct. 15, 18, 1935.

[16]Ross, "Social Distance," pp. 164, 178; Los Angeles Japanese Association, Committee Reports, Feb. 21, 1930, Jan. ?, 1931.

[17]*Rafu Shimpo,* Feb. 16, 1930; Central Japanese Association Minutes, Feb. 10, 1933.

[18]*Rafu Shimpo,* Apr. 24, 1938; *Kashu Mainichi,* May 15, 1938.

[19]*Rafu Shimpo,* Mar. 22, 1935, Dec. 23, 1938, Feb. 4, 1940; Lloyd H. Fisher and Ralph L. Nielsen, "Japanese in California Agriculture," in Tolan Committee, *National Defense Migration Hearings,* pt. 31, 77th Cong., 2nd sess. (1942), p. 11816.

agricultural education could open new farming and organizational methods beyond the competence of the first generation. Beginning as early as 1926, the Central and local Japanese Associations worked with farm organizations and the vernacular press to convince Nisei to ''return to the farm as their strong foothold in the economic life of the race on the coast.'' Oratorical and essay contests urged the theme. Nisei were assured of a good start and attractive opportunities by the Southern California Japanese Farm Federation, which offered an industry well regulated in behalf of security, and some urban amenities in a rural recreation center. In time a Nisei Farmers' Cooperative was established to take up the theme, designing itself in the ''interest of agriculture'' as an ''intermediary in joining the isseis and the American [i.e., Nisei] farmers.'' Similar plans proliferated in both generations throughout the 1930's.[20]

With Issei successes behind them, and less obvious Caucasian opposition before them, the first generation expressed enthusiasm about their children's farm opportunities. Their economic ambitions for the next generation involved a grander version of the Issei achievement:

> The nisei can go further by extending into the cattle, cotton, wheat, corn, dairy products industries. Their future is a hopeful one especially in view of the fact that farmers of other races are abandoning their farms for the cities. By not only [not] limiting themselves in production alone, but by advancing into distribution, transportation, and marketing there are numerous avenues of vocation that agriculture offers to the nisei. There should be a gradual diminishing of the so-called problem of the lack of vocations for the second-generation people.[21]

What did this dream imply in terms of the relationships of Nisei to the white majority, and of Japanese-American culture to Anglo culture? The answer is that insofar as Issei clung to such visions, they anticipated—and even welcomed—continued racial separation. The color line was an essential and almost welcome element of this vision,

---

[20]Central Japanese Association Minutes, Mar. 6, 1926, Feb. 26, 1930; Los Angeles Japanese Association, Committee Reports, Feb. 27, 1930; *Rafu Shimpo,* Feb. 23, 1930, Oct. 1, 1933, Jan. 21, 1937, July 30, 1939; *Kashu Mainichi,* May 1, 1937.

[21]Kamata Ota, president of Cooperative Farm Industry of Southern California, at Nisei farm forum. *Rafu Shimpo* of Dec. 1, 1935, was an issue devoted in large part to the back-to-the-land theme. In fishing, a less hopeful tone prevailed. The secretary of the Fishermen's Association was quoted in 1935 as complaining about the desertion of the industry by the second generation. ''They want to run a little fruit business up town, or something like that. You know. Something soft.'' Timothy T. Turner, ''Japan—One Hour Away,'' *Los Angeles Times Sunday Magazine,* Apr. 28, 1935, pp. 11, 18.

accepted and converted from a socially irrational discrimination to an economically valuable advantage. The horizontal and vertical integration of general agriculture, made possible by residential compactness and ethnic division of labor, could permit a great enlargement of the first-generation economic beachhead at the expense of the individualistic white American farmer. The promise of America, even for one's children, had thus been narrowly defined.

Of course, matters did not progress this far. The Nisei generation neither abandoned nor concentrated upon farming. The Depression weakened truck farming in Los Angeles more than it did animal husbandry and field crops. Nevertheless, Japanese farms in Los Angeles County increased in acreage between 1930 and 1940, while acreage farmed by whites decreased. But Japanese remained almost exclusively in truck and berry production. For the Nisei, the farms remained what they had been: places where, in reasonable security and with a minimum of interference, they might be left alone to make their livings. By the time of relocation more than half the Japanese acreage in Los Angeles was in the hands of Nisei managers or proprietors, mainly through inheritance or assignment; in part, heightened international tensions and the more precarious legal position of the aliens explained the shift of farms into Nisei hands.[22]

Matters were not much different off the land, although some of the more sophisticated urban Nisei began to see that the first step toward emancipation was to wrest business leadership from their parents.[23] It was in this atmosphere that the Nisei Business Bureau was established, and that Nisei businessmen bought ads in the *Rafu Shimpo* English-language section to wish "CONGRATULATIONS AND BEST WISHES ITANO BROS., HOME APPLIANCES ANOTHER NISEI STORE," or to exhort: "This is a competitive world and the survival of the fittest is the foremost code of the day. Still, the nisei must bear in mind the co-operative spirit. Help others! Give freely! If in your neighborhood a nisei starts a new business, you as a nisei should give him first consideration in patronizing his new venture."[24]

[22]"Value of Agricultural Production in Los Angeles," compiled by Agricultural Department, Los Angeles County Chamber of Commerce, folder "Agriculture," Box 68, Clements Papers; Tolan Committee, *Fourth Interim Report*, p. 129; *Census 1940 Al*, p. 691.

[23]References to changes which rendered the aliens less competent than their children to lead the Japanese community veiled the fact that Nisei wished the Issei to abdicate for other reasons. See for example columnist Tad Uyeno in *Rafu Shimpo*, Aug. 7, 1938.

[24]*Rafu Shimpo*, Feb. 19, 1939, Aug. 18, 1937; Tad Uyeno in *Kashu Mainichi*, Mar. 13, 1938.

For hemmed-in Nisei, the fruitstand was the bitterest of all symbols of their frustration. Nisei in need of jobs had long availed themselves of retail produce as a relatively sure resort, where their ethnic stereotype would be an advantage rather than a hindrance. By the late 1930's, however, the trade had become a realization of defeat for their increasingly urgent ambitions to break out of the ethnic mold. The manifold pressures upon the Nisei were focused with particular intensity upon the fruit-and-vegetable trade, perhaps the more so because of the incongruity between the mundane business and the heightened emotions of the participants. Constraint by whites here intersected with parental concern, demography, Depression economics, and the renaissance of organized labor in Los Angeles. For large segments of the Los Angeles Nisei, the turmoil that was to develop over the Japanese fruitstands raised the question of a new definition of their community.

Even in strictly numerical terms, any change in the retail produce industry was important to the Nisei. By Pearl Harbor no less than one in five second-generation Japanese employees worked in the Japanese-owned retail produce stands and produce concessions in larger markets. Of these 1,500 to 2,000 workers, between a third and a quarter were women.

The Japanese retail produce industry had been growing by fission since the mid-1920's, when Nisei first achieved majority in meaningful numbers. As long as the stands could multiply, family or community connections could provide hard-to-find jobs for younger Nisei, whose cheap and theoretically grateful labor in effect subsidized the new stands begun by ambitious and experienced Nisei. By 1941 half of the Japanese retail produce proprietors and managers in Los Angeles were Nisei, and this proportion was rapidly rising; but the continued pressure to accommodate the abundant recruits was pushing the Japanese produce industry toward economic irrationality. For once, Los Angeles Japanese may not have been in advance of public demand—rather, they were anticipating the growth of a demand that was relatively inflexible. And any threat to the trade was construed as a threat to the economic health of the entire Japanese community of Los Angeles.[25]

The Japanese most desperately wanted to convert labor into income, as their experience with farming demonstrated. Their fruitstands competed not so much in price as in service and quality, with

[25]On the background of the produce business, see the fifth chapter, above, and Bloom and Riemer, *Removal and Return*, p. 18; Thomas, *The Salvage*, pp. 35 (n. 54), 603; WCCA, *Bulletin No. 10*, p. 5; *Rafu Shimpo*, Dec. 12, 1934.

meticulous efforts taken to maintain the freshness of carefully selected produce. The workday of the Japanese fruitstand employee was long, and a fussy concern for his merchandise was required, not least to impress his Caucasian customers. The work was neither unpleasant nor inspiring.[26] The hours—up to seventy-two a week —were vexing to the workers, but were generally accepted as the price that had to be paid in order for the business to flourish.

But Nisei in the industry and other community members gradually grew concerned over the distinct air of defeat which surrounded many Nisei working on the fruitstands. The least ambitious seemed somehow un-Japanese in their apparent hedonism and distaste for work; on the other hand, neither irony nor faith prevented the more ambitious from believing that fruitstand work was a perversion of the hopes nurtured by their American upbringing. One Nisei wrote in the English-language section of a local vernacular newspaper:

> I am a fruitstand worker. It is not a very attractive nor distinguished occupation, and most certainly unappealing in print. I would much rather it were doctor or lawyer . . . but my aspirations of developing into such [were] frustrated long ago by circumstances . . . [and] I am only what I am, a professional carrot washer. . . . The little optimism that is left in me goads me on with the hope that when I have a few shekels saved that I can call my own, and only God knows when that may be, I will invest it in an enterprise which will be, through habit and familiarity rather than choice, most likely another market.[27]

The system, of course, did not exist in isolation, despite its tightly ethnic organization. The Depression seems to have inspired a sharp increase in shopkeeping in Los Angeles generally, since small proprietors could at any rate avoid outright unemployment. Moreover, in view of the generally depressed state of consumer indexes, the retail fruit and vegetable trade in Los Angeles held up remarkably well at first. But by the mid-1930's temporary small gains of retail produce outlets were halted, as the new supermarkets made their first rapid inroads into the traditional market.

Although no more than 129 experienced Japanese retail produce workers in Los Angeles reported their unemployment to the Census Bureau in 1940, the figure is deceptive: only two-thirds of all Japanese workers in food retailing had worked a full twelve months in

---

[26] A good description of the work from an employee's point of view is contained in a case history in Thomas, *The Salvage,* esp. pp. 420–22.

[27] Taishi Matsumoto, "The Protest of a Professional Carrot Washer," *Kashu Mainichi,* Apr. 4, 1937.

1939, and periods of unemployment were long. Inexperienced men could often get no jobs at all; nevertheless, unemployment rates for "other races" in retail trade and sales were less than half those of whites.[28] The outlook was not bright, however, and concerned Japanese in the industry began to ask why. Some even blamed the industry's difficulties upon Jews, who to anxious Nisei sometimes seemed to be "proving more than a match for the Japanese in the managerial end." Others condemned such superficial responses as "the cheapest form of racial hatred and prejudice."[29] Seen correctly, the multiple threats to the delicate economic balance established by their parents revealed the precariousness of Issei accommodation—but it also suggested that, in a period of change, an escape might be at hand.

Even had the industry continued to grow despite Depression and competition, a threat from within had developed: unionization. Fruitstand entrepreneurs and the leaders of both first- and second-generation groups deeply distrusted the idea that workers—Nisei workers—might have an interest distinct from that of their employers, when those employers were Japanese. Unionization was anathema to the now-conservative Japanese leaders in Los Angeles in the late 1930's. Early in the century Japanese had frequently struck, to their considerable advantage—but almost invariably along ethnic lines against Caucasian employers. Now, with the Japanese in entrepreneurial positions and dependent upon abundant and cheap labor, the situation had changed. In dealing with Nisei workers, the older generation recalled the kind of paternalistic employer-employee relationship that predominated in Japan, and reacted with horror to the idea of Nisei joining unions, sometimes with responses shading into Red-baiting.

[28]*Census 1930 P4*, p. 162; *Census 1930 B1*, p. 192; *Census 1935 B1*, p. 145; U.S. Bureau of Foreign and Domestic Commerce, *Consumer Market Data Handbook, 1936* ("Market Research Series," No. 15), p. R-53; U.S. Bureau of Foreign and Domestic Commerce, *Consumer Market Data Handbook* (1939), p. 30; *Census 1940 B1*, p. 91; *Census 1940 P3*, pp. 244–47, 351, 360; Ralph Cassady, Jr., and Wylie L. Jones, *The Changing Competitive Structure in the Wholesale Grocery Trade: A Case Study of the Los Angeles Market, 1920–46* (Berkeley and Los Angeles: University of California Press, 1949); Max M. Zimmerman, *The Super Market* (New York: McGraw-Hill, 1955), pp. 48, 54, 60–65, 131; Rom J. Markin, *The Supermarket: An Analysis of Growth, Development and Change* (Pullman: Washington State University Press, 1963), pp. 6–17; Lucius P. Flint, "The Los Angeles Super," *Chain Store Age* (Grocery Managers' Edition) 26 (June, 1950): J34–35; *Census 1948 B1*, p. 421.

[29]Thomas H. Yamate, quoted in *Rafu Shimpo,* July 16, 1939; James Oda, "What's Wrong with Japanese Fruit Markets," *Doho,* Sept. 5, 1939.

A year of frequent strikes and unquestionable resurgence for traditionally feeble organized labor in Los Angeles, 1937 was a high point of statewide organization in retail sales and clerical occupations.[30] The activity provided such a striking contrast to the usual lassitude of local labor that the potent anti-union advocates in Los Angeles were forced to establish front groups to explain labor's aggressions to the public. Local and state anti-picketing initiative measures were proposed, designed to prevent picketing by any but current employees of a struck firm. Los Angeles voters approved their version in September, 1938, though the state measure went down to defeat in November.[31]

The union ferment was felt strongly in the produce industry of the city. In wholesale, unionization came quickly and with great impact. Centralized and dependent upon the daily delivery of bulky produce, the wholesale markets found themselves confronted in 1936 with a newly formed AFL local, the Market Workers Union. Six months of bickering led to intensive negotiations in April, 1937. The union gained general recognition, increased wages, and an eight-hour day for its members.[32]

The Market Workers Union initially omitted Japanese from its membership, despite the many Japanese workers in that industry. Almost two decades earlier, however, a similar union had failed because of competition from unorganized Japanese workers, and almost immediately the Market Workers began to proselytize among the Nisei. Alarmed Japanese wholesalers decried " 'strong arm' tactics" and tried to foster a parallel ethnic union, but the organization they started quickly disavowed pretensions to union status or to rivalry with existing unions. Its president, Robert K. Sato, declared that the group was devoted merely "to studying the situation more thoroughly." After a week of such study, Sato received a written nondiscrimination pledge from the Market Workers Union, and his group affiliated with the white workers. By autumn the local had joined the Teamsters as Local 630, Produce Drivers and Employees

[30]California, Department of Industrial Relations, Division of Labor Statistics and Law Enforcement, *Biennial Statistical Report to the Legislature, 1939–40*, pp. 46, 55; Richard Norman Baisden, "Labor Unions in Los Angeles Politics" (Ph.D. dissertation, University of Chicago, 1958), pp. 160–66; Louis B. Perry and Richard S. Perry, *A History of the Los Angeles Labor Movement, 1911–1941* (Berkeley and Los Angeles: University of California Press, 1963), pp. 442–91.

[31]The Los Angeles measure was declared unconstitutional within a year. Perry and Perry, *History of Los Angeles Labor*, pp. 423–41, 498–501; La Follette Hearings, part 57, p. 20949.

[32]*Kashu Mainichi*, Apr. 23, 1937; *Los Angeles Citizen*, Apr. 30, 1937.

Union. Under it, a union shop was established in the downtown wholesale produce markets.[33]

The retail produce industry was less vulnerable to unionization because of small units, diffuse sources of supply, nepotism in hiring, and paternalism in labor management. But New Deal hopes still encouraged a concerted attempt to organize the retail food industry of Los Angeles on the part of the Retail Clerks Protective Association. Before 1937 the International had had a highly indifferent record of success in Los Angeles, and nationally it was only waking from decades of torpor.[34] A new group was chartered in early 1937 that would eventually organize the markets of Southern California and become the most powerful local in the International: Local 770, Retail Food Clerks. After some indecision, 770 settled on a highly pragmatic and vigorously self-assertive approach. Prime exponent of this strategy was Joseph De Silva, who came to the fore as business manager and leader of the anti-"radical" faction of the local in late 1937.[35]

The Japanese community displayed great alarm at the developments in the local labor movement. The wages-and-hours policy which had encouraged the growth of the fruitstands was viewed as indispensable to the survival of the Japanese industry, while the AFL had not shed the threatening aura arising from its earlier persecution of the local Japanese. At this time the Los Angeles AFL was playing an opportunistic game with the Japanese, retaining their essential antipathy but lowering official barriers to Japanese membership "sufficiently so that . . . they could be taken into our unions," in the words of the secretary of the Central Labor Council. This practice was followed mainly in industries where Japanese were already so well represented that they might prove a threat if left unorganized. Although prior to 1937 some Japanese had been admitted to membership in various AFL locals in Los Angeles (some of which, like the

[33]*Rafu Shimpo,* May 3, 11, 12, 15, 16, June 4, 1937; *Kashu Mainichi,* May 12, 15, 1937; *Los Angeles Citizen,* Feb. 11, 1921 (minutes of the Los Angeles Central Labor Council, Feb. 4, 1921), Sept. 3, 1937; interview with Robert K. Sato, Los Angeles, May 2, 1968.

[34]Their weakness in Los Angeles in the mid-1930's is gauged by examining the frequency with which the multitude of new and weak Los Angeles locals appear in the delinquency lists published in *The Retail Clerks International Advocate* 34–36 (1934–37); also Michael Harrington, *The Retail Clerks* (New York: John Wiley, 1962), pp. 6–7.

[35]*Retail Clerks International Advocate* 36 (Mar., 1937): 19; *Los Angeles Citizen,* July 2, Sept. 17, 1937; Lee Quick, "History of Local 770," *Voice of 770* 1 (Jan., 1942): 14–15.

Japanese and Oriental Hotel and Restaurant Workers' Union, were segregated), their experiences did not greatly modify the group's suspicion of the AFL.[36] Minor AFL concessions, however, could conceivably have developed toward a more substantial understanding.

When Produce Drivers 630 succeeded in organizing the wholesale produce markets and brought Japanese workers into the fold, the Japanese community immediately launched a preemptive counterattack. Some 450 Nisei fruitstand workers, calling themselves the Southern California Retail Produce Workers Union, established a union of their own. President and leading force in the union was Thomas Hiromu Yamate, a buyer. Membership was limited to Japanese workers in retail produce, and was to include all such workers. SCRPWU's articles of incorporation omitted all mention of strikes and collective bargaining. The SCRPWU was only "to assist" the workers "in obtaining adequate compensation for their services." Within two weeks, with no controversy, recognition came from the all-Japanese Retail Market Operators' Association.

Though the Nisei union was not—as 770 repeatedly charged—a company union pure and simple, it did possess most characteristics of that type of organization. To the SCRPWU, the immediate interest of the Nisei worker was decidedly of secondary importance. When necessary, the union would suppress his grievances in order to assert ethnic solidarity in the face of changes which went far beyond the ethnic group and the industry. Never could the Union credibly define its relationships to management as even potentially conflictual. Instead ethnic consensus was sought, so that a unified effort might hold off 770 and maintain the traditional basis of the Japanese industry. Yamate's role was neither that of a labor leader, nor that of a "stooge." In fact, he was an ethnic group leader.[37]

For its part, Local 770 shortly began a two-pronged attack upon ethnic dual unionism. One prong was aimed at the Japanese em-

[36]*Rafu Shimpo,* Sept. 13, 17, 1933; *Los Angeles Citizen,* July 23, 1937; quotation from John Buzzell, in HUAC, *Investigation,* pt. 15, p. 9287.

[37]Yamate ran in 1938 for the position of first vice-president of the local Citizens League (*Doho,* Dec. 5, 1938). "Articles of Incorporation of Southern California Retail Produce Workers Union," filed Aug. 3, 1937 (but dated May 28, 1937), California, Secretary of State, Corporation Number 172,404; *Makita et al.* v. *Three Star Produce Co., Ltd.,* Superior Court, Los Angeles County, Docket No. 431741 (1939), "Brief of Plaintiff," p. 2; *Rafu Shimpo,* May 16, 17, 27, 1937; *Kashu Mainichi,* May 17, 1937; *Doho,* Sept. 1, 1938; *Los Angeles Citizen,* May 21, Sept. 17, 1937; La Follette Hearings, pt. 66, pp. 24354–355. All citations to these hearings in this chapter, except when otherwise specified, are to memos and letters subpoenaed from the files of the Neutral Thousands, a local white anti-union group, printed as exhibits.

ployers and was intended to convince them that present arrangements would not bring industrial peace, even if Nisei employees were ready to accept them. The other was aimed directly at the Nisei worker. As De Silva prepared his union to face Safeway, giant among California grocery chains, he was simultaneously working to undercut the hastily but rather successfully established claims of the SCRPWU, which enrolled over 1,000 members in its first week.[38]

On July 4, 1937, Local 770 addressed an open letter in the vernacular press to their "Dear Brothers and Sisters" on the Japanese fruitstands and concessions. Maintaining that the ethnic union served only the Japanese employers, 770 challenged the individual Nisei worker to place class interest above ethnic interest, thus supporting what 770 considered to be the American Way.

> We believe that the Japanese and white workers should unite and work together. We recognize no national or racial difference. The 'Company Union' that your employers have asked or told you to join, has been for the purpose of isolating and segregating the Japanese workers from the white . . . that they may, and can keep you under their thumbs . . . that they can, and will, work you longer hours for less pay. We have not set up a separate wage and hour scale for the Japanese worker, while the 'Company Union' proposes to do this very thing.
>
> If you are real Americans, why don't you fight for the American standard of living? This is made possible only by joining our union.
>
> United in one organization, working and fighting together for the same purpose, employers will have to listen to us. WHY SHOULD JAPANESE FRUIT STAND WORKERS WORK LONGER HOURS AND ACCEPT LESS PAY THAN WHITE WORKERS IN THIS SAME INDUSTRY? WE SAY 'NO!' WE WILL NOT LET THIS HAPPEN! YOUR PLACE IS WITH US! JOIN NOW![39]

The extent to which such arguments—and the scarcely veiled threat of the "real Americans" phrase—moved the Nisei workers is unclear. The skittish state of the industry, combined with lingering doubts about the ultimate intentions of the AFL, hardly suggest this as the point for a radical Nisei departure from the cautious and defensive patterns of group survival developed by their parents. De Silva later attributed the failure of his recruiting effort to the "prejudice" of most Japanese toward the AFL and their fear of "co-mingling" with whites. Other white labor leaders explained the failure in terms of the Nisei's blind obedience "to the advice of their oldsters . . . when they went home to talk about it," or to fear of sanction by the

---

[38]*Kashu Mainichi*, May 19, 1937. The controversy with Safeway was to last intermittently for three years. The local emerged victorious.

[39]*Ibid.*, July 4, 1937.

Japanese Association. On the whole, the white union leaders subscribed to the current stereotype of a monolithic Japanese community, failing to recognize that the generations hardly saw eye to eye or that the Nisei themselves were greatly disarrayed. They certainly did not understand that the idea of an adversarial union challenged hallowed bases of Japanese-American group organization. As far as 770 was concerned, the question had been put publicly to the Nisei, and their public answer had been no.[40]

Local 770, of course, was mainly intent upon establishing what it sometimes called an ''American'' standard of living for white workers. If Nisei workers were willing to throw in their lot with the ''American'' workers—and this meant primarily adhering to a high wages-and-hours standard—benefits would be shared, and 770 would treat the Nisei as allies. But to the extent that the Nisei sought special treatment for the Japanese portion of the industry, they were to be condemned as enemies of American labor. Since white-run concerns could not concede a substantial advantage in labor costs to their Japanese competitors without suffering losses in trade, Local 770 believed that they could not ignore the Japanese if they were to organize the white portion of the industry.

In the meantime, 770 was working directly on some of the larger Japanese employers of Nisei retail clerks. The union began by picketing the Three Star Produce Company, the largest chain of Japanese retail markets, with about forty concessions and well on the way to establishing the first wholly owned Japanese supermarket.[41] When Produce Drivers 630 respected the picket line, Three Star quickly capitulated, signing a contract with 770 which called for the union shop, higher wages, and shorter hours to go into effect as soon as 770 succeeded in gaining the adherence of half the remaining Japanese retailers in Los Angeles.[42] But after an injunction was secured which removed the danger of further 770 picketing, few retailers were converted. Still, the threat of economic strangulation had evoked a general shudder in the Japanese community.

In December, 1937, Yamate widened the conflict on behalf of the SCRPWU. When his ability to protect the Japanese industry was

[40]Joseph De Silva to John Modell, Mar. 14, 1968; Buzzell in HUAC, *Investigation*, p. 9287; interview with O. I. Clampitt, Retail Clerks Local 1442, Santa Monica, Calif., Mar. 23, 1968.

[41]*Rafu Shimpo,* Oct. 1, 1940.

[42]*Los Angeles Citizen,* Nov. 26, Dec. 3, 1937, Feb. 11, Apr. 29, May 13, 20, 1938; *Rafu Shimpo,* Feb. 7, 1938; La Follette Hearings, pt. 57, p. 21244 (communication of Buzzell to Committee); pt. 66, pp. 24354–465.

threatened by 770 picketing, he spoke out in a Los Angeles City Council meeting in favor of a proposed anti-picketing ordinance; the measure was intended by its sponsors to restore the previous feeble position of organized labor in Los Angeles.[43] What De Silva thought of workers who would support a step like this can easily be imagined. The conflict between the Japanese union and 770 had driven both parties to new and more extreme positions. The arguments which Local 770 was readying about the Japanese workers and their employers were more than dimly reminiscent of the old brand of AFL anti-Orientalism. For its own part, the Nisei group was assuming the stand of a militantly anti-labor organization, stressing ethnic ties to the exclusion of all others.

De Silva soon announced a further weapon which had been forged for other reasons but which was a potent reminder of the capacity of organized white America to strangle the Japanese-American economy. Banding together with the Teamsters and other unions in an "AFL Food Alliance," the Food Clerks stated their goal: the closed shop in all food markets, restaurants, and cabarets. The Food Alliance, De Silva announced, would be able to "stop sources of supply within forty-eight hours."[44]

Almost immediately 770 was able to report a success: a Japanese produce concessionaire caved in after one day's picketing of his establishment. Japanese employees there had followed the lead of James Oda, Japanese organizer for 770, and Produce Drivers 630 had respected their line.[45] But within two months this encouraging 770 victory had evaporated. A legal fiction transferred the outlet to another Japanese concessionare, who fired the organized employees and refused to honor his predecessor's AFL contract. Leaflets distributed by 770 reflected their ire at this trick, demanding that the public bypass the market and thus "SUPPORT AMERICA."[46] The Japanese merchant was granted a temporary injunction, however, when his employees gave a deposition stating that they were satisfied

[43]Los Angeles *Times,* Dec. 11, 1937.

[44]Los Angeles *Examiner,* Feb. 4, 1938.

[45]*Los Angeles Citizen,* Feb. 11, 1938; Buzzell to Committee, La Follette Hearings, pt. 57, p. 21244.

[46]The leaflet proclaimed the produce section was unfair to the Retail Food Clerks and urged: "*Do not aid a Japanese controlled company union.* Support American Standards of Labor and Wages." Exhibit in *Nakanishi, etc.* v. *Retail Food Clerks Union, etc.,* Superior Court, Los Angeles County, Docket Number 427106 (1938). See also "Plaintiff's Brief," "General Demurrer and Answer" of Ray Porter (President of 770), and "Affidavit of Robert Minami *et al.*" (employees of Nakanishi).

with the terms of their employment, and 770 dropped its interest in the matter.[47]

In like manner, the AFL at Three Star had experienced a potential victory more than an actual one, for operation of the contract was dependent upon the local's future organizing successes. When the SCRPWU denied 770 such successes, a new factor entered the situation. Previously, the confirmed foes of labor organization within the Japanese community had prudently supported the SCRPWU as the best available compromise. Now Susumu Hasuike, president of Three Star Produce, decided the time had come to reassert an even more adamantly paternalistic outlook on labor relations, and he attacked both 770 and the SCRPWU. Hasuike, who interpreted his own considerable success as typifying what was possible for the ambitious in America, seems to have bewildered both Yamate and De Silva with his quirks.

After late April, 1938, Hasuike moved rapidly to take advantage of the fact that Three Star employees were theoretically covered by a closed-shop agreement with 770. He purged employees who made a point of their continued adherence to SCRPWU, and even refused them permission to communicate with Yamate.[48] With jobs scarce, after a few weeks Hasuike forced a vote in which his 300 employees signified that they wanted nothing to do with SCRPWU; he publicly interpreted the vote as signifying that his men knew that he knew best how to care for their welfare.[49] This move, in turn, led to the absurd situation in which the SCRPWU threatened to blacklist Three Star employees who refused to reaffirm their SCRPWU memberships. The blacklist was to be honored by other Japanese markets.[50]

This bizarre contretemps undermined the whole basis of worker support for the SCRPWU, which was quite obviously powerless in the face of Hasuike's obduracy. What had failed was the very solidarity of the Japanese community which Yamate had considered his strongest advantage and indeed the raison d'être of his union. Now he had to fall back upon those outside the ethnic community who were willing to lend assistance. By no accident, aid was found among strongly anti-labor whites who had earlier been intrigued by Yamate's unusual stand in support of the anti-picketing ordinance.

The Neutral Thousands, devoted to making Los Angeles once again an open-shop haven by encouraging so-called independent unions, was enlisted to try to bring Hasuike around. What Yamate

[47]Some kind of compromise was apparently reached, for in about a month Local 770 took the market off its unfair list. *Los Angeles Citizen,* May 20, 1938.

[48]La Follette Hearings, pt. 66, pp. 24354–56.

[49]*Rafu Shimpo,* May 4, 10, 1938.

[50]*Kashu Mainichi,* May 5, 1938.

had in mind was almost undoubtedly economic pressure, for to an extent Hasuike was the prisoner of the white proprietors of markets in which most of the Three Star Produce concessions were located. The Neutral Thousands promised to try to exert such pressure, and in return asked Yamate to secure signatures of SCRPWU members to get the anti-picketing measure on the ballot as an initiative.[51] Yamate readily agreed, offering also to deliver the endorsement of the Nisei Voters League and the Citizens League, once the initiative measure appeared on the ballot.

Although the Neutral Thousands contacted the secretary of the Allied Food Industries, who promised "that he would take the matter up with some very influential people he knew," Hasuike could not be reached.[52] In September, 1938, Yamate reversed gears: in contravention of the proposed anti-picketing initiative, he placed pickets around a few of the Three Star locations. Yamate declared that working conditions at Three Star were a "shameful blot" and brought civil suit against Hasuike, with the officers of Local 770 as co-defendants. The suit charged a conspiracy of the AFL local and the anti-union employer to compel SCRPWU members who worked at Three Star to resign from the union.[53] Their joint goal, Yamate charged, was "eventually to disrupt and destroy the same [SCRPWU] . . . and to cause said employees to become members of the defendant local." The charge went on to detail the firing of three of the eighty SCRPWU men who had openly refused to leave the union.[54]

Both sides believed that, in the last analysis, their disagreement hinged upon differing definitions of ethnic-group policy. The primacy of ethnic solidarity was common to both definitions; at issue was the question of the relative rewards of labor and capital—or Issei and Nisei—within a consensual ethnic group. Hasuike and Yamate asked the community to arbitrate the struggle. By pitching the argument in terms of the broader issues at stake, they left immediate bread-and-butter issues mainly unspoken.

Hasuike put forth his clearest statement a few days after the picketing of Three Star had begun. In an open letter which had been solicited by the English section of *Rafu Shimpo* he explained:

> I am very close to the nisei. I have worked with you as an employee and fruit stand clerk myself. . . . The welfare of the Japanese community is at vital stake. It means much to the Three Star company. We are all

[51]La Follette Hearings, pt. 66, pp. 24417–19, 24424, 24354–57. The Neutral Thousands was also making use of other Japanese splinter unions in their campaign.

[52]*Ibid.*, 24357–60; *Kashu Mainichi*, Sept. 12, 1938.

[53]*Rafu Shimpo*, Sept. 2, 4, 1938; *Kashu Mainichi*, Sept. 4, 1938.

[54]*Makita et al.* v. *Three Star Produce Co.*, "Brief of Plaintiff."

affected by it. That is why we of the Three Star company fail to understand why one Japanese organization that claims to be interested in community welfare is trying to attack, disrupt and tear down another Japanese business organization. . . . The Three Star company is an expanding concern. We are far from the goal. I sincerely believe that when my firm expands, I am cooperating with the great goal of the J.A.C.L. Development Program in opening new outlets of employment for the nisei. By doing this I believe that the Three Star company is making a far more concrete and real contribution to the nisei welfare and community progress.[55]

Together, the phrase "concrete and real contribution" and the juxtaposition of Three Star with the SCRPWU as two "Japanese business organizations" indicate Hasuike's view of the Japanese community and its future. His was a dense, unified conception of the situation of the Japanese in Los Angeles, in which economic growth (especially in competition with white society) should direct the course of affairs. What was best for the Japanese community was best for the individual Japanese. Farsighted organizations like the Citizens League saw this and encouraged the development of ethnic business for the same reason. By contrast, selfish reasons led SCRPWU to disregard the fact that Hasuike was bringing money into the Japanese community and generating new jobs. That these jobs were for "professional carrot washers" bothered ex-clerk Hasuike not at all, for this pursuit had sustained the Japanese of Los Angeles. To object was factionalism.

To counter Hasuike's line of argument, Yamate had to justify the actions of his own union in an unanticipated conflict, but without embracing 770's viewpoint that class outweighed ethnic loyalties. He also had to counter Hasuike's claim that his personal success gave him the authority to define ethnic-group policy without seeming to challenge the not dissimilar entrepreneurial drives that possessed other leaders of both generations, including, no doubt, his own constituents.

> We are fully aware that the outcome of the present dispute will determine whether the efforts of thousands of Nisei to better their working condition and to protect the Japanese industry will succeed or fail. . . .
> Before this union was organized long hours and low wages were the accepted condition in the industry, not because of the unscrupulousness of one individual or a group of individuals, but because such conditions were taken for granted.

[55]*Rafu Shimpo,* Sept. 7, 1938.

Today, through the efforts of our union with the aid of the civil organizations in our community, we have been able to bring order and reason into the fruitstand industry. Our objective rises above the mere employer-employee dispute and takes in consideration of the welfare of the Japanese people as a whole. With this broad perspective in mind, we started to negotiate with all Japanese fruitstand owners. In our negotiation we were aware that the circumstances and condition among the Japanese people, with a different traditional background from other races, called for a modified form of workers' organization. . . . Why is Mr. Hasuike refusing to cooperate with our organization and with the Japanese people as a whole? Why is Mr. Hasuike obstructing the progress of the Nisei?

Yes, why? Because of the selfishness of one man who cannot see that by giving Nisei a square deal he will be helping to build a brighter future for the second generation in America. There are many workers in Three Star company who would like to attend high schools to learn better trades, so that they can open new fields of employment to the Nisei. But who can better themselves when they must work twelve, thirteen hours every day?[56]

Like Hasuike, Yamate described his position as being the one that took the Japanese community into consideration. Like Hasuike, he described his opponent's position as narrowly self-interested. In the opinion of both, the Japanese community and economy could afford little internal conflict. Both Yamate and Hasuike agreed that the future was with the Nisei, but that momentary economic stringency clouded that future. Neither chose to consider the part that accommodation to the caste line played in the crisis, or to speculate about the possibilities of breaching it. And, of course, neither suggested the cooperation with 770 which might open such a breach.

A clear-cut decision between these two points of view was not to be reached before the war. Formal reconciliation between Yamate and Hasuike was achieved about two weeks after picketing began. Yamate merely announced that ''Mr. Hasuike has agreed to work in close harmony with our union. . . . With the cooperation of the Three Star employees with our union, [we] are definitely on our way to fulfill our function.'' Hasuike probably let Yamate off the hook by permitting Three Star employees to have token membership in SCRPWU, but without materially altering the conditions of their employment.[57]

Soon De Silva resumed his attack. Accustomed to little Nisei cooperation, he now turned to a boycott, which he promoted with

[56]*Kashu Mainichi,* Sept. 7, 8, 9, 1938.
[57]*Rafu Shimpo,* Sept. 17, 1938; *Doho,* Nov. 20, 1938.

undisguised racial appeal. "DON'T BUY JAPANESE," read handbills put out by 770. "Support the organized RETAIL FOOD CLERKS. Do not contribute to unemployment, Low Wages. Long Hours[.] Do not let us compete with un-American standards of living[.]"[58] His boycott was "not one of racial prejudice," De Silva explained, but was a "humanitarian action" designed to bring down the Nisei union which had "divided the workers so that they suffer and trust no one." He argued: "The Japanese Association through its agent, the Company Union, has so incensed the Japanese workers against the American Labor movement, they have withdrawn into a world of their own. . . . These anti-labor merchants are practicing a dictatorship within our democracy, and are set to destroy, with keenest competition, the little we have accomplished."[59] De Silva insisted during the course of the boycott that "there is no discrimination nor feeling against the rank and file Japanese workers," and that Nisei employees were "free and welcome" to affiliate with 770.[60]

The ineffective and listless boycott promptly led De Silva one long step further toward the final solution of the Japanese problem: the Japanese retail produce industry must be strangled, for reasons of economic nationalism, by and on behalf of the caste of "real Americans."

> Almost every economist and leading citizen of the country today admits the reason we cannot come out of the depression is because there is a lack of circulation of money. All Americans can contribute substantially to this cause if they would only make it a practice to Buy American when they spend their hard-earned wages. 'Buy American' and 'Buy Union.' Let us make this our sacred creed as other people do. Support the American merchants that are Union and keep the American dollar in American channels of trade.[61]

These words added their weight to a growing clamor against resident Japanese, based on fear of subversion. But their slight economic effect upon the fruitstands was absorbed, along with the cost of a brief downturn in the business, by the Nisei workers, whose wages were reduced. In early 1939 Yamate complained to his allies at the Neutral Thousands that the passage of the anti-picketing ordinance, which he had supported, had left the union weaponless in the face of employers who were determined to impose a wage cut on

---

[58]*Los Angeles Citizen,* Feb. 24, 1939; *Rafu Shimpo,* Mar. 10, 19, 1939. The last reproduces a photograph of one such broadside.

[59]*Los Angeles Citizen,* Mar. 3, 24, Apr. 28, 1939.

[60]*Doho,* Sept. 20, 1939.

[61]*Los Angeles Citizen,* Apr. 28, 1939.

those workers who were reluctant to picket in their own behalf for fear of losing their jobs. "We acted for the best interests of our members, as well as the preservation of our organization, but many members felt that the passage of the ordinance had done more harm than good." The union accepted a wage cut to the minimum of $20.25 for a sixty-hour week for experienced men in 1939 and agreed to settle for the same again in 1940, though they managed a dollar-a-week raise late in the year.[62]

What had occurred was a classical self-fulfilling prophecy. Earlier experience had taught the Japanese elders to fear the AFL and to stay safely within the ethnic economy. As a reflex, Nisei had been led to reject the overtures of the Retail Clerks, which, though clearly tactical in purpose, had raised the possibility that the Nisei might develop there a modicum of power for themselves, to hold off the Issei proprietors and perhaps to develop an opening beyond the ethnic community. This rejection encouraged the recapitulation of organized labor's old patterns of denunciation of "un-American" Oriental labor, which again cemented solidarity within the Japanese community.

By late 1940 Yamate had quietly retired from his post and visited Japan, reportedly to "sell some rubber patents." Members of his union were more and more troubled by its lack of militancy and by the far more satisfactory wage-and-hour scales attained by white clerks. The situation was ripe for change. Wishing to relieve the aggressive De Silva of a burden while depriving him of a chance to increase his power base, officials of the Retail Clerks International called upon the Nisei unionist Robert K. Sato to take out a charter and organize the Nisei retail fruit-and-vegetable workers.[63]

In March, 1941, the Retail Clerks International leadership handed Sato a charter establishing the "Fruit & Vegetable Store Employees' (Japanese) Union, Local 1510," with jurisdiction over all Japanese employees in retail fruit-and-vegetable stores in Southern California.[64] With both Yamate and De Silva out of the picture, members of the SCRPWU quickly and unanimously consented to their old or-

[62]La Follette Hearings, pt. 66, p. 24361: *Rafu Shimpo,* Jan. 31, 1939, Feb. 1, Sept. 19, 1940.

[63]Thomas, *Salvage,* pp, 422–23: *Rafu Shimpo,* Sept. 19, 1940; *Doho,* Apr. 1, Aug. 14, 1941: *Retail Clerks International Advocate* 40 (May–June, 1941): 26; interview with Robert K. Sato, May 2, 1968.

[64]Interview with Sato, May 2, 1968; *Rafu Shimpo,* May 3, 11, 12, 15, 16, June 4, 1937; *Kashu Mainichi,* May 12, 15, 1937; *Los Angeles Citizen,* Sept. 3, 1937. Also Charter of Local 1510, Mar. 27, 1941, and C. C. Coulter to Robert K. Sato, Mar. 28, 1941, both in possession of Robert K. Sato.

ganization's immediate demise, and the transfer of membership lists (and two officers) to Local 1510. Relieved at escaping the unsympathetic De Silva, the Japanese merchants soon granted union contracts with terms identical to those previously won by 770.[65] Membership in 1510 grew slowly, however, and certain Japanese merchants—notably Hasuike—were reluctant to live up to the terms of their contracts. Relations with 770 were strained and formal. Although De Silva was one of eight labor leaders who addressed the charter-installation ceremony of Local 1510, it was not until two months later that "All Japanese Markets" were taken off the official unfair list of the Los Angeles Central Labor Council. Just two months before Pearl Harbor, 770 threatened unofficially to take over its segregated fellow local if it continued to show tendencies toward company unionism.[66]

How are we to gauge the outcome of the fruitstand union episode? Did it constitute a victory for the Nisei in their battle for independence? Or a defeat in that battle? Or was the issue not truly joined at all? Was ethnic solidarity threatened by 1510, or buttressed by it? Was integration furthered, or set back, or was this question ignored by all concerned? Answers to these questions never appeared, for the consequences of the unionization episode were thoroughly obscured by World War II.

The most fitting assessment of the episode probably would emphasize the state of uncertainty and flux in which many Los Angeles Japanese Americans found themselves before the war. The Issei had been challenged on their own ground, but the challenge had failed when the Nisei had to consider repudiating the ethnic economy in favor of the theoretically wider promises of the white community. But we cannot say whether whites were prepared to follow through on their promises of non-discrimination, because the Nisei were unwilling to risk their parents' economic edifice to make the test.

To their refusal, an appropriate afterword is more certain. When the war was over, many Japanese Americans returned to retail produce in Los Angeles; as a matter of course they joined Local 770, for 1510 had expired with the relocation. But a common union did not mean an end to segregation: within retail produce Japanese were limited to certain job categories, not necessarily the lowest, but with

[65]*Rafu Shimpo,* Mar. 26, Apr. 6, 1941: *Kashu Mainichi,* Apr. 2, 1941; *Doho,* Apr. 15, 1941.

[66]*Rafu Shimpo,* Apr. 27, May 14, 1941; *Doho,* June 1, Aug. 1, Oct. 5, 1941; *Los Angeles Citizen,* Aug. 8, 1941; Tanaka, "Journal," Aug. 20, 1941; Joseph De Silva to John Modell, Mar. 14, 1968.

an effective quota and a ceiling to attainment.[67] In short, within retail produce the definition of the Nisei survived the war, in its essence at least. And this was despite the decline of Issei power within the ethnic group, and the collapse of the ethnic economy.

[67]Scott Greer, ''The Participation of Ethnic Minorities in the Labor Unions of Los Angeles County'' (Ph.D. dissertation, University of California, Los Angeles, 1952), p. 59.

7

The Nisei Dilemma: Defining a Generation

When group policy called for them to be pressed into service as strikebreakers, Nisei were expected to answer the call. Their parents, accustomed to the confines of the ethnic community they had constructed, simply assumed that fidelity and a real intermingling of interest between the generations would lead to their children's natural cooperation. And so it was, in the matter of the Mexican farm-labor strike. But the subsequent fruitstand-union episode indicated that cooperation was becoming problematic.

Questions of economic policy were generally beyond the immediate comprehension of a group as young as the Nisei. Indeed, the second generation arrived on the scene most suddenly, an echo of the intense period of childbearing that had so alarmed the white majority when Japanese women had first arrived and the Issei established their families. As Tables 7.1 and 7.2 show, the Nisei came of age as an adult generation in the 1930's. By approximately 1940 Nisei constituted one-third of all Japanese adults in Los Angeles City. There was a notable lack of age-peers to breech the cultural gaps between the two generations when the young Nisei came of age. Only for the 1905–9 birth cohort was there a real mix of generations. The native-born generation, of course, was constantly replenished by newly born Japanese Americans—by 1940 some were even children of Nisei—while at the same time Issei, especially the males, were dying or returning to Japan in retirement. By 1945 half of the adult Japanese Americans in Los Angeles would be Nisei. Already by 1940, moreover, most Nisei men and women twenty-five or older were married. Over a thousand young Nisei men (13 percent of all Nisei) were heads of households that year, and 21 percent of all Japanese households in the city had Nisei heads.

Japanese-American demography intensified a situation already fraught with difficulties, even when Nisei and Issei could agree upon a common definition of the Japanese-American community as an economic entity. In cultural matters, intergenerational tensions sometimes caused anguish for each group. In coping with the wishes of

E 7.1. Age and Sex by Nativity, Los Angeles City Japanese, 1930 and 1940

| | Males | | Females | |
	American-born	Japan-born	Japan-born	American-born
Under 21	177	4,342	154	4,268
21 or over	7,547	531	3,987	275
Under 21	54	4,717	60	4,479
21 or over	5,330	2,972	3,282	2,427

: *Census 1940 P2*, p. 630.

their parents' generation, the Nisei realized that many of their aspirations were distinctly American, requiring a fulfillment different from, and perhaps in conflict with, that chosen by the immigrants.

To be sure, the Nisei were not so ignorant of things Japanese as were their Caucasian neighbors. The quasi-official Nisei position expressed by the English-language pages of the vernacular newspapers clearly encouraged interest in Japanese culture, and for many years urged a sympathetic outlook toward the Japanese side of international questions. Successful athletes from Japan were featured, notably "wiry-muscled" ones—compensating perhaps for Nisei shame at their slight builds. Included were stars like Don Sugai Matsuda, professional wrestler "from Japan," who employed jiu-jitsu to subdue Dangerous Dan McShane and Mysterious Mr. X at the Hollywood Legion Auditorium in 1937. Rather more authentic local displays of Japanese culture, many featuring traditional costume or ceremonies, were frequently reported in the English sections of the vernaculars. Other favorite topics were descriptions of Japanese

TABLE 7.2. Native-Born Japanese Population of Los Angeles City, 1940, by Year of Birth

Year of birth	Native-born Japanese	Percentage of age group native	Cumulative percentage of native-born population
Pre-1900	190	3	1
1900–4	304	18	3
1905–9	783	56	9
1910–14	1,824	91	21
1915–19	2,981	96	42
1920–24	3,039	98	63
1925–29	2,200	99	78
1930–34	1,570	99	88
1935–40	1,707	99	100

Source: *Census 1940 P4*, p. 99.

artistic efforts, such as an exhibit of block prints at the University of Southern California, which combined "the typical Japanese perfections in balance with the beauty of the colors," as well as accounts of lectures explaining aspects of Japanese culture to Nisei. Travelers in Japan regularly submitted informative accounts of old-country ways, and *Kashu Mainichi* regularly reprinted English translations of articles from Japanese periodicals, with a similar purpose.[1]

The Nisei, of course, were American citizens by birth *jus soli,* and as such gave their allegiance to America. School and other contacts with white Americans made this allegiance emotional as well as legal. Although their children's legal Americanness was a blessing to the first generation in dealing with the Alien Land Law, the cultural side of this allegiance was harder to deal with. When identified as "Japanese," even shared values were sometimes poisoned for the Nisei. One Los Angeles investigator discovered that four-fifths of the high school juniors and seniors he queried about "Japanese customs or ideas" denied that they "liked" such unexceptionable traits as "sincerity" and "loyalty."[2] In contrast to the close approximation of the Japanese value of hard work to the "innerworldly asceticism" of Protestant America, the family in Japan was based on values of filiality, obedience, and unquestioning respect, which clashed strongly with American values. So did the traditional hierarchical relationship of husband and wife. Young Nisei men commented frequently upon how differently they would treat their own wives, just as they remarked upon how they would choose them. The Japanese-American daughter, if somewhat less independent than her brother, was different from him only in degree. The upset of family patterns thus posed to the first generation a personal threat more immediate than any characteristic of white America.

A value shared by Japanese and American, Nisei and Issei alike, was formal education. Into this most potent agency of extra-familial socialization Japanese immigrants entrusted their children, fully recognizing how far beyond "school subjects" their education would extend. Parents and organizations within the ethnic community together impressed the young with the importance of formal schooling. How involuted this complex of values and motives could become is seen in the reported admonition of a Los Angeles fisherman.

[1]*Rafu Shimpo,* Mar. 4, Apr. 15, May 5, 1937; *Kashu Mainichi,* Mar. 30, Apr. 6, 1937.

[2]Kanichi Kawasaki, "The Japanese Community of East San Pedro, Terminal Island, California" (Master's thesis, University of Southern California, 1931), p. 95. The interpretation is my own.

If you graduate from college, I will proudly meet our ancestors in Heaven. . . . Until today I have never felt I was living in a free land because of two reasons: one was the racial problem, the other that I was ignorant of English. I do not wish to put you in the same social status in which I have lived in the past. Continue with American higher education, and show the Americans your ability. Son, this is your duty to your parents.[3]

Los Angeles Nisei were exemplary students. Invariably they were described as quiet, attentive, prompt, and neat, with generally high participation in group activities and with many examples of leadership.[4] School authorities and teachers placed great stock in the observation that Japanese boys were good boys—a stereotype that the Nisei seem to have deserved, recognized, and sometimes courted. A 1930's survey of 400 Los Angeles teachers revealed that they believed that the Nisei were not exceptionally bright students; rather, their will to please and achieve was responsible for their academic success. A study of white teachers' "attitude grades" at the almost all-Japanese Terminal Island elementary school, where attendance was phenomenally high and group social control at a maximum, showed that teachers almost invariably ranked their students with the angels. Nine-tenths of the attitude grades for a sample of Japanese students said that the young people were more obedient, dependable, courteous, clean, and thrifty than average students. A Los Angeles probation officer in 1933 declared that of some 10,000 truancy cases handled in the preceding year by his department, only one involved a Japanese American.[5]

Their grades reflected this approbation. Japanese students in Los Angeles junior and senior high schools almost never failed a subject, and they received better grades than other students. Reginald Bell's comparison of grades based on school records from the late 1920's and early 1930's shows a pronounced tendency, however: starting in junior high, Japanese grades declined toward the average received by all students, until by graduation Japanese grades were slightly below

[3]Quoted *ibid.*, pp. 109–10.

[4]George Howard Freeman, "A Comparative Investigation of the School Achievement and Socio-Economic Background of the Japanese-American Students and the White-American Students of Gardena H.S." (Master's thesis, University of Southern California, 1938), pp. 50–53.

[5]Marion Svensrud, "Some Factors Concerning the Assimilation of a Selected Japanese Community" (Master's thesis, University of Southern California, 1931), p. 85; John Mills Richardson, "A Comparative Study of Japanese and Native American White Children" (Master's thesis, University of Southern California, 1937); *Rafu Shimpo,* Mar. 31, 1933.

average.[6] It is hard to imagine this striking pattern being attributable to the Japanese students' behavior, but one can readily imagine how it might result from the perceptions of white teachers about what constituted excellence. For older students this standard clashed with Japanese demeanor, rather than fitting it as neatly as it did for younger students. In 1940 only 39 percent of the Los Angeles City Nisei twenty-five or older had failed to complete high school, as compared with more than half of the native whites.

A strong kinship network, a stable position within a community, and a well-established pattern of generational succession within the "corporate family" had all lent support to the family unit in Japan. Even Little Tokyo Nisei grew up without these institutional restraints and supports; thus they were more attuned to their teachers and peers. Parents were often unable to comprehend the choices that faced Nisei, and were likewise unable to comprehend their own inability to raise their children properly. Parents often charged their hard-working and obedient Nisei progeny with being lazy or incorrigible, even when in fact they exercised considerable control over their children's behavior. Because authorities had recognized this strict control, they generally left Japanese youth to the discipline of their parents, reinforced within the Japanese community by the power of gossip, an influence dreaded by children.[7] In such matters as educa-

[6]Reginald Bell, *Public School Education of Second-Generation Japanese in California* (Stanford: Stanford University Press, 1935), pp. 38, 46, 52–60.

[7]A social-psychological study of a declining Los Angeles neighborhood in 1938 found that the Japanese-American family was three times as likely as the native white to be in the highest quartile on "influence of primary family" upon their youth. Everett W. Du Vall, *Relative Influence of Primary Groups on Underprivileged Children* (Los Angeles: University of Southern California Press, 1938), p. 9; Sidney R. Garfield, "Los Angeles County Jail Records of Mexicans, Japanese, Chinese, 1923," typescript in Governor Young's Mexican Study Papers, California State Archives, Sacramento; Walter G. Beach, *Oriental Crime in California* (Stanford: Stanford University Press, 1932), p. 85; Edwin M. Lemert and Judy Rosburg, *The Administration of Justice to Minority Groups in Los Angeles County* (Berkeley and Los Angeles: University of California Press, 1948); H. K. Misaki, "Delinquency and Crime," in Edward K. Strong, Jr., *et al.*, *Vocational Aptitudes of Second-Generation Japanese* (Stanford: Stanford University Press, 1935), p. 156; Catherine Holt, "Interview with Miss Esther B. Bartlett of the Y.W.C.A. International Institute," Dec. 17, 1924. Broom and Kitsuse, in their elaborate case-history study of Japanese-American families, conclude that "the Japanese family in America rarely participated as a unit in the larger society. . . . The differential participation of its members in the dominant institutions created a wide range of acculturation in the population. Within the ethnic enclaves the family was a major conservative influence, and in most families acculturation of the Nisei was accompanied by conflict." Leonard Broom and John I. Kitsuse, *The Managed Casualty: The Japanese-American Family in World War II* (Berkeley and Los Angeles: University of California Press, 1956), p. 9 and *passim*.

tion and hygiene the official Japanese community played an explicit and potent role.[8] Social control of this kind, however, was far from answering the needs of the first generation.

Nisei responded to parental care with gratitude and affection, but the kind of wholehearted and unquestioning filial obedience expected in Japan was not to be had in the American setting. The pathos of the parents' position did not far exceed that of their children, as the two faced one another over such pressing questions as the appropriateness of dancing. The author of this early example of Nisei journalism could not decide whether the four-hour all-Issei Japanese Association meeting deserved scorn, satire, praise, or appreciation.

> Characterizing the spirit of the gathering, and the core of the conference, one thing stood out above all the petty arguing and disagreements. That was the fact that the leaders were trying to find a way out from the misunderstanding between the two generations. . . . Long have we been in need of a clearing-house of misunderstanding [*sic,* but not meant to be humorous]. . . . Foremost among the subjects under discussion was that concerning the social life of the young people. . . . The whole gamut of social life problems was brought to view. Long-winded discourses of the evils of the dance, in fact all of the lighter activities and frivolities of the younger set, were brought before the august gathering. Devotees of terpsichore took the challenge and upheld the art of dancing. The Flaming Youth took too many joyrides, saw too many movies depicting the gay life, and in short made the existence of the older folk dwindle into obscure shadows in comparison was the contention of a few of the speakers. The freedom of their children seemed to be a worry to some parents who feared only the worst for their liberty-loving progeny.[9]

First-generation parents turned in their anxiety to the Japanese community for the most basic kind of support. In and from the community grew new institutions to defend old values that reinforced the family. Difficulties besetting the Japanese-American family in Los Angeles were often explained as a "lack of communication" between generations, sometimes literally referring to the imperfect overlap of language skills. With this in mind, the first generation established an institution which they hoped would bridge the gap—the Japanese-language school, or *Gakuen.* The *Gakuen* was more than a language school, narrowly understood; there a morality compatible with (though not necessarily identical to) that of Japan might

---

[8]Edna Carew Jennings, "A Study of the Nutritional Work in the Elementary Schools of the Los Angeles School District" (Master's thesis, Univeristy of Southern California, 1931), p. 75; Central Japanese Association Minutes, Feb. 5, 1919, Mar. 29, 1924, Feb. 15, 1926.

[9]*Rafu Shimpo,* Apr. 4, 1927.

be developed through the study of Japanese language, geography, and history, and through careful shepherding by a specially trained teacher from Japan. An observer in the mid-1920's described the "ultimate purpose" of the *Gakuen*—apart from Americanization, which was simultaneously emphasized—as being "to teach the Japanese language in order to increase the understanding between parents and children so that they may all enjoy their home life. Through the use of the language at home, parents and children are kept in harmony and proper control is exercised by parents."

The *Gakuen,* in fact, was an embodiment of cultural pluralism. Among the teacher's duties was to explain to the parents of his pupils the over-all educational context in which their children were growing up. The schools were utterly unsubversive, both in effect and in political content. Their philosophy was explained by the president of the Southern California Japanese Language School Association: "Although the moral training of the children can be greatly accomplished by the presentation of good Japanese racial traits, we must not forget that we are educating American citizens. We must study more diligently in order to select character traits which will be suitable to the American nationality."[10]

The first Los Angeles *Gakuen* opened in 1911 and was followed by at least three more before the end of the decade, in addition to branches in outlying districts. The Central Japanese Association quickly took an interest in the Language School Association and maintained a close relationship with it. Throughout the 1920's new *Gakuen* were formed under Buddhist, Protestant, nonsectarian, and even Roman Catholic auspices. In 1933 the Japanese consulate reported that fully 4,000 students were attending *Gakuen* in Los Angeles County.[11]

But the *Gakuen* had reached the peak of their influence. Classes, once five days a week after school, had already been reduced in frequency to forestall student restiveness. Without calling for the

[10]Sakae Tsuboi, "The Japanese Language School Teacher," *Journal of Applied Sociology* 11 (1926–27): 163–64; Kohei Shimano, quoted in Tamiko Tanaka, "The Japanese Language School in Relation to Assimilation" (Master's thesis, University of Southern California, 1933), p. 57. The Educational Department of the Central Japanese Association recommended in 1918 that the *gakuen* urge their charges to attend public schools faithfully, and that they make certain that all contradictions in content between their textbooks and those used in the public schools be rectified in favor of the latter. Hoisting the American flag was also part of the curriculum. Central Japanese Association Minutes, June 8, 1918, Feb. 27, 1926.

[11]Tanaka, "Japanese Language School," pp. 26–28; Chotoku Toyama, "The Japanese Community in Los Angeles" (Master's thesis, Columbia University, 1926), p. 22.

outright abolition of the *Gakuen,* Nisei wished to modernize both the administration and the curriculum of their parents' cherished institution. By 1935 the Japanese-language schools had begun to fall victim to the criticism of those for whom they had been designed to create a cultural bridge. A leading Nisei lawyer of Los Angeles declared that, for older Nisei, the *Gakuen* had become as potent a symbol as they were for their parents. "The first generation just drift along. They try to keep their children in Japanese [language] schools, but here in America their children won't mind them so if they quit Japanese school and refuse to go back it's just too bad. There is nothing to be done. They just throw up their hands in despair."[12]

Church, too, struck many of the older generation as an institution that could help them close the generation gap. Community resources of time and money were lavished upon church activities, for common ground between Japanese and American ways might be found in the right conduct they taught. Sunday schools proliferated, involving more than half of all Japanese-American children.[13] But complicated Japanese-language services were nearly meaningless to Nisei; to hold their interest, English-language services had to be offered and church activities had to bear obviously upon the American interests of the young members. "We tell him [the pastor] he should have something to keep the young people interested," a Los Angeles Nisei girl complained in 1925, "and he is always making promises, but he

[12]Quoted in Robert Howard Ross, "Social Distance as It Exists between First and Second-Generation Japanese" (Master's thesis, University of Southern California, 1939), pp. 81–82; H. Fukuoka, "Mutual Life and Aid among the Japanese in Southern California" (Master's thesis, University of Southern California, 1937), pp. 69–70; Tanaka, "Japanese Language School," pp. 73–81; *Rafu Shimpo,* Oct. 6, 20, 1935. Strong's 1930 California survey noted that about seven in ten Nisei had attended *gakuen;* the mean period of total attendance was about five years for both boys and girls. Although two of Strong's interviewers who spoke Japanese judged the Japanese-language performance of the Nisei typically to be good or excellent, 75% of Nisei queried preferred English to Japanese; the figure rose to 82% among Japanese-American high school students and 97% among those in college. Strong, *Vocational Aptitudes,* pp. 116–20.

[13]Buddhist groups initially were somewhat slower to form than Christian. Donald H. Fujiyoshi, "A Study of the Educational Program of the Church School of the Japanese Christian Church and Institute of Los Angeles" (Master's thesis, University of Southern California, 1942), p. 24; Norio Osaki, "A Survey of Interdenominational Cooperation within Each of Three Japanese Religions in Los Angeles, Shinto, Buddhism, and Christianity" (Master's thesis, University of Southern California, 1941), pp. 47, 75; Kyojiro Takahashi, "A Social Study of the Japanese Shinto and Buddhism in Los Angeles" (Master's thesis, University of Southern California, 1937), p. 124; Gretchen Tuthill, "A Study of the Japanese in the City of Los Angeles" (Master's thesis, University of Southern California, 1924), pp. 66–67.

never does anything. . . . If they want the young people to stay there, they should have something to keep us interested."[14]

Usually the churches tried to comply with such demands. The Los Angeles Japanese Methodist Episcopal Church in 1935 reported a total of eleven young people's organizations, including the "Friendly Indians" and the "Tokiwa," each with its own Nisei group leader. But in pleasing the youth, the church organizations offended the parents, who began to feel that some church activities—notably the "church social"—violated their understanding of the purposes of a religious institution and created, rather than reducing, misunderstanding between generations. In reaction, churches sometimes resorted to desperate and hopeless exhortation: "Stand up, young people! Take courage, Japanese-American citizens! You have the key to the future of the Japanese race. Keep awake, our brothers."[15]

At first the parents hoped that Nisei groups could be set up formally separate from their Issei counterparts but functionally interrelated with them, offering an independence along lines that could encourage the growth of deeper intergenerational understanding. The original *kenjin-kai,* supported by localistic attachments to home prefectures, had served the Issei need for mutual assistance and for a bridge to the culture they had left in Japan. To Nisei these motives were quite irrelevant; so, therefore, were the junior *kenjin-kai* proposed by their parents. The purposes of the junior *kenjin-kai* were explained by a member of the senior organization in 1932:

> The junior body will . . . study civics, politics, economics, and other subjects, hold social meetings for the mutual understanding and friendship, and further, through occasional joint meetings with the senior body, learn the ways of the parents and copy whatever good points they have. By the way, the senior body may have many good points to learn from the junior body as well. . . . Mutual understanding . . . is particularly sought by the parents. To remedy this fault is one of the objects of the organization of the junior members of Okayama [prefecture] people.[16]

In 1939 the fourteen junior *kenjin-kai* which had been formed in the previous decade united in a federation—a contradiction in terms from the first-generation standpoint. The federation became just another of the panoply of Nisei organizations in Los Angeles. By the late 1930's

[14]Catharine Holt, "Interview with Miss Chiyoe Sumi," Feb. 21, 1925, Major Document 299, SRR Papers.

[15]*Japanese American Directory of Young People's Organizations,* pp. 12–13; Catharine Holt, "Interview with Teru Miyamoto," SRR Papers; Masao Dodo, "Report on 'Young People's Week,' " Minor Document B-445, SRR Papers.

[16]Dr. P. Suski, quoted in *Rafu Shimpo,* Jan. 31, 1932.

the junior *kenjin-kai* were an embarrassment to most Nisei; to some they even seemed "un-American and detrimental."[17]

The *Gakuen* failed because they were scarcely relevant to the American situation in which Nisei saw themselves; the church organizations fell prey to a tug-of-war between the wishes of the two generations; the junior *kenjin-kai* proved hollow. The first generation attempted to direct their children's wishes for independence, ultimately a forlorn hope. By accommodating themselves to a hostile environment by organization and by tireless labor and undying patience, the Issei had in a sense won their own battle with white America; at least, they had achieved an equilibrium which they deemed satisfactory. But in their struggles to make the Nisei way of life into a variant of their own, especially in view of their continued dominance of the ethnic economy, the seeds of discontent were sown. The discontent provided a major dynamic in the Japanese-American community of Los Angeles until its dispersal by World War II.

As Nisei began to arrive at maturity, the new generation developed a growing preoccupation with their unique problems.[18] Their discontent was attributed to the constraints placed upon them by white Americans and by their parents. Nisei adopted a number of different stands toward the community which their parents had built, and toward the white community which attracted but refused Nisei entrance. "Nisei problems" were public problems, and public discussion was lavished upon them. Most Nisei simply accepted what was. But from more vocal minorities three widely held positions appeared.

The simplest argument subtly or bluntly attacked the first generation or even rejected it outright, in favor of Nisei Americanism. According to proponents of this viewpoint, their parents were in conflict with the Nisei for the same reasons that they had been in conflict with the whites: they were simply not Americans. In 1936 a meeting of forty Nisei leaders discussed the difficulties of intergenerational relationships, concluding that the older generation had "neglected" their children "due to the lust for material gain" and by sending too much money to Japan.[19] Another young Nisei made the point even more clearly, speaking at an interracial meeting of the World Council on Youth in Pasadena: "The first Orientals in Califor-

[17]*Ibid.*, Sept. 9, Oct. 19, 23, 1939; Togo Tanaka, "Journal," July 14, 1941, folders A 17.06 and A 17.07, JERS Collection.

[18]Bill Hosokawa, *Nisei: The Quiet Americans* (New York: William Morrow, 1969), though uncritical, contains some interesting details on the emergence of the Nisei generation. See esp. pp. 152–89.

[19]*Kashu Mainichi,* June 6, 1936.

nia were of the poorest class. They wore dirty clothes and were ignorant, so it is not strange that prejudice against them and circumstances, I think the 1924 Exclusive Act was a fine law. Before the law, the Japanese had not been good citizens and were here only to make enough money to take home, but now there is a group which is truly loyal to this country.''[20] Such offhand, shallow, and inaccurate treatment was neither isolated nor meaningless. It represented many Nisei's deeply felt wish that their parents would be (or had been) less Japanese and more respectably white American. The element of fantasy within the Nisei community was in this respect the mirror image of their parents'. Each generation berated the other for not fitting into ''America,'' but while Issei leaders accepted the caste line as a not unbearable part of reality, to prominent Nisei caste and democracy were incompatible.

A second common Nisei attitude, cutting somewhat less cruelly, denied the relevance of alien parents to the ''American'' problems faced by the Nisei. According to this view, the aging generation was a problem to be coped with gently and responsibly. Solicitude, condescension, and emotional convenience combined in this outlook. ''True, the Issei live in a world of their own. True, they speak another language of their own. True, they have their peculiar way of looking at things. But it is also true that they are human.'' The author of the above sentiments, which appeared in a feature article in *Rafu Shimpo,* wrote in the conviction that ''it is about time the nisei begin to understand the issei.'' Such understanding, according to a *Rafu Shimpo* editorial, could result from ''Issei-Nisei good will banquets and programs'' and '''Issei nights' sponsored by the J.A.U. [Nisei] Basketball League.''[21]

Only the most thoughtful and courageous Nisei accorded value, without condescension, to the accommodation their parents had made and the community they had created. Kazuo Kawai, though legally an Issei rather than a member of the Nisei generation for whom he was an early cultural spokesman,[22] was able to achieve this outlook only after grief and confusion. Because Kawai has recorded the evolution

[20]Jimmie Nakamura, quoted in Los Angeles *Times,* Aug. 23, 1932. It is interesting to note that the *Times* gave this example of Nisei group self-rejection a featured position in the article. An earlier speech by Nakamura, declaring that race was of no concern in an internationalist world, is one of many early Nisei efforts (mainly valedictories) printed in Paul T. Hirohata, ed., *Orations and Essays by the Japanese Second Generation of America,* 2nd ed. (Los Angeles: Los Angeles Japanese Daily News, 1935).

[21]Tsuyoshi Matsumoto, ''Issei Are Human,'' *Rafu Shimpo,* Dec. 18, 1938; editorial, *ibid.,* Feb. 26, 1939.

[22]Kawai, though born in Japan in 1904, clearly thought of himself as a spokesman for the American-born Japanese. By virtue of his youthful arrival in America, he

of his position, and because this evolution points up some of the difficulties of being socialized to American values while living within the bounds imposed by the Issei accommodation, his views serve our purposes especially well.

Kawai did not become aware of the caste line until high school. When white high school classmates "simply ignored" him, "I turned for the first time to Japanese friends. . . . By common isolation, we became close friends." Kawai was a new breed: "I [had] thought I was an American, but America made a foreigner out of me—not a Japanese, but a foreigner." Kawai explicitly rejected the first-generation solution of passive accommodation to American standards as a "cheaply optimistic, goody-goody idea that if they stay in their place, work hard and please the Americans and remain happy in the position where God has placed them, surely the Christian Americans, out of the generosity of their hearts, will throw out to them a few more crumbs."

Instead, Kawai insisted that the Nisei position was one of opportunity:

> Neither Oriental nor Occidental, yet both Oriental and Occidental, embodying within me the clash and the adjustment and the synthesis of the East and the West, a microcosm reflecting the world problem of race and culture. I am both East and West made into one whole. I had at last found my field. The peculiar work for which I had been ordained was to be just myself: my very self is an interpretation of the East and West.

Because he recognized his marginality, Kawai could function more smoothly in each of the two worlds which were tangential to his own: "My decision to be an interpreter [of cultures] has improved my relations with both races. I am happy because I don't try to be a poor imitation of a genuine Japanese. I am simply what I am. I don't try to imitate either, so I am never disappointed when I feel myself excluded by either side."

The risk of being forced to be "a generation of fruitstand keepers" by white discrimination and by unquestioning allegiance to the established Japanese-American way could be avoided only by embracing

belonged to the Nisei in all but legal status. In an interview by the Survey of Race Relations and a life history which Kawai prepared for the Survey (neither intended for publication), Kawai's alien status was brought out. But in an article which Kawai wrote for publication in *Survey Graphic* (an issue prepared by the Survey on Race Relations), his Japanese birth is suppressed and the article is subtitled "An American-Born Japanese Looks at Life." Quotations from Kawai will be from these sources. William C. Smith, "Interview with Kazuo Kawai," Aug. 7, 1924, and untitled life history appended, Major Document 8, SRR Papers; Kawai, "Three Roads and None Easy," *Survey Graphic* 19 (1926): 164–66.

marginality, and remembering "to keep ever before us the vision of what we might accomplish. . . . Then we shall be so dissatisfied with existing conditions that we shall be working continuously to change them."[23] Kawai argued that it was "a privilege to be a Japanese in America, because we have to do so much more than the average person to win recognition"— one variation on a theme heard often in the prewar Nisei world.[24]

As Nisei struggled for self-definition, they joined with their parents in a profoundly ambivalent and highly symbolic struggle to redefine the Japanese-American community in a more "American" style. Its proponents believed that a new style would propitiate outside hostility, as well as allowing ethnic community practice to reflect demographic shifts. In this light, the meaning of the inward-facing Nisei and Issei "causes" of the 1930's may be understood.

One such cause was the regeneration of Little Tokyo. The area served as the concrete metaphor—understood alike by whites, Issei, and Nisei—for the accommodation the Japanese had made to the American environment. As early as 1931 the Los Angeles Japanese Association expressed concern that their downtown was becoming commercially vestigial. This was to some extent due to the middle-class shopping habits of the Nisei, who preferred the greater variety and lower prices of white department stores to the Japanese atmosphere of Little Tokyo. A "Committee on the Development of the First Street Nihonmachi [Japantown]" reported that the imminent decline of the area could be halted by better management of commodities, better service, and the development and adoption of an approach to merchandising that would attract Caucasian customers by being distinctly Japanese yet not frighteningly foreign.[25]

Nisei support was even more crucial. An essay contest was planned to elicit Nisei opinion; the approach offered first-generation leaders a

---

[23]Kawai attended Stanford University, receiving an A.B. in 1926 and a Ph.D. in history in 1938. His goal in history was to interpret East-West relationships to Westerners. After teaching at UCLA from 1932 to 1941, he went to Japan as an editor of the *Nippon Times*. Caught there by the war, Kawai remained until 1949, when he returned to American academic life.

[24]For example, one heard it frequently with an economic emphasis. "I know I am a 'Jap' and the whites look down on us. I don't beg them to treat me as a man to man. I wish to show them that I can do something. If I can make money, they will come to me." Chiko Sayeki, "A Life History of an American-Born Japanese," n.d., Major Document 353, SRR Papers; William C. Smith, "Interview with Seiichi Nobe," Aug. 11, 1924, Major Document 78, *ibid.* I have made a fuller analysis of prewar Nisei "ethnic ambivalence" in my introduction to Charles Kikuchi, *The Kikuchi Diary: Chronicle from an American Concentration Camp* (Urbana: University of Illinois Press, 1973).

[25]Los Angeles Japanese Association, Committee Reports, June 25, 1931.

sense of communication with the Nisei and the comforting right to choose the winner. The complexities and near-contradictions of the essay selected as the best reveal the emotions enveloping the seemingly mundane economic issue of the shopping area. The author, with more passion than control, advised that Nisei delay further acculturation until the final parting of the older generation, that Little Tokyo business strive for the white trade by "constant advertising and a good publicity agent," and that the Nisei trade be recaptured by adopting American sales methods. "They say business is bad. Yet what do they do about it? Sales, yes, but what sales! Clothes that have been stuck in the stock room for the past two years are dragged out to the counter with prices that might have been attractive then."[26]

"Nisei Week" was another typical campaign of intragroup public relations, designed to reacquaint Nisei with Little Tokyo. The first serious proposal for a Nisei Week came in 1934, the by-product of a struggle for Nisei support between the Los Angeles Japanese Chamber of Commerce and the (Japanese) Southern California Chamber of Commerce and Industry.[27] The Nisei at first were justifiably suspicious, but they were assured by *Rafu Shimpo*'s promise of "thirty-four second generation mercantile clerks . . . there to greet the nisei customers," and of the "remarkable change in the make-up of the display in the windows of the Lil Tokio stores."[28] The stage was set for Eddie Holden's "Frank Watanabe." Little Tokyo continued to decline, but Nisei Week has survived to today. With growing Nisei domination of the event, the participation and admiration of the white population were increasingly solicited, and the intergenerational and economic aspects were pushed into the background.

The second generation, however, was too imbued with their parents' values not to declare independence by emulation. No more symbolic example can be found than the vehicle chosen to prove their maturity: the rehabilitation of the Japanese Children's Home. Established in 1914, in its early years the Home had been one of the most formidable of the Japanese mutual-assistance projects, its governing board including at one point whites along with immigrant Japanese. By 1934, however, the Home had fallen into disrepair, apparently

[26]Taishi Matsumoto, "A Preface to Greater Lil' Tokio," *Rafu Shimpo*, Aug. 12, 1935. Another essay contest three years later similarly failed to halt the decline of Little Tokyo. *Kashu Mainichi*, July 17, 1938.

[27]The competition between the two Japanese Chambers was so heated that the Japanese consul had to decide which organization was to open relationships with the Nisei; he ruled in favor of the Chamber of Commerce. *Rafu Shimpo*, June 26, July 2, 3, 1934.

[28]Editorial, *ibid.*, Aug. 12, 1934.

through the lack of interest and energy of the first generation. With a deliberate flourish of extraordinary enthusiasm, Nisei collected about $4,000 to rehabilitate the home, including a 5,000 yen contribution from the Emperor of Japan:

> Undaunted by rebuffs and reversals, the second generation have answered the challenge of youth with a temerity and zeal that can only end in ultimate success. The eyes of the world are focused today upon the Japanese Americans [that is, the Nisei] as they take the spotlight in a humanitarian cause that has hardly been equalled in the past. . . . The benefits of the movement may not be counted in the medium of dollars but in the realization of duty that has been instilled in youthful minds. Many a young boy or girl will realize some of the responsibilities of coming citizenship. Many a youth will understand for the first time that "it is more blessed to give than to receive." In short, the movement may herald the coming of a new era—in which the niseis have come of age.

The Emperor's donation points directly at the awkwardness of the Nisei position: asserting the competence of the American generation as against the failing hand of their Japanese parents, they gracefully accepted a contribution from the invested symbol of their parents' foreignness.[29]

But the leadership that planned such projects was not a mere carbon copy of that of their parents' generation, even when they shared Japanese pride in group self-sufficiency. The Issei leadership had placed a great stress on economic success; in pursuit of that goal, Issei had been reluctantly willing to suffer quietly the small, daily indignities of being segregated. Such was not the position of the Nisei leadership. Although they controlled few economic resources, they possessed generally superior education, and their desires were far more "middle class" than those of their parents. The identity, goals, and methods of the leadership in the prewar years were seen most clearly in the Japanese American Citizens League.

Los Angeles was slow to form its branch of the Citizens League. Not until 1928—seven years after Seattle—was a chapter formed there, and it folded shortly afterward. Nevertheless, the idea had taken root in the Nisei community and, with some help from the Japanese Association, a new and permanent version of the Citizens League was instituted in the following year. By virtue of the generality of its interest, and by its preeminent claim to Nisei loyalty in the political realm, the Citizens League was a central institution in the

[29]City of Los Angeles, Social Service Commission, *Annual Reports*, 1917–24; *Rafu Shimpo*, Feb. 4, 22, Apr. 28, 1934.

growing Nisei subcommunity. Yet from the start it was plagued by apathy, poor finances, and factionalism. As late as 1932 the Los Angeles branch was so poor that it could not afford to send delegates to the national JACL convention without soliciting the financial assistance of their parents. Four years later, despite the fact that Los Angeles was much the largest Japanese community in the continental United States, the national JACL turned down a suggestion that the national office be moved there. The Los Angeles chapter, which had enrolled no more than 400 members, had experienced "too many coup d'etat [*sic*] and other shenanigans"[30] for the national organization's taste.

The stakes were probably larger than most Los Angeles Nisei recognized, for the Citizens League did offer the opportunity for developing a genuine and concerted Nisei voice with which to address both the whites and the Issei. Yet most Nisei rejected this possibility, leaving the organization prone to expressing minority interests. One reason why the organization was not embraced by all Nisei was that from the first its leadership represented only the most "respectable" segment of the community: the League was initiated by a lawyer in 1928, resuscitated by another lawyer in 1929, and generally run by college graduates. Before the war it seemed that the Los Angeles JACL legislated for the Nisei largely without their active consent or involvement.

The Citizens League scored a tactical success in gaining approval of the Jefferson Park plat, and the league was to be spokesman for the Japanese-American community during World War II. Even though their political apprenticeship was a trying, often humilitating, one, the fledgling efforts of the JACL to define a position for their generation beyond their parents' quiet accommodation deserve recognition. But likewise their failure in the prewar period bespeaks the costs of powerlessness.

Some of the 800 city Nisei of voting age must have winced at the contradiction between early Citizens League policy and performance. The "one thing the citizens of Japanese ancestry can do," the League had announced, was to reward friends and punish enemies. But real friends were hard to find in Southern California politics, and even such formerly outspoken anti-Japanese as Sheriff William Traeger and Buron Fitts were given favorable publicity by the League in 1930 in the vain hope of a taste of patronage. Three years later Mayor John C. Porter gained endorsement by the Citizens League for

<hr>

[30]*Rafu Shimpo,* Oct. 15, 29, 1928, Apr. 29, May 13, 1929, Mar. 20, 1932, Dec. 3, 1933, Feb. 6, 1936, Aug. 16, 1936.

"his interest in and friendship toward us and our people." Yet Porter had merely flattered a Citizens League meeting by delivering a routine "business administration" speech.[31] The Citizens League recognized the rhetoric of politics, but powerlessness bred fantasy.

Only as more Nisei came of age and their leaders matured did political action in Los Angeles make any meaningful impression upon either the white or the Japanese community. The breakthrough occurred in 1938, when one Assembly candidate became convinced that the Nisei might constitute a swing vote in his district. Clare Woolwine, the candidate, responded with a verbal generosity to which the Los Angeles Nisei were unaccustomed. "With the voting strength you now have," he told them, jobs should be made available. Once elected, Woolwine would "let everyone—from the Governor down—know that you are here."[32] The absence of references to Japanese in Woolwine's personal papers suggests that he made no special project of the Japanese, but merely courted their vote in the course of his campaign. Nevertheless, many of the most influential members of the Nisei community—lawyers, doctors, businessmen—soon gathered to form the Nisei Voters' League, or, more precisely, the Japanese-American branch of the Republican party in Los Angeles.[33]

The Voters' League spurred the Young Democratic Clubs of California to form a counterpart group among the Nisei. Before the 1938 campaign was over, the Los Angeles Japanese Young Democrats were organized, and had support enough to stage a Little Tokyo rally. For the first time Los Angeles Japanese Americans were participating in the Rooseveltian world of minority-group politics; they were elated to score a triumph when they helped force through a clause in the State Youth Commission bill which granted at least one of seven seats to a minority-group member.[34]

[31]*Ibid.,* July 21, Aug. 25, 1930, May 25, 1933.

[32]*Kashu Mainichi,* July 12, Aug. 23, 1939; *Rafu Shimpo,* Aug. 16, 1938. Shortly before election day a Nisei political commentator maintained that increased political interest was encouraging, and that the growing belief that politics contained a pay-off for the group was a healthy one. Nevertheless, he warned against blatant bloc voting, which "may result in giving opportunistic politicians a temptation to use the Nisei as an issue or a target of attack." Indeed, the California Joint Immigration Committee remarked on the Woolwine campaign with considerable displeasure. Les Kurihara, "Political Sizeup," in *Kashu Mainichi,* Nov. 6, 1938; California Joint Immigration Committee, Progress Report, Nov. 9, 1938, typed copy in folder "CJIC-1938," Box 2, JERS Collection.

[33]*Rafu Shimpo,* Sept. 1, Oct. 24, 1938.

[34]*Kashu Mainichi,* Oct. 28, Nov. 1, 2, Dec. 12, 1938; *Rafu Shimpo,* Dec. 11, 1938.

Nisei leaders, beginning to find a forum, were also beginning to counter adversaries. At the state Young Democrat meeting, they called various anti-Japanese measures into question and challenged Assemblyman Samuel Yorty to justify his anti-alien fishing bill.[35] In the succeeding year the Young Democrats forced John Dockweiler, candidate for district attorney (against Buron Fitts), to recant outright his earlier anti-Japanese statements. "There will be no arousing of public hysteria, so that under a smoke-screen of anti Fifth Column drives, those [Nisei] civil rights will be abrogated," Dockweiler now promised. By this time, too, Nisei had found a friend and advisor in John Anson Ford, a white Los Angeles reform politician. But the Nisei vote was too insignificant to win much in the way of jobs or favors, or anything like a reversal of the trend toward increased hostility toward local Japanese, as Japan's international aggressions increased.[36]

The Citizens League, however, had other rows to hoe than the political. It led the way in countering white hysteria as Pearl Harbor approached. But group loyalty was in the last analysis impossible to prove, as the events of 1942 were to show. Yet another local public-relations effort bore an even more intimate relationship to the Nisei leaders' self-image and community image. It reveals the pathos of the Nisei position, and the inability of the leaders to conceive of any appropriate group solution to the dilemma in which their parents' accommodation and their own tastes placed them.

It was with considerable pride that the Nisei Business Bureau, another face of the local American-born elite, announced in early 1940 "the first nisei demonstration even held in the United States" of the Dale Carnegie method of personal relations.[37] The Business Bureau announcement informed their public that they "feel every adult nisei has something to gain from a greater knowledge of how to apply his knowledge and educational training in this important sphere of human relations." The public-relations push was one more fantasy, a hope that the "method" could overcome the disability of their racial heritage. Nisei could use Carnegie to expunge the stigma of association with foreignness—at least as far as their faces and Japanese and American definitions of military necessity would permit. Both as an aid to group equality with whites and as a road to individual success across the caste line, Carnegie's approach seemed

---

[35]*Rafu Shimpo*, Dec. 13, 1938, Feb. 21, 26, 1939.
[36]*Ibid.*, Nov. 3, 1940; Kay Sugihara to Togo Tanaka, Feb. 9, 1939, copy in folder "Racial Problems," John Anson Ford Papers, Huntington Library, San Marino, Calif. (All subsequent citations to this collection are to this folder.)
[37]*Rafu Shimpo*, Feb. 25, 1940.

crucial to the Nisei Business Bureau. "The Japanese community has so much to gain from just such a thing as this. We are establishing valuable contacts with the larger American community by becoming part of a truly national business group trained in effective leadership."[38]

The vocal leadership of the Nisei group envisioned the embourgeoisement of the generation. For them the struggle for gentility was coequal with the struggle for racial equality with Caucasians, the latter in part deriving its importance as a component of the former. Militancy and gentility were incompatible; accordingly, the Bureau was anything but militant. When a local Negro filed a suit to open the facilities of a local riding academy to members of his race, the Nisei Business Bureau found "significance in the fact that while a Negro suit charging discrimination was on file in the courts, the owner of Silver Glen Stables, adjoining Griffith Park where the defendants stable was located made a personal call on the Bureau to find out how he could get the nisei to ride from his academy." The Bureau concluded that such discriminations "call for positive effort by prospective Nisei targets of discrimination, to make themselves welcome should they desire to rent from private riding academies."[39]

Those who had a different vision or order of proprieties were in a lonely position, and in fact were for the most part shut out of the vernacular press. Even though *Doho,* the leftist sheet, argued against the fundamental importance of small business for the Nisei, it shared the Bureau's parochial view of the group economy.[40] The first generation had stressed group prosperity; their children stressed a variant, gentility. Though the leaders of each generation meant different things by success, they agreed that the Japanese in Los Angeles had a chance of attaining it. Such a chance was not to be risked, no matter how the immediate outlook might rankle, or how much the realities of the local situation might impinge upon the dream.

[38]*Ibid.,* Feb. 28, 1940. The course was successful enough to warrant a second one. *Ibid.,* Sept. 22, 1940.
[39]*Ibid.,* Apr. 1, 1940.
[40]*Doho,* June 15, 1939.

8

Toward Relocation

The temporary remission of labor union enmity in the 1930's exemplified the racial peace that prevailed once the caste line had been peacefully established between Anglos and the Issei-led ethnic community. Adaptive mechanisms denying harsher aspects of the situation proliferated. Japanese-American veterans of the World War were encouraged to form the all-Japanese Admiral Perry Post, Number 525, American Legion, and the Japanese-American drum and bugle corps which they sponsored "created a sensation with their exhibition" in 1935. Little Tokyo became a minor tourist haven: Claudette Colbert was one distinguished visitor who came "to satisfy her hunger for that international renown [*sic*] dish sukiyaki." Nisei Week flourished, and even the Central Labor Council's *Los Angeles Citizen* plugged "the exotic spring festival dream fantasy" put on at Nisei Week in 1937.[1]

But tranquillity was not to prevail, for the racial accommodation achieved by the Issei and accepted with reservations by the Nisei preserved a strong popular association of Japanese Americans with the government of Japan. An old anti-Japanese bugaboo, the Japanese-American fisherman, was again recalled, and legislative harassment was threatened. Earlier, the Japanese fisherman had posed an economic threat; now he seemed the agent of a skillful and aggressive military foe. As military considerations gained importance and citizen support grew, Southern California took over sponsorship and the agitation acquired a more promising aspect.

Initially, the attack upon the Japanese fishing fleet was just one incident of a Depression-born nativism which affected aliens from all nations. In Los Angeles, old groups like the Native Sons, and new ones like Leo V. Youngworth's "Anti-Alien League of Americans," challenged non-citizens. In a few years Youngworth would turn his

[1]*California Legionnaire*, June 15, Dec. 15, 1935; *Rafu Shimpo*, Jan. 17, Feb. 8, 1935; *Los Angeles Citizen*, Apr. 23, 1937.

energies toward permanent elimination of the menace of disloyal Japanese residents.[2]

The first important ammunition with which to harass the Japanese fisherman was developed in 1934 by Lail Kane, whose self-chosen mission was to abate the fishing menace. When the House Special Committee on Un-American Activities was conducting brief hearings in Los Angeles on Brown Shirt and Silver Shirt activities, Kane assured committee members that "no structural changes" would be necessary to convert the Japanese fishing boats to make them "suitable for the use of laying mines . . . [or for] torpedo vessels." The boats, Kane said, were known to fly the Japanese flag when at sea, raising the American flag only when they neared harbor.[3] In 1935 his draft of an anti-alien fishing bill was endorsed by the California Department of the American Legion.

The bill never left committee, but it was the opening salvo in a seven-year public relations effort which concluded by defining the resident Japanese, including the Nisei, as the enemy. Spies (sometimes real, sometimes dubious, sometimes nonexistent) were forever being hunted. Kane was constantly gaining more "evidence" of the fishing menace. New figures with some political influence, like Assemblyman Sam Yorty of Los Angeles, were learning for the first time that Japanese fishermen had been "decorated for destroying the Russian Naval Fleet. They have worked the same old trick they are working now and we have been . . . sound asleep." Yorty pushed this theme enthusiastically; after an abortive fishing strike in 1938 which was betrayed by Japanese fishermen who deserted the CIO to join the non-striking AFL, he introduced a bill to deny fishing licenses to aliens ineligible to citizenship. The Central Labor Council of the AFL in Los Angeles opposed the bill on the grounds that it infringed "upon people's right in the profound sense of humanity,"

[2]Los Angeles *Times,* May 5, 1938, July 3, 1939; Clarence Hunt, "Grizzly Growls," *Grizzly Bear,* Sept., 1938, p. 10.

[3]Kane's testimony was given in executive session and, along with other testimony considered confidential, was sealed. No mention of Kane's appearance can be found in newspaper accounts. However, bits of the sealed testimony were subsequently revealed by the man who chaired the subcommittee when it sat in Los Angeles; Representative Charles Kramer (from Los Angeles) later became obsessed with the fishing menace himself. U.S. House of Representatives, Committee on Merchant Marine and Fisheries, *Americanization of Fisheries, Hearings,* 76th Cong., 1st sess. (1939), pp. 3–9; Clarence Hunt, "Grizzly Growls," *Grizzly Bear,* May, 1936, p. 23; *Rafu Shimpo,* Feb. 16, 1935; Togo Tanaka, "Pre-Evacuation Pressure Group Activity in Southern California," p. 11, manuscript dated May 30, 1943, in folder 16.20, JERS Collection; *Congressional Record,* 76th Cong., 1st sess. (1939), pp. 4411–12, and 78th Cong., 1st sess. (1943), p. 6269 (H. Resolution 254).

and accused the CIO of egging Yorty on.[4] Although he never made good on his promise to disclose details of such espionage in Los Angeles, Yorty brought naval intelligence officers to Sacramento to testify in executive session, and to announce navy support for his bill. A series of sensational articles in the short-lived weekly magazine *Ken* began to bring the Japanese fishing menace to national attention.[5]

By 1940 "numerous and extended conferences with Government naval and merchant marine authorities" led to House approval of a bill designed to drive the alien Japanese off the seas "for purposes of national defense." The legislation limited ownership of even very small boats to American citizens and to corporations in which no stockholder was an alien; crews even on small fishing vessels had to consist almost entirely of American citizens. The bill died in Senate committee, but within months the California legislature passed a "Spy Curb" law requiring detailed registration of all commercial fishermen, with special notice of intentions to take out citizenship. Even optimistic Los Angeles Issei saw how those in the fishing trade were being harassed, and what little bargaining strength they had.[6]

From the mid-1930's until Pearl Harbor, Japanese anxieties expanded in response to growing white American suspicions. The public relations efforts of the first generation to prove loyalty and harmlessness were badly botched: their instinct was to defend their fatherland, a tendency which confirmed the prejudices of white Americans. Maintaining that "one of our duties . . . is to make the people clearly understand the present situation of the Far East," the

[4]At this time Yorty was only a few months away from his ideological trek from the left to the right wing of the Democratic party; therein he discovered "the laxity of our laws designed to curb treason and foreign espionage." "State Relief Investigation Progress Report," in California, *Journal of the Assembly,* 53rd (extraordinary) sess. (1940), pp. 814–64; Sacramento *Bee,* Apr. 4, 1939; *Los Angeles Citizen,* Mar. 17, 1939 (Central Labor Council minutes of Mar. 10, 1939).

[5]Ed Ainsworth, *Maverick Mayor: A Biography of Sam Yorty of Los Angeles* (Garden City, N.Y.: Doubleday, 1966), pp. 88–90; Sacramento *Bee,* Apr. 1, 28, 1939; Los Angeles *Times,* Apr. 22, 1939; *Kashu Mainichi,* Jan. 6, Feb. 17, 1939; *Congressional Record,* 76th Cong., 1st sess. (1939), pp. 4411–12. The *Ken* series was published in four installments in mid-1939, without attribution of authorship or explanation of how the material was gathered. See esp. "The Strange Actions of Furtive Japs in the U.S.," and "The Secret Menace to the Safety of the U.S. Fleet," *Ken* 5 (July 20, July 27, 1939), each pp. 9–11.

[6]U.S. House of Representatives, *Citizen Ownership of Vessels,* 76th Cong., 3rd sess. (1940), H. Rept. 2917; U.S. House of Representatives, *Citizenship Requirements for Manning of Vessels,* 76th Cong., 3rd sess. (1940), H. Rept. 2918; *Congressional Record,* 76th Cong., 3rd sess. (1940), p. 12856; *Rafu Shimpo,* Oct. 2, 1940.

Japanese Chamber of Commerce of Los Angeles detailed "China's oppressive policy toward the Japanese" in a 1931 English-language pamphlet. Probably reflecting consular advice, the Chamber emphasized that the purpose of Japanese military action in Manchuria was "purely to protect the life and property of our countrymen . . . for we possess no political ambition."[7] The Japanese residents of Los Angeles, in the quasi-official view of the Central Japanese Association, quite expected that they would be treated by white Americans as though they were representatives of Japan. The Association urged its adherents to expect white hostility, which they should accept "without being perturbed" while practicing ever more thrift and diligence "with the spirit of mutual assistance."

As late as 1937 another Chamber propaganda pamphlet on the Asian war, though written by a white American public relations man and including touches like an acknowledgment of the "debt of deep gratitude" felt by alien Japanese "for the privilege we are enjoying living in this great republic," was again blatant Japanese propaganda. Togo Tanaka recalled that white editors "laughed it out of print." But even so, in 1938 the Central Japanese Association held that "our duty as Japanese living overseas" was to collect money to aid the Japanese war effort, with donors' names being forwarded to the homeland to be honored.[8]

The Nisei had not yet dissociated themselves from their parents' understandable pro-Japanism, but when they finally did so, they made an all-out effort. As late as 1937 Tanaka was exhorting the Nisei readers of *Rafu Shimpo* to look beyond "Chinese propaganda" and urging each Nisei to think of "himself as an instrument for preserving the peace and neutrality of this country." But in mid-1939 Nisei newspapermen began to contradict rather than support Japanese policy. As Tanaka reflected, "This was a conscious effort. It was an insistent message that soon drowned out every other theme in the editorial mill."[9]

The Nisei press was filled with pathos as America and Japan moved toward war. "This is only a little story made up for friendly

[7]Los Angeles Japanese Chamber of Commerce, *The Present Situation in Manchuria and Shanghai* (Los Angeles: By the Chamber, [1931]), pp. 4, 8.

[8]Los Angeles Japanese Chamber of Commerce, *Japan's Position in the Shanghai and North China Hostilities* (Los Angeles: By the Chamber, 1937), p. b and *passim;* Togo Tanaka, "Journal," Dec. 2, 1941, folders A 17.06 and A 17.07, JERS Collection; Central Japanese Association, Resolution, in Minutes, Feb. 21, 1933; also Minutes, July 23, Oct. 1, 1938.

[9]*Rafu Shimpo,* Mar. 25, Sept. 5, 1937; Togo Tanaka, "The Vernacular Newspapers," folder A1.11, JERS Collection, pp. 38–46.

relationship on Hina Matsuri [Girl's Day, a Japanese holiday]. Please read it over and see if it will be good enough to print in Sunday's *Rafu Shimpo*. If it is, I would appreciate it, so it will improve people's foreign relationships. I am only 13 years old, but I want to see America and Japan as No. 1 friends," wrote a Nisei in 1937.[10]

The desperation of the Nisei is apparent in their efforts to throw off the "dual citizen" epithet.[11] This issue was faced simultaneously with the SCRPWU, Jefferson Park, and Dale Carnegie episodes— and with the heartfelt entreaties like the one just quoted. "Dual citizenship" for their children was never the intention of Issei parents when, following tradition, they enrolled their children in the home village registers. Such registration certainly had no practical relationship to loyalty. The attacks of Phelan and others on dual citizenship had earlier led Japan to make provision for renunciation of it; however, most parents and children had never considered such a highly abstract action worth the effort. In the late 1930's nervous and hostile whites began to ask why most Nisei had retained Japanese citizenship.

By then Nisei leaders felt pressed to eradicate the source of this embarrassment. The Citizens League and the Young Democrats stood in the vanguard, aided by the alarmed first-generation leadership. Emblem of the campaign was a cartoon first published in the Los Angeles *Examiner,* showing a black knight with a shield labeled "Divided Allegiance" with bar sinister (lettered "Hyphen American"). *Rafu Shimpo* headed the cartoon "*Time to Take Heed!*" and repeated it on several occasions. "American public sentiment today," the newspaper exhorted, has "no place for hyphenated Americans." "Gay-clad kimonos, samurais and other atmospheric symbols of Nippon" would be banished from their 1940 Rose Bowl float, they decided. "Americanism"—"Nisei beauties in American formal gowns"—would instead be shown.[12] The Equality Committee lectured draft-age Nisei who were fearful of being treated as expendable cannon-fodder: "True patriotism is never qualified by doubt or fear of unequal treatment regardless of circumstances. Nisei loyalty to their native land must be based upon a willingness to and a desire to

[10]*Rafu Shimpo,* Mar. 21, 1937.

[11]An excellent history of the dual-citizenship question as it has affected Japanese Americans is in U.S., Department of the Interior, War Relocation Authority, *Wartime Exile* (Washington: U.S. Government Printing Office, [1946]), pp. 30–43; James Fisk, typescript memorandum to California Joint Immigration Committee, Aug. 11, 1939, in folder "Misc. CJIC Materials," Box G2, JERS Collection; *Rafu Shimpo,* June 8, 22, 25, Dec. 22, 1939; *Doho,* June 15, 1939.

[12]*Rafu Shimpo,* Dec. 19, 1940.

make the supreme sacrifice without reservation.''[13] Others professed even more perfect loyalty. A Los Angeles Nisei girl wrote in *Rafu Shimpo:* ''Since our faces so loudly seem to proclaim 'I am a Japanese—' even if we aren't, why shouldn't our clothes at least pronounce our Americanism? We should very much like to see some clever nisei girl design a dress with this motif worked out on the dress in embroidery or some decorative type of stitching . . . The nisei should start it first before anybody else does.''[14]

By 1941 the Equality Committee proposed not only to promise, but to assure and prove loyalty. A meeting was arranged (at whose initiative is unclear) between the Committee and Kenneth Ringle, a lieutenant commander in the navy, and other members of naval intelligence. Los Angeles Sheriff Biscailuz was invited, and Ringle urged that the Nisei provide as much publicity as possible. After the meeting the ''Bay District Plan'' was issued. The plan greatly and intentionally exaggerated the capacity of its authors for performance. According to its terms, the Southern District Council of the Citizens League pledged to report disloyal acts (presumably by members of their parents' generation), to counsel against innocent but suspicious ones, and to translate and investigate any cases that might be turned over to them by the authorities. In return, the Nisei hoped that Japanese aliens would be spared the kind of harassment which Martin Dies's Special House Committee on Un-American Activities was preparing.[15]

In the summer of 1941 the Dies Committee publicly announced its certainty that ''thousands of Japanese on the west coast'' were available for subversion at the Emperor's command, that the Japanese fishing fleet was prepared ''to dynamite and bomb,'' that it already

[13]*Ibid.,* Sept. 25, Dec. 1, 1940.

[14]Mary Oyama, in *Rafu Shimpo,* Aug. 21, 1941. See also *ibid.,* Dec. 1, 1940. Nowhere was this outlook stated more eloquently than in the ''Nisei Creed.'' Written by Mike Masaoka, national secretary and field executive of the Japanese American Citizens League, the Creed was published first in January, 1941. It states, in part: ''Although some individuals may discriminate against me I shall never become bitter or lose faith, for I know that such persons are not representative of the majority of the American people. True, I shall do all in my power to discourage such practices, but I shall do it in the American way: above-board, in the open, through courts of law, by education, by proving myself worthy of equal treatment and consideration.'' *Ibid.,* Jan. 26, 1942; *Congressional Record,* 77th Cong., 1st sess. (1941), Appendix, p. A2205.

[15]*Rafu Shimpo,* Mar. 16, 22, 23, 1941; Memo, Francis X. Riley to John W. Abbott (about meeting with Ringle), copy in folder A 12.051, JERS Collection; conversation with Joe Grant Masaoka, nominal author of the Bay District Plan, July 22, 1968; ''An Intelligence Officer [Kenneth Ringle],'' ''The Japanese in America,'' *Harper's* 185 (1942): 489–97.

had "sensational evidence" about subversive activities by Japanese consulates on the west coast, and that it was about to call at least twenty witnesses who would reveal even more. Dies's repeated enticing news releases, together with the utter lack of substantial information (or even clever staff work), were revealed in his "Yellow Book" as finally released after Pearl Harbor; they make clear his manipulative intentions. Available evidence suggests that he made only a slight impression upon public opinion, but his attacks did bring the Nisei to even greater professions of loyalty.[16]

In early 1941 John Lechner, a professional patrioteer with a local reputation as a tireless orator and close ties with the California Department of the American Legion, approached the Los Angeles Nisei leadership with a plan for a "bang-up public relations job" whereby they could "convince the public that you fellows are just as good Americans as I am." Central to Lechner's plan was a "huge patriotic mass meeting of the Japanese Americans in this community," to be co-sponsored by the Citizens League and by Lechner's Americanism Educational League. The Nisei with whom Lechner dealt at first suspected mercenary motives behind Lechner's eagerness, but they submitted to the logic of his contention that the rally would be the "dramatic means by which the message of nisei loyalty to America would be used in effectively spreading better understanding of the group."[17] In a sense, the Nisei were Lechner's ideal clients: defensive, unmoved by radicalism, economically self-reliant, politically uncommitted, and clamoring for a more complete expression of citizenship. Lechner hoped to become an apostle to the Nisei, leading them by hortatory techniques which he had perfected at countless meetings, helping them to discover a way of expressing the loyalty their faces seemed to deny.

Under Lechner's guidance, the Nisei mass meeting was held in May, 1941, at the Hollywood Legion Stadium. Among the many who endorsed this extravaganza were the American Legion, the "I Am an American" Foundation, and the California Women of the Golden West. The rally was endorsed by Dr. George Gleason, then of the

[16]Los Angeles *Evening Herald and Express,* July 22, 1941; Los Angeles *Times,* Aug. 1, Sept. 3, 14, 1941; *Rafu Shimpo,* June 10, 1941; HUAC, *Investigation,* Appendix, pt. 6, pp. 1723–31. That appendix, published after Pearl Harbor, is Dies's "Yellow Book," for those interested in the vagaries of the American governmental process.

[17]*Rafu Shimpo,* Apr. 15, 19, 29, 1939; Tanaka, "Journal," Mar. 27, 1941; Fred Tayama to Mike Masaoka, May 15, 1943, folder A 16.213, JERS Collection; Edward Edell, *An American with Guts* (Los Angeles: Cole-Holmquist Press, 1961), p. 32. This last is an almost incredibly adulatory biography of Lechner.

Committee for Church and Community Cooperation, and Dr. R. E. Farnham, executive secretary of the Church Federation of Los Angeles. John Anson Ford expressed his pleasure that "those among the Japanese who still have dual citizenship . . . [will take advantage of the meeting to] publicly take steps to renounce their allegiance to Japan." Nisei leaders urged attendance at the event; so did the Japanese Chamber of Commerce.[18]

The program included Lechner, Issei and Nisei speakers, a pledge of allegiance, and a ceremonial renunciation of dual citizenship; the assembly joined in the singing of "God Bless America" led by Mamie Stark, "America's only feminine baritone." The Nisei bore witness to their loyalty: the American Legion, Lechner, and those who believed deeply enough in the importance of Americanism listened. County Legion Commander Bob Snyder urged "the nisei to come to [the] Legion for any help they desired." Lechner privately reported to a follower that the meeting had been "a huge success . . . [and] did a lot of good," a feeling officially concurred in by Nisei leaders. But a letter from a member of the audience to the editor of *Rafu Shimpo* came closer to the mark: "I was quite disappointed to see the comparatively few Caucasian Americans present. Did the group which Dr. Lechner represents attend the rally?"[19] The simple answer was that Lechner really represented no one. The corollary was crushing to Nisei hopes.

Public relations had been offered by the powerless in place of power, with minimal results. No amount of posturing, whether guided by John Lechner or by Dale Carnegie, could budge the essential fact of the caste line: the Nisei were, in the public mind, "Japanese," and would prosper or suffer along with that stereotype. Lechner soon drew back from his disappointed Nisei clients; by the middle of the war, no more vocal hater of Japanese Americans was to be found in Los Angeles. And whereas the Japanese menace twenty years earlier had especially impressed Northern Californians, now Southern California, with its larger Japanese population, became most exercised. A poll of Pacific Coast opinion taken in the second

[18]Program of the pageant, *Rafu Shimpo,* May 10, 1941; Los Angeles *Evening Herald and Express,* May 10, 1941; Ford to Col. J. R. Ruggles, Apr. 29, 1942 [1941], Ford Papers.

[19]*Kashu Mainichi,* May 10, 1941; Lechner to Haan, May 14, 1941, folder "Haan," Americanism Educational League Files, Knott's Berry Farm, Buena Park, Calif.; Fred M. Tayama to Lechner, May 12, 1941, folder "Nazism on the Pacific Coast (Lechner)," *ibid.;* letter of Kiyoshi Hara in *Rafu Shimpo,* May 18, 1941. The AEL treated my inquiries with an openness hardly consistent with the notion of right-wing "paranoia."

week of February, 1942, showed that even before the evacuation one out of three people in Southern California wished to see the Nisei placed in concentration camps, as compared with only one out of seven elsewhere on the Coast. Three-quarters of Southern Californians but just under half of Northern Californians thought this was a good idea for alien Japanese.[20] That the greatest suspicion of a perfectly loyal and harmless group occurred among people who had best "known" them—as a caste—tells us about something more than the failure of the frantic Nisei efforts to stave off catastrophe. It speaks eloquently to the argument, whether separationist or segregationist, that a distinguishable group can remain unmolested "in its place."

The Japanese-American "test case" should have been singularly unexplosive. The immigrants were never deemed inferior; they themselves were well organized, with customs and institutions that ideally suited them to exploit any economic opportunities granted by the majority. Their control over their children was such that prewar Nisei political consciousness issued only the mildest challenges to "their place" as accepted by their parents. Yet so urgent were demands for culturally nationalistic unity that neither Issei nor Nisei were treated in Los Angeles as a fully legitimate group. Working their own garden was somehow not enough. Social values of the majority demanded of the local Japanese deeds which American racial definitions had not given them much chance to perform.

Whether their slim chances of avoiding definition as an alien group were fully exploited cannot be answered unequivocally. Surely both Issei and Nisei were, properly considered, ornaments to the places they inhabited—"superlatively good citizens," in Roger Daniels's words.[21] But one must wonder whether more aggressiveness within the Japanese accommodation to Los Angeles might have brought

[20]The February questions (in the field Feb. 7–13, 1942) were: "Taking all the Japanese aliens around here as a whole, which one of these statements comes closest to the way you feel we ought to treat them?" and "Which of these same things on the card comes closest to the way you feel we ought to treat the Japanese here who are citizens of the United States?" (Note the "we" in these questions, and the description of the Nisei.) A set of questions posed by the same polling agency *after* the relocation had begun showed a massive crystallization of opinion in support of what was now government policy. Office of Facts and Figures, Bureau of Intelligence, Polling Division (in Collaboration with National Opinion Research Center, University of Denver), "Pacific Coast Attitudes toward the Japanese Problem," typescript report no. 7, Feb. 28, 1942, and "The Japanese Problem," typescript report no. 19, Apr. 21, 1942.

[21]Roger Daniels, *The Politics of Prejudice* (Berkeley and Los Angeles: University of California Press, 1962), p. v.

about more varied and knowledgeable contacts between whites and Japanese. Even if such contacts had been wary, they might have made the indeterminate-loyalty stigma according to which the Japanese were evacuated seem as ridiculous to contemporaries as it is to us today.

Such a prescription would imply many, perhaps impossible things: the active challenging of the kindly paternalism and racial presumptions of the churchmen who early supported the Japanese American; less stress on "Americanization," coupled with an insistence on the validity of the Japanese-American mixed culture; willingness to risk growth of the ethnic economy by diverting capital into economic alliances with whites in diverse ventures; greater readiness to dicker with De Silva in the 1930's; Nisei politics less fearful of charges of "bloc voting." Each or all of these prescriptions may pretend an unrealistically wide range of possibilities within the culture of the immigrants and their children. But as it was, it was all too easy to pack off the Japanese, with the general approbation of Los Angeles.

Well before Pearl Harbor the FBI raided first-generation organizations, gathering a "truckful of records" in a vain search for evidence of disloyalty.[22] The Central Japanese Association issued a credo, calling attention to their "honor of being the most law-abiding people in the community" and pledging "full cooperation and support"— not only to legally constituted authorities, but also to "patriotic organizations, and other worthy agencies for the promotion and maintenance of national unity." Their closest tie to America, the immigrant group stressed, was the Nisei: "Here we bring up and educate our children in the hope that they may become good Americans. It is gratifying to see that these children are living up to our expectations. Many of them have already . . . proved their loyalty to America by joining cheerfully and enthusiastically the armed forces of the United States."[23]

Alien Japanese could not properly wave the American flag themselves, but they hoped their citizen children could do it for them. Time, however, was running out. "Indications are: it's safer to be geared in *expectation* of war conditions," Tanaka warned Japanese-American businessmen in late November.[24]

---

[22]*Rafu Shimpo,* Oct. 6, 1941; Los Angeles *Times,* Nov. 13, 1941.

[23]"Statement of the Central Japanese Association of America," in *Congressional Record,* 77th Cong., 1st sess. (1941), appendix, pp. A5325–26.

[24]Tanaka, "Journal," Nov. 29, 1941. For internal consumption—though with some effort to publicize the fact among whites—the Central Japanese Association had earlier produced a booklet on Americanization for Issei, featuring Japanese language translations of the Declaration of Independence, Pledge of Allegiance,

Among the many reflexes aroused by Pearl Harbor, few were faster than those of the Los Angeles Nisei. Within hours an Anti-Axis Committee was formed, composed of the most influential Nisei in Los Angeles. The committee faced an uncertain situation which seemed to dictate a strategy of complete openness about the activities of their community.[25] Various federal, state, and local agencies reacted in the week after Pearl Harbor by picking up and detaining suspicious aliens, preventing Japanese-American fishermen from sailing, shutting down the fruitstands, and suspending liquor licenses held by Issei.[26] The official actions, however, were usually temporary.

When Los Angeles authorities first turned to the Japanese question after Pearl Harbor, their position showed compassion. Two days after the attack the County Board of Supervisors expressed concern lest innocent Nisei schoolchildren be attacked as scapegoats. They requested school superintendents to ''take every practical step'' to encourage in their schools ''a real American spirit toward American born children of Japanese blood and their parents.'' Mayor Fletcher Bowron of Los Angeles, who had earlier been attacked by political opponents for permitting Nisei to gain city jobs through civil service, continued his distantly friendly attitude.[27]

Only about a month after Pearl Harbor did more threatening thoughts become foremost in the minds of Los Angeles officials. On January 5, 1942, Colonel Wayne Allen, the efficient chief administrative officer of the County Board of Supervisors, wrote to John Anson Ford expressing humanitarian concern about economic dislocations to be suffered by local Japanese: ''Doubtless, public opinion will reduce the amount of trade with these people.'' Allen concluded

Nisei Creed, and Bill of Rights. *Rafu Shimpo,* May 7, 1941; Matsumoto, ''History of Resident Japanese in Southern California,'' trans. Togo Tanaka, typescript, p. 38, in Tanaka, ''Journal,'' at entry for Aug. 25, 1941.

[25]*Rafu Shimpo,* Dec. 7, 1941. Also mimeographed sheet dated Dec., 1941, from County Committee for Church and Community Cooperation telling ''The Citizens of Los Angeles County'' of the composition and aims of the Citizens League; Fred M. Tayama to Ford, Jan. 15, 1942, both in Ford Papers.

[26]Leonard Bloom and Ruth Riemer, *Removal and Return* (Berkeley and Los Angeles: University of California Press, 1949), p. 163; *Kashu Mainichi,* Dec. 10, 1941; U.S. Department of the Interior, War Relocation Authority, *Wartime Exile* (Washington: U.S. Government Printing Office, n.d.), pp. 98–100.

[27]Los Angeles County Board of Supervisors Minutes, Dec. 9, 1941, Ford Papers; Robert Gerhart Lane, ''The Administration of Fletcher Bowron as Mayor of the City of Los Angeles'' (Ph.D. dissertation, University of Southern California, 1954), p. 56; Morton Grodzins, ''Political Aspects of the Japanese Evacuation'' (Ph.D. dissertation, University of California, Berkeley, 1945), p. 164.

that because "it may be quite difficult to pick any of these people up on relief. . . some means" had to be found to "care for these people on a national basis."[28]

The local burden of dealing with the suspect group increasingly weighed upon public officials. Chief C. B. Horrall of the Los Angeles Police Department complained in mid-February that resident aliens (including other aliens than Japanese, but also indicating Nisei) made "constant police patrols and a constant investigative check" necessary. These tasks were taxing to Horrall, because of "the limited personnel that this department has at the present time." But the federal government refused to subsidize a police department plan for using propaganda and other persuasive techniques "to get control of the American-born Japanese and see what we could do to keep them in line."[29]

Practical considerations, like ending the alarming Japanese presence on Terminal Island without destroying the important cannery business there, began to worry Mayor Bowron. His own motives, as he would claim, may have had no mercenary component. He was, however, under some pressure of a decidedly self-seeking kind, as reflected in letters, such as one from a local produce broker who complained of the "bitter pill" he had to swallow when the Japanese Americans continued business as usual "while they carry on their faces a smirking smile."[30]

In late January Allen was in Washington, trying to convince the federal government that Los Angeles simply could not handle the manifold problems caused by its large Japanese population. His position continued to be ambiguous: while he was appealing to the federal authorities for immediate assistance to local Japanese in financial difficulties, he was reminding the Board of Supervisors that "it must be considered that Japanese aliens are a possible danger to

[28]Wayne Allen to Ford, Jan. 5, 1941 [1942], Ford Papers.

[29]Letters of the police chiefs were among the responses to a questionnaire sent to law enforcement authorities by California Attorney General Earl Warren in early 1942. Photostats are in folder A 15.04, JERS Collection. Horrall's response is printed in Tolan Committee, *Hearings,* pt. 29, pp. 10988–89. The plan to exhort Los Angeles Nisei is discussed by a member of the Los Angeles Police Commission in HUAC, *Investigation,* pt. 15, pp. 9210, 9213.

[30]Ray D. Wall to Bowron, Jan. 24, 1942, folder A 16.201, JERS Collection. Other such letters can be found. Bowron later insisted that his actions before relocation were not influenced by the pressure upon him, although he was aware of the public hostility to the Japanese. "At the time, we were acting, not under pressure, but largely in the dark. . . . Those of us in official position . . . felt that we owed a distinct duty to the people we represented to insure their protection in time of war." Bowron to John Modell, Aug. 16, 1967.

our interests." He wanted the Board to draft a resolution "urging the President, Congress and the Federal Bureau of Investigation to provide housing and subsistence for Japanese nationals."[31] The supervisors so resolved on the following day, concluding that "Japanese aliens [should] be transferred from coastal areas to inland points." Copies of their resolution were sent to the War Department, California congressmen, the FBI, and the newspapers.[32]

On the day of that resolution, Los Angeles County and City exacerbated the Japanese-American community's straits by retiring civil servants of Japanese extraction. Bowron ambiguously expressed the "earnest wish . . . that no advantage of any kind be taken of the Japanese people. This should be true even though [when?] a person of Japanese race feels he owes his first loyalty to Japan." On the same day, the mayor told the general public that although the city's action "is not to be construed as an indication that any of them [the Nisei civil servants] is dangerous or that their loyalty has been questioned. . . . We feel that we would be derelict if we did not take every precaution for the full protection of life and property of the people of this city, and we further feel that all that has been done has been strictly a proper municipal affair."[33] American-born Japanese were now officially stigmatized.

Government provided a mold within which public opinion was crystallized. A year later a Los Angeles County official proudly recalled that official actions were "immediately followed by expressions from other organized groups for prompt government action to remove the menace, which the Japanese population here was believed to present." The Native Sons' predictable commendation for the Board of Supervisors' resolution was echoed more significantly by the County Republican Central Committee, which wrote that "the feeling is general that no chance should be taken." Defense overrode the question of rights, and "those [Japanese] who are citizens and have the interest of our country at heart would be glad to subject themselves to whatever the requirements would be." Some days later the grand jury of Los Angeles County concurred.[34] Having

[31] Allen to Board of Supervisors, Jan. 26, 1942 (2 letters), Board of Supervisors File 740.18/63.25 ("Relocation and Return"), Ford Papers. These two letters, identically dated, were somewhat different in emphasis.

[32] Text in Los Angeles *Examiner,* Jan. 28, 1942.

[33] "Statement of Mayor Bowron to the Japanese People of Los Angeles—January 28, 1942," typescript copy in folder A 15.14, JERS Collection; Los Angeles *Illustrated Daily News* and *Los Angeles Daily Journal,* both Jan. 28, 1942; HUAC, *Investigation,* pp. 9210–12.

[34] Only one other grand jury, that of neighboring Orange County, declared likewise. A. H. Campion (acting chief administrative officer, Los Angeles County

accepted a large measure of self-segregation in the past, the Los Angeles Japanese were now asked to stand for worse.

The semi-official Los Angeles County Defense Council devised a relocation scheme in early February. According to the plan, citizen Japanese could easily be encouraged to move "voluntarily" from the area if their alien parents were compelled to leave. Dominant in formulating the Defense Council's Japanese policy was Paul Shoup, president of the Merchants and Manufacturers Association, whose actions typified what Morton Grodzins called "the multiple roles played by certain individuals in fostering evacuation." The Los Angeles County Chamber of Commerce was also very active and influential at this point; through its Washington office, the Chamber worked directly upon California congressmen and indirectly through the relocation efforts of the Los Angeles County Board of Supervisors.[35]

County District Attorney John Dockweiler expressed typical frustration at the stodgy legalism which forbade authorities to abate the dangers they perceived: "You can't tell the difference between a Jap, whether he is native born or a citizen. . . . I am astonished that there is not more sabotage. I am astonished that they haven't done more. . . . We have got to make a drive to do something about the American born Japs, not the alien Jap, but the American born. He is

---

Board of Supervisors) and Earl Kudell to Morton Grodzins, Jan. 21, 1943, folder A 15.12, JERS Collection; Walter H. Odemar (Grand Trustee, Native Sons) to Board of Supervisors, Jan. 28, 1942; William F. Campbell (chairman, Republican Central Committee) to Roger Jessup (chairman, Board of Supervisors), Jan. 30, 1942, last two in Board of Supervisors File, Ford Papers; Jacobus ten Broek, Edward N. Barnhart, and Floyd W. Matson, *Prejudice, War and the Constitution* (Berkeley and Los Angeles: University of California Press, 1952), p. 380, n. 102.

[35]Grodzins, "Political Aspects," pp. 49–55; mimeographed copy of telegram, Paul Shoup to Hiram Johnson, Feb. 13, 1942, folder A 16.03, JERS Collection; Morton Grodzins, interview with Harold Kennedy (executive director, Los Angeles County Defense Council), Mar. 2, 1942, folder A 12.051, JERS Collection; testimony of members of Defense Council in Tolan Committee, *Hearings*, pt. 31, pp. 11678–94; statement of Paul Shoup, Feb. 13, 1942, including resolution of Los Angeles County Defense Council, printed as exhibit in Tolan Committee, *Hearings*, pt. 31, pp. 11866–70; Rudolph Van Nostrand (director of public relations, Merchants and Manufacturers) to Edward N. Barnhart, July 22 and Aug. 1, 1949, folder A 16.03, JERS Collection; "Grodzins in Washington," typewritten notes of interview with James C. Ingebretsen (Washington representative of Los Angeles Chamber of Commerce), Oct. 14, 1942, folder A 12.04, *ibid.;* "Grodzins in Washington, #15," Oct. 15–17, 1942, and Grodzins, interview with James Read (Los Angeles Chamber of Commerce), July 20, 1942, both typescripts in folder A 16.204, *ibid.*

the danger. He is the smart guy, he is the fellow who went back to Japan and learned his tricks there."[36]

On February 5 Fletcher Bowron employed his weekly radio broadcast to pressure the federal government with an aroused local public opinion. As mayor, he was "directly responsible to the people of this area for the protection of life and property," but this responsibility was impossible to fulfill on a local level without proper federal policy. In the federal realm, Bowron saw only "confusion as to what to do with the Japanese in California." "We in Los Angeles have been . . . somewhat impatiently waiting for some kind of action. . . . We are the ones who will be the human sacrifices." Although there had been no overt act of subversion in Los Angeles,

> common sense and reason dictate that if there are enemy agents in our midst who will be useful in a plan as well worked out with such diabolic cunning and perfidy as characterized the attack on Pearl Harbor . . . then such persons, to be most valuable to Japan, would endeavor to mislead all of us—to avert suspicion by any means in their command. The most natural thing would be for the most dangerous of them to condemn the Japanese war clique.

Only "sickly sentimentality" would deny that all Japanese had to be removed, lest Americans "lose the very thing we are fighting for—a right to demonstrate brotherly love and to be nice to everybody in time of peace."[37] In a supplementary statement to the press, Bowron explained Washington's "slowness and apparent indecision" in terms of an inability

> to distinguish between Japanese and other enemy aliens. The Japanese, because they are nonassimilable, because the aliens have been denied the right to own real property in California, because of the Alien Exclusion Act, because of the marked difference in appearance between Japanese and Caucasians, because of the generations of training and philosophy that made them Japanese and nothing else—all of these contributing factors set the Japanese apart as a race, regardless of how many generations may have been born in America.[38]

Bowron insisted that public opinion "with hardly a dissenting voice say[s] that the Japanese, both alien and American-born must go." He feared that federal authorities might order only partial

---

[36]"Proceedings, Conference of Sheriffs and District Attorneys Called by Attorney General Warren on the Subject of Alien Land Law Enforcement," Feb. 2, 1942, typescript verbatim minutes, pp. 69, 114–15, folder A 15.02, JERS Collection.

[37]*Congressional Record,* 77th Cong., 2nd sess. (1942), pp. A 457–59.

[38]*Ibid.,* p. A 459.

evacuation, combined with a brief and local application of martial law. Though a limited policy of this kind would be more in keeping with "sentimental" interpretations of the Constitution, it might injure Los Angeles commerce; more important, it would forfeit a unique opportunity to solve for once and for all the city's Japanese problem.[39]

Bereft of influential allies and hounded by public officials claiming the joint spurs of military necessity and public opinion, the outlook for Japanese Americans was dark indeed. Soon Bowron could remark publicly that "our problem is solved. . . . It has been solved by the United States Army."[40] For by March, 1942, the relocation of Japanese Americans, alien and citizen alike, was occurring under army auspices, with President Roosevelt asking only that the procedures be "as reasonable" as "possible."[41] Bowron, and most local people, correctly recognized that Washington did not much care to restrain their enthusiasm for their experiment in forced migration and enconcentration.[42] In 1942 Bowron expressed to Congress the hope that his constituents were correct in their understanding that the Japanese problem had been resolved "for keeps—at least for the duration." In missionary tones he emphasized that "the people of the Nation must be aroused and must be unrelenting in a determina-

[39]*Ibid.*, pp. A 653–54; Bowron to Representative John Costello, typewritten copy, Feb. 14, 1942, folder A 15.14, JERS Collection.

[40]Tolan Committee, *Hearings,* pt. 31, pp. 11642–53.

[41]Quotation in Roger Daniels, *Concentration Camps, U.S.A.: Japanese Americans and World War II* (New York: Holt, Rinehart, and Winston, 1971), p. 65, which also provides the best narrative account of the events leading to the relocation. For events of local significance to Los Angeles, see Morton Grodzins, *Americans Betrayed: Politics and the Japanese Evacuation* (Chicago: University of Chicago Press, 1949).

[42]Bowron's reading of Los Angeles opinion was essentially correct. The "Los Angeles Research Jury" conducted a survey of unknown size in December, 1943, which included the item: "Should there be a constitutional amendment after the war for the deportation of all Japanese from this country, and forbidding further immigration?" The Jury reported that 64% of those who answered "yes" to the questions included American-born Japanese in their ban. Of all respondents, 65% answered "yes," 21% "no," and the balance did not know. Wage-earners and lower economic classes were somewhat more in favor of the ban—69% compared with 59% for others. An identical question was asked again in March and September, 1944, to cross-sections of 1,000 Los Angeles County residents. The March inquiry yielded identical results, but by September a major shift from the "don't know" category brought the figures to 74% favoring deportation. Los Angeles Research Jury, "Survey of Public Opinion Regarding Post-War Problems, Los Angeles County," report in folder "Los Angeles—Economic Conditions," Haynes Collection; Los Angeles *Times,* Oct. 2, 1944.

tion to wage an all-out war in which human sympathy can play no part''—a racial war, in other words.[43]

The Japanese had "succeeded" economically in Los Angeles; as a "model minority" they had responded resourcefully to the Depression; they had held their adult unmarried men in check; they had instructed their children in proper respect for the authorities and kept them out of trouble. But these deeds did not protect them. In fact such admirable behavior, though not unnoticed by the white majority, entered popular consciousness as part of a racial stereotype. The Anglo image of the Japanese Americans pigeonholed information far too neatly, and inhibited other than superficial understanding.

Thus an often beneficial view of the model minority turned harshly destructive when "Japanese behavior" was taken to include Nisei, Issei, and perfidious Japan herself. Always eager and self-contained, "the Japanese" now threatened in the international arena. The daring and innovative agricultural enterprise of the Japanese Americans, and their frequent employment of cooperative action to further it, could be seen as the fulfillment of a "Japanese" plan to gain a foothold on this side of the Pacific. Their fishing enterprise, similarly conducted, must be similarly motivated. The failure of the Nisei work force to distinguish its interest publicly from that of the Issei entrepreneurs demonstrated that ties of blood were thicker than the ties of birthplace, school, and daily "American" milieu.

As of Pearl Harbor, the Nisei were only coming into their own within the ethnic economy; they had had little opportunity to develop it in a way that might have brought them into broader contact with whites. Their political action had been limited both by the size of their voting population and by their group's inability to coordinate its voting, owing in part to internal socioeconomic variation. Nisei leadership as of 1941 was, understandably if unequivocally, much involved in cosmetic exercises. They misread their situation. The plasticity which their professions of competence, gentility, and loyalty suggested to whites merely served to reinforce their stereotype.

Yet the stereotype did not necessarily suggest an acute danger from the Nisei or their parents. Even though Pearl Harbor was a sneak attack, in keeping with white fears, it did not bring the vigilantes to Little Tokyo. Instead, the sanction of public officials was called for—and was offered, after a while. The sanction came because

[43]HUAC, *Investigation*, pt. 15, pp. 8989–98, 9202–9; U.S. Senate, Committee on Military Affairs, Subcommittee on Japanese War Relocation Centers, *Subcommittee Report*, 78th Cong., 1st sess. (1943), pp. 92–98.

under the circumstances it relieved officials of one anxiety they shared with many other Americans, and because the solution involved virtually no political cost. Official action in turn enflamed public opinion, which then encouraged even stronger official action. The components of this process were, taken individually, more unfortunate than malign. But the process itself was a perversion of American democracy—arguably the more so for the offhand manner in which it occurred.

The generation that has passed since these horrors has, by and large, been more aware of the moral ambiguities of cultural and racial nationalism; one need hardly continue to decry the malignancy of racism. But Japanese Americans and other Americans alike have on the whole neglected the part played by minorities in accommodating to the limitations *and* opportunities of their situations. The foregoing is an account of the accommodation of one minority to racist America, and some of the benefits and costs implied by that minority's strategies.

Census Code Titles

Publications of the United States Bureau of the Census and of its predecessor, the Census Office, have titles which vary from decade to decade, and which are usually both lengthy and confusing. The code titles listed below with the full citation of the publications to which they refer have been used invariably in the notes and tables.

FULL CITATION	CODE TITLE
U.S. Census Office. *Eleventh Census: 1890. Report on the Statistics of Agriculture in the United States.*	*Census 1890 A1*
———. *Compendium of the Eleventh Census: 1890, Part I: Population.*	*Census 1890 P1*
———. *Compendium of the Eleventh Census: 1890, Part II: Population.*	*Census 1890 P2*
———. *Report on Population of the United States at the Eleventh Census: 1890,* Part II.	*Census 1890 P3*
———*Twelfth Census, 1900,* Vol. V: *Agriculture,* Part I.	*Census 1900 A1*
———. *Twelfth Census, 1900. Census Reports,* Vol. 1: *Population,* Part I.	*Census 1900 P1*
———. *Twelfth Census, 1900. Census Reports,* Vol. 1: *Population,* Part II.	*Census 1900 P2*
———. *Twelfth Census, 1900. Special Report, Occupations.*	*Census 1900 P3*
U.S. Bureau of the Census. *Thirteenth Census, 1910,* Vol. VI: *Reports by States (Agriculture).*	*Census 1910 A1*
———. *Thirteenth Census, 1910. Abstract of the Census . . . with Supplement for California.*	*Census 1910 P1*
———. *Chinese and Japanese in the United States 1910. Bulletin 127.*	*Census 1910 P2*
———. *Thirteenth Census of the United States,* Vol. IV: *Population 1910, Occupation Statistics.*	*Census 1910 P3*
———. *Thirteenth Census of the United States,* Vol. II: *Population 1910, Reports by States . . . Alabama-Montana.*	*Census 1910 P4*
———. *Thirteenth Census of the United States,* Vol. I: *Population 1910: General Report and Analysis.*	*Census 1910 P5*

————. *Fourteenth Census, 1920,* Vol VI, Part 3:   *Census 1920 A1*
Agriculture, The Western States.
————. *Fourteenth Census of the United States,*   *Census 1920 C1*
1920. Compendium.
————. *Fourteenth Census of the United States, 1920,*   *Census 1920 P1*
Vol. III: *Population, 1920, Composition and*
Characteristics of the Population by States.
————. *Fourteenth Census of the United States, 1920,*   *Census 1920 P2*
Vol. IV: *Population 1920 (Occupations).*
————. *Fourteenth Census of the United States, 1920.*   *Census 1920 P3*
State Compendium, California.
————. *Fourteenth Census of the United States, 1920.*   *Census 1920 P4*
Vol. II: *Population, 1920, General Report and*
Analytical Tables.
————. *United States Census of Agriculture, 1925,*   *Census 1925 A1*
Part III: *The Western States.*
————. *Fifteenth Census of the United States; 1930.*   *Census 1930 A1*
Agriculture, Vol. II, Part 3: *The Western States.*
————. *Fifteenth Census of the United States: 1930.*   *Census 1930 A2*
Agriculture, Vol. III: *Type of Farm,* Part 3.
————. *Fifteenth Census of the United States: 1930.*   *Census 1930 B1*
Distribution, Vol. I: *Retail Distribution,* Part 2.
————. *Fifteenth Census of the United States,*   *Census 1930 B2*
Manufactures: 1929, Vol. III: *Reports by States.*
————. *Fifteenth Census of the United States: 1930.*   *Census 1930 P1*
Population, Vol. II: *General Report, Statistics,*
by Subject.
————. *Fifteenth Census of the United States: 1930.*   *Census 1930 P2*
Population, Vol. III, Part 1: *Reports by States.*
————. *Fifteenth Census of the United States: 1930.*   *Census 1930 P3*
Population, Special Report on Foreign-Born White
Families . . . with an Appendix . . . for . . .
Japanese Families.
————. *Fifteenth Census of the United States: 1930.*   *Census 1930 P4*
Unemployment, Vol. I.
————. *Fifteenth Census of the United States: 1930.*   *Census 1930 P5*
Unemployment, Vol. II.
————. *Fifteenth Census of the United States: 1930.*   *Census 1930 P6*
Population, Vol. VI: *Families.*
————. *Census of American Business: 1933.*   *Census 1933 B1*
Wholesale Distribution, Vol. VII.
————. *United States Census of Agriculture: 1935.*   *Census 1935 A1*
Reports for States, Second Series, Vol. II, Part 3.
————. *United States Census of Agriculture, 1935,*   *Census 1935 A2*
Part III: *The Western States.*
————. *Census of Business: 1935. Retail Distribution,* *Census 1935 B1*
Vol. II.

―――. *Sixteenth Census of the United States: 1940.*   *Census 1940 A1*
Agriculture, Vol. I, Part 6: *Statistics for Counties.*
―――. *Sixteenth Census of the United States: 1940.*   *Census 1940 B1*
Census of Business, Vol. I: *Retail Trade: 1939,*
Part 3.
―――. *Sixteenth Census of the United States: 1940,*   *Census 1940 P1*
Population, Vol. II, Part 1: *United States Summary.*
―――. *Sixteenth Census of the United States: 1940.*   *Census 1940 P2*
Population, Vol. II: *Characteristics of the*
Population, Part 1.
―――. *Sixteenth Census of the United States: 1940.*   *Census 1940 P3*
Population, Vol. III: *The Labor Force,* Part 2.
―――. *Sixteenth Census of the United States: 1940.*   *Census 1940 P4*
Population, Characteristics of the Nonwhite
Population by Race.
―――. *Japanese Population of the Pacific Coast*   *Census 1940 P5*
States by Sex and Nativity or Citizenship, by
Counties: 1940. Series P-3, No. 25.
―――. *Population: Japanese Population by Nativity*   *Census 1940 P6*
or Citizenship in Selected Cities in the United
States: 1940. Series P-3, No. 24.
―――. *Sixteenth Census of the United States: 1940.*   *Census 1940 P7*
Population and Housing, Statistics for Census
Tracts, Los Angeles-Long Beach, California.

Index

demographic detail on, 17–22; comparison of Japanese and non-Japanese, 19, 20, 30; non-Japanese, 19, 20, 28–29, 30; reasons for, 19, 98; position of Los Angeles Chamber of Commerce on, 37; picture brides, 87. *See also* Immigration Act of 1924; Immigration Commission; Population
Immigration Act of 1924, 164; exclusion clause, 32, 83; effects, 88n55, 100
Immigration Commission, U.S., 69, 115
Initiative Proposition 1. *See* Alien Land Law of 1920
Integration of business, 114–17, 137–38
Irwin, Wallace, 2, 3–4, 5n8, 108
Italian Americans, 19, 70, 125n69
Iwata, Masakazu, 100, 102, 103

Japan America Society. *See* Los Angeles Japan America Society
Japan-U.S. Treaty of 1911, 101
Japanese American Citizens League (Los Angeles Chapter), 142n37, 147, 148, 179; and Nisei Day festival, 1; Equality Committee, 14, 15, 177–78; Anti-Axis Committee, 15, 183; response to racism, 15, 171; endorsement of strikebreaking, 123, 124; formation and membership, 168–69; problems, 168–69; political connections, 169–70; and dual citizenship, 177
Japanese American Citizens League (national), 75, 169, 178n14
Japanese and Korean Exclusion League, 31, 34
Japanese Association (Los Angeles). *See* Los Angeles Japanese Association
Japanese Association of America, 14; response to racism, 11–12, 83, 101; and picture bride dispute, 87n53
Japanese Associations (local): formation and role, 80; encouragement of farming, 135
Japanese Chamber of Commerce, Los Angeles, 77n23, 123, 180; and war bonds, 84; formation and purpose,

88; activities, 88–89, 93, 118, 120; merger with Los Angeles Japanese Association, 88, 118; competition with (Japanese) Southern California Chamber of Commerce, 167; defense of military actions of Japan, 176
Japanese Children's Home, 167–68
Japanese Farm Laborers Association, 126
Jefferson Park development, 14–15, 75, 169, 177
Jews, 10n21, 20
Jim Crow legislation, 65–66
Johnson, Hiram, 38, 39n33
Joint Anti-Asiatic Committee. *See* Los Angeles County Anti-Asiatic Society

Kane, Lail, 174, 175
Kashu Mainichi, 156
Kawai, Kazuo: as cultural spokesman for Nisei, 164–66
Ken (magazine), 175
Kenjin-kai, 89–91; original function, 162; junior, 162, 163

Labor movement, 78; anti-Japanese activities of (white) organized, 31–36, 37, 52n65, 145, 149–50, 151; "bunk-house" farm organization, 68–69; work patterns of Japanese, 83–84, 95, 96–99, 138; El Monte strike of 1933, 121–23; 1936 strike, 124–26; fishery strikes of 1917 and 1938, 125n69; unionization of Japanese, 139–44. *See also* Employment; Retail Clerks Protective Association; Three Star Produce Company
Lechner, John, 179–80
Legal questions, court cases: efficiency of Japanese farmer, 7; housing, 75; Los Angeles Japanese Association election, 87n54; Alien Land Law (1920), 100, 101, 103n23; floral markets, 115n38; SCRPWU suit, 147. *See also* Legislation, discriminatory
Legislation, discriminatory: Alien Land Law of 1913, 31, 32, 38, 97; alien land legislation in other states, 32n11; school tuition bill, 33n12; anti-alien